# HUNGER IN
# THE BALANCE

# HUNGER IN THE BALANCE

The New Politics of International Food Aid

**Jennifer Clapp**

*With a New Preface*

CORNELL UNIVERSITY PRESS    ITHACA AND LONDON

First published 2012 by Cornell University Press
First printing, Cornell Paperbacks, 2015
Printed in the United States of America

Library of Congress Cataloging-in-Publication Data

Clapp, Jennifer, 1963–
    Hunger in the balance : the new politics of international food aid / Jennifer
Clapp.
        p. cm.
    Includes bibliographical references and index.
    ISBN 978-0-8014-5039-6 (cloth : alk. paper)
    ISBN 978-1-5017-0065-1 (pbk. : alk. paper)
    1. Food relief—Political aspects.    2. Food relief—International cooperation.
I. Title.
    HV696.F6C515    2012
    363.8'83—dc23        2011037594

Cloth printing            10  9  8  7  6  5  4  3  2  1
Paperback printing        10  9  8  7  6  5  4  3  2  1

*For Eric, Zoë, and Nels*

# Contents

# Illustrations

## Preface to the Paperback Edition

Food aid can be an important lifeline in times of crisis, providing a vital source of nourishment for those who cannot access food by other means. The importance of food aid in response to recent crises—such as the conflict in South Sudan, the Ebola outbreak in West Africa, and the earthquakes in Nepal—underscores this point. But food aid, though well intended, is not uncontroversial. Indeed, food aid policies and practices have sparked heated debate in recent years, especially policies that put the needs of the donor country above those of recipients. Most donors have at one time or another tied their food aid donations to food commodities grown in their own country. Such practices, referred to as "tied" food aid, can have undesirable impacts. Large shipments of food sourced in donor countries can create disincentives for local farmers in recipient countries. Tied food aid also tends to be highly inefficient, reaching fewer people than other types of assistance.

In this book I tell the story of the politics involved in trying to reform food aid policies in a way that enhances the effectiveness of that aid while minimizing its potentially harmful impacts. I focus in particular on efforts to encourage the untying of food aid and the adoption of policies that enable donors to provide cash, vouchers, or food that is sourced locally or within the region where it is needed. Policy reforms along these lines can help to ensure a backstop for those most in need but without the problematic side effects associated with tied food aid.

Reform efforts with respect to food aid have wide-reaching implications, particularly for the world's poorest and most hungry people who rely on this form of assistance. The process of reforming food aid policies also reveals important lessons for policy change more broadly. As I argue in this book, no one factor can explain how the food aid reform process has unfolded in different donor countries. Ideas on how to improve the delivery of food aid matter a great deal in shaping policy outcomes. But so do the powerful interests that have a stake in the way food aid is delivered. The institutions through which reform occurs also have an enormous bearing on whether appropriate reforms are possible to secure, and if so, what they might look like in practice.

The European Union, Canada, and Australia, all traditional donors, have adopted policies to untie their food aid over the past twenty years. These donors no longer require the food assistance they provide to be delivered in the form of commodities grown in, and shipped from, their own country. Instead, they now provide cash assistance for the purchase of food that is grown closer to the source of hunger and provide vouchers and cash payments to those in need. The process of reform in these cases, outlined in chapter 3, was unique to each donor country. But in each case, the ideas for reform were pushed by a domestic coalition of civil society groups and policymakers at key moments, just as shifts were taking place among economic interests with a stake in the policy. As a result, institutional changes that favored reforms were easier to adopt.

The United States has been a holdout with respect to the reform of food aid policies, and it remains out of sync with the other major donor countries. Its food aid is still nearly 100 percent tied to commodities grown in the United States, and it requires that a significant portion must be shipped to recipients via U.S.-flagged ships. This is not to say that efforts are not under way to change U.S. policy. But compared with other donors, the U.S. process has been exceedingly slow. Despite the promotion of the idea of reform from several quarters, the economic interests that prefer the old way of doing things—namely the U.S. shipping industry and some food aid delivery organizations—wield an enormous amount of power, and they ultimately influence how decisions regarding food aid reform are made.

As the later chapters of the book highlight, the divergence of approaches to food aid between the United States and other traditional donors has led to political skirmishes on the international stage over the past decade. These include flare-ups over genetically modified organisms (GMOs) in food aid, over how trade rules at the WTO deal with food aid, and over global governance mechanisms that address food aid.

Since 2012, there have been continued attempts to reform U.S. food aid policies, with some incremental progress. At the same time, the international community of donors has adopted a new Food Assistance Convention, changing some of the rules and norms that donors have pledged to follow. New donors have also become increasingly important in terms of the amount of food aid they provide, though often under policies that include aid tying rather than reformed modes of aid delivery.

## Reform Efforts in the United States

There have been several small steps toward untying U.S. food aid since 2012, and there appears to be considerable momentum for bolder reforms as of early 2015. In 2012, an important shift occurred in the cargo preference rules for U.S. food aid, when the amount of aid earmarked to be carried on U.S.-flagged ships dropped from 75 percent to 50 percent. There had been attempts in the past to change the cargo preference requirement, but it was particularly difficult to achieve given the strength of the shipping lobby, which shut it down every time, as explained in chapter 4. This recent shift in policy is noteworthy, in that Congress slipped it into an unrelated transportation bill at the final moment and voted on it without debate, or even the shipping lobby's knowledge, until it was already passed into law. The move was not intended as a food aid reform per se but rather as a way to recover funds by shifting government spending away from an inefficient practice to pay for activities in the transportation bill. The shipping lobby was taken by surprise and has since attempted to reinstate the 75 percent requirement. So far it has been unsuccessful.

The shift in the cargo preference rules occurred around the same time that the negotiations on a new U.S. Farm Bill (to replace the 2008 Farm Bill that expired in 2012) were heating up. In early 2013, the Obama administration proposed major changes to U.S. food aid policy as part of its 2014 fiscal year budget proposal. The reform proposal was put forward despite a plea earlier that year from some seventy organizations to retain the current structure of the food aid program. The administration's proposal asked to shift the food aid budget from the Farm Bill to three different accounts in the U.S. Agency for International Development (USAID). The proposal included flexibility for up to 45 percent of that aid to be spent on cash, vouchers, and local and regional purchases of food aid, while still requiring 55 percent to be spent on U.S. commodities and transportation. The proposal also called for an end to both monetization and the cargo preference rules for food aid. With respect to the last item, however, the proposal also included a $25 million payment to the U.S. Maritime Administration, to come from the efficiency gains from the reforms and to be used to help retain U.S. flag vessels and maritime jobs. This was a bold proposal that sought to change the institutional framework for food aid in a way that took it out of the hands of regular congressional renewals and put it into the administrative bureaucracy of USAID. Shifts in food aid administration from agriculture ministries to aid agencies had also occurred in the other major donor countries, which unlocked the door to subsequent reforms to untie food aid.

The main components of the president's budget proposal for food aid were incorporated into the Food Aid Reform Act, brought to the U.S. House of Representatives by Representative Ed Royce (R-Cal) as an amendment to the Farm Bill, which was under negotiation at the time. Still stung from the changes to the cargo preference rules for food aid a year earlier, the shipping lobby came out in full force against the proposal. Both Cargill, a major grain supplier, and the National Farmers' Union supported the reform legislation, but the bill was very narrowly defeated in mid-2013 by a vote of 220 (against) to 203 (for). Despite this defeat, the issue gained considerable notice. It was the closest that reform advocates had gotten in their efforts to bring significant change to U.S. food aid legislation. The administration, through this proposal, had put down a clear marker for the direction and extent of reforms for which it was aiming, and this helped to galvanize further reform initiatives.

The Farm Bill, which was eventually passed in early 2014, included some changes to U.S. food aid legislation, albeit more minor reforms than the administration had initially requested. The pilot project for local and regional purchase that had been incorporated into the 2008 Farm Bill was regularized, and the allocation for this type of food aid increased from $40 to $80 million annually over the 2014–2018 period. These changes were modest compared with the 2014 budget request and Food Aid Reform Act provisions, but they provided a wedge into the issue by legally allowing that up to 5 percent of U.S. food aid could be untied.

Reform efforts continued in the 2015 and 2016 budget requests from the administration. For both years, the requests were more modest, asking for the flexibility to use up to 25 percent of Title II aid for cash-based food assistance programs, rather than the 45 percent initially proposed. They also still included the $25 million transfer out of efficiency savings to the Maritime Administration. At the same time, a significantly more comprehensive reform proposal, the Food for Peace Reform Act, was put forward by senators Chris Coons (D-Del) and Bob Corker (R-Tenn) in mid-2014 and was reintroduced in early 2015 with the new Congress. The proposal calls for the transfer of food aid authority from the Farm Bill to USAID and allows full flexibility for both U.S. commodity aid as well as local and regional purchase and other cash and voucher tools—with the stipulation that USAID use the most cost-effective type of aid in each instance. It would also exempt food aid from cargo preference rules and eliminate requirements for monetization. How this proposed legislation will fare in Congress remains to be seen. Thus far, there is a great deal of support from reform-minded NGOs, and there has not been much by way of organized opposition as of April 2015.

Efforts in the United States during the 2012–2015 period reveal that the reform initiative remains robust. Reform advocates have actively sought to counter the claims made by interests seeking to maintain the status quo. They have pointed out repeatedly that over the 2002–2011 period, food aid constituted less than 1 percent of U.S. agricultural exports and accounted for at most 1.41 percent of farm income, indicating that change would have a minimal impact on farmers and exporters. Further, they stressed that cargo preference rules cost on average $50 million more per year than would be the case with a competitive selection of shippers and that ending the practice of monetization would save $30 million per year. Those promoting new ideas for reform have also highlighted that U.S. food aid could feed many millions more people if the proposed policy changes were made. Together, these arguments provide a powerful message of efficiency, cost savings, and human lives saved, a message that has played particularly well with the public given the strained government budget.

The recent reform efforts in the United States have some similarities to activity in other countries that were successful in reforming their food aid policies.

Although a unique set of circumstances enabled a policy shift toward untying in each case, some common elements are evident. In each case a domestic coalition of civil society actors and sympathetic policymakers pushed the idea of reform. In each case the voice of private corporate interests that wanted to keep food aid tied had become weakened in relation to the state interest in reducing costs by making aid programs more efficient. And in each case, the authority over food aid policy shifted from ministries of agriculture to ministries of development aid. The relative weight of interests has started to shift in the United States, and reform advocates have seized this moment to push for institutional changes—to move food aid policymaking out of the clutches of the agricultural policymaking setting of the Farm Bill and into the development policymaking arena of USAID. Without this institutional shift, it is unlikely that U.S. food aid will be untied.

## Adoption of the Food Assistance Convention

In December 2010, the Food Aid Committee, chaired by Canada, began negotiations to redraft the 1999 Food Aid Convention, as discussed in chapter 7. Negotiations proceeded throughout 2011 and early 2012 in a largely secretive process that took place among donors only, behind closed doors. In April 2012 the Food Aid Committee announced a new agreement that brought important changes to international rules for food assistance. Civil society groups have welcomed some of these changes and have raised concerns about others.

In an important move, the committee renamed the convention the Food Assistance Convention (FAC), reflecting changes in the agreement that allow donors to count multiple forms of food assistance in addition to the commodity food aid and seeds that were included in the 1999 agreement. The new FAC allows for donors to count cash, vouchers, and other items such as agricultural tools and livestock, as well. The agreement also emphasizes that food aid should be provided primarily in grant form and, reflecting the reforms in many donor countries that have untied aid, underscores the importance of purchasing food and other components of food assistance locally or regionally whenever possible and where appropriate. The new agreement also shifts its stance on monetization away from the 1999 agreement, which openly endorsed the practice, to stating that monetization should be utilized only when deemed necessary. This shift regarding monetization reflects growing research that demonstrates the potential market-distorting impact of that practice.

The most significant changes to the agreement are that it dispenses with the minimum floor for donations (collectively provided by all donors) and the multiyear commitments from donors denominated in tonnes of grain or its equivalent, components that had been central to each of the earlier Food Aid Conventions. The intent had been to provide predictability and a basic minimum amount of aid to enable forward planning and to provide recipients with the security that even if food prices rose sharply they would not be left without assistance. The new agreement, however, allows donors to pledge their commitments in financial amounts, in their own currency, and pledges are renewed on an annual basis with no guaranteed collective minimum amount.

These changes to the structure and requirements for commitments reflect the fact that several donors have untied their food aid in the past twenty years. The ability to pledge donations in cash rather than tonnes of grain provides donors with more budgetary certainty regarding their commitments, something they had wanted to achieve with the new agreement. But these changes introduce new uncertainties because they transfer the price risk to receiving countries. The new commitment structure also creates difficulty in tracking the overall amounts of food aid pledged because pledges are now denominated in different currencies. In general, however, it is becoming increasingly challenging to isolate food aid from the broader category of aid. Although it introduces more uncertainty, in some ways this convergence can be viewed as a positive development because it gets away from the commodity-focused nature of food aid, which caused so many problems in the past.

The new treaty also incorporates some changes to its governance structure, signaling a move toward possibly greater transparency and participation of stakeholders. Thus far, the new FAC has been open to including more stakeholders, including civil society organizations, at its regular meetings. But to date, the FAC website does not contain much information regarding members' deliberations, a weakness also evident with the previous agreement. The new FAC retained the location of its secretariat in the International Grains Council in London, despite encouragement from civil society groups to relocate the FAC in Rome to situate itself closer to the UN Committee on World Food Security (CFS).

The new Food Assistance Convention gained enough signatures to become legally binding as of January 1, 2013, and has since picked up additional members. There are now fourteen donor members.

## New Donors and Old Challenges

A third area in which updates are worth noting concerns the role and impact of new donors of food aid. In the past, the United States, the European Union, Canada, and Japan were the primary donors. Today, China, Brazil, and Russia have emerged as important donors. Together, China and Brazil's contributions are nearly equal to the EU's in terms of the volume of food aid they provide and are on par with donations from Canada and Japan. What is interesting about these new donors is that their food aid contributions are nearly 100 percent tied to commodity sourcing in the donor country. In 2012, for example, Brazil provided over 300,000 metric tonnes of food aid, a major jump in its provision of this type of assistance, and it was 100 percent tied. Russia moved from being a minor player during the 2004–2011 period, increasing its aid to over 50,000 metric tonnes in 2012, all of it tied. China's aid, at 240,000 tonnes in 2012, was also nearly 100 percent tied.

The arrival of these new donors means that on the global stage, the United States no longer stands out as unusual with its tied aid policy. In 2012, the global percentage of direct-transfer food aid increased to 62 percent after declining for several years, and the amount procured locally and regionally decreased. Even Japan has increased the degree to which it ties its food aid over the past decade. With these trends, the future might bring more tied food aid rather than less. If so, there may be a return to the familiar problems of inefficiency and lack of effectiveness that civil society groups have worked so hard to root out. Although there is currently strong reform momentum in the United States, as noted above, it may be stalled by these developments, which may reduce the pressure on the United States to reform its food aid policies further.

Although in recent years these new donors have increased the amount of assistance that they provide, their donations from year to year remain largely unpredictable. With the exception of Russia, these new donors are not members of the new FAC. If the FAC moves its secretariat to Rome to better coordinate with the CFS, where developing countries have better representation than they do in the International Grains Council, there might be an increased desire on their part to join the agreement.

## Little Movement at the WTO and on GMOs

In addition to the updates above, it is worth noting the areas in which there has been little change. One is the Doha Round of trade talks. As of early 2015, the Doha Round has not been completed, and the text on food aid discussed in chapter 6 is still in the draft format negotiated in 2008. As the food aid text has sat gathering dust, we have witnessed a continuation of extreme food price volatility, the adoption of the new FAC, and some reforms in U.S. food aid policies. There has been some movement on food security more generally at the WTO, with a major flare-up over the issue between India and the United States at the Bali Ministerial meeting in late 2013. This flare-up intensified further over the course of 2014, as India sought to bring clarity to rules on domestic food assistance policies in developing countries in the face of concerns on the part of the United States regarding the potential trade impacts of those policies. Given these developments, it may well be that some changes will need to be made to the WTO draft text on food aid disciplines, which may further stall the completion of the Doha Round.

There has also been little change with respect to donor policies regarding GMOs in food aid. Although it is likely that GMOs will continue to be present in food aid shipments, there have been few political clashes over the issue in recent years. However, in late 2012, Kenya took steps to ban the import of genetically modified foods, including in the form of food aid. As of early 2015, there was mounting pressure from several quarters within the country to reverse the ban.

## Final Reflection

Developments since 2012 demonstrate the continued relevance of the key arguments advanced in this book regarding how and why food aid reform unfolds in the way it does in different donor countries. Untying food aid requires the right balance of ideas, interests, and institutions in each donor country. As the U.S. case shows, although interests and institutions worked against the idea of reform in the early 2000s, interests have shifted since 2012, opening space for the promotion of ideas as well as institutional changes that could unlock further, more comprehensive reforms. The new FAC reflects the power of ideas to lead to reforms but is also shaped by donor interests as well as its institutional framework. And with new donors on the scene, there may be a push to embrace reform to food aid policies in those countries as well. The story of reform in these locations, if embraced, will no doubt unfold in unique ways.

*Preface = written 2015*

# Acknowledgments

My interest in this topic dates back to 1989, when I was in Guinea, West Africa, conducting field research. I was studying the political and economic impact of structural adjustment reforms on the agricultural sector and was especially interested in how local rice markets were affected. It was in the course of this research that I learned of a shipment of U.S. food aid rice that had been sent in response to a shortage in 1988, during the country's "hungry season"—the months just prior to the domestic rice harvest. Unfortunately, the food aid arrived late and coincided with the harvest. Prices on local markets plunged, and the sudden glut of rice meant that local farmers saw their incomes drop. This was my first introduction to the ways in which food aid programs of donor countries could have profound impacts on local economies. A decade later, I began to teach a course on the global political economy of agriculture and food, and not surprisingly, I regularly included a week on the political economy of food aid. In the early years of teaching this course, I became even more fascinated with the political dynamics surrounding international food aid, especially as those dynamics changed with the advent of agricultural biotechnology, agricultural trade liberalization, and fluctuating food prices. I began to focus my research on this topic in 2003, supported by several grants from the Social Sciences and Humanities Research Council of Canada. This book is my attempt to explain the "new" politics of food aid.

There are many people to whom I am deeply grateful for their insight, wisdom, and support as I researched and wrote this book. For outstanding research assistance at various points, I thank Kim Burnett, Taarini Chopra, Sam Grey, Brittney Martin, Ryan Pollice, Christopher Rompré, Linda Swanston, and Justin Williams. I also thank the people who took time out of their busy schedules to talk or correspond with me, including Chris Barrett, Jayne Bates, Mary Chambliss, Stuart Clark, Edward Clay, Marc Cohen, Charles Hanrahan, John Hoddinott, Allan Jury, Gawain Kripke, Dan Maxwell, Thomas Melito, Andrew Natsios, Leslie Norton, Julie Shouldice, Emmy Simmons, Alessandra Spalletta, Philip Thomas, David Tschirley, Patrick Webb, William Whelan, and Richard Woodhams. Thanks are also due to colleagues who helped to point me in the right direction when I got stuck. They include Andy Cooper, Robert Falkner, Derek Hall, Matias Margulis, Sophia Murphy, Osamu Nakano, Ian Rowlands, Susan Sell, John Shaw, Luke Simmons, and Simron Jit Singh. I also owe thanks for feedback to the Waterloo Food Issues Group and Engineers Without Borders Waterloo, two groups to whom I gave presentations on this topic while the research was under way. I am extremely grateful to the two anonymous readers of the manuscript for useful comments, as well as to Roger Haydon, Ange Romeo-Hall, Jamie Fuller, and Mahinder Kingra at Cornell University Press for shepherding the book through the publication process. Finally, but not least, I owe my deepest thanks to my family for putting up with me during the course of this project. Special thanks go to my husband, Eric Helleiner, who listened to me for many hours and made helpful suggestions along the way.

# Abbreviations

| | |
|---|---|
| AFA | Alliance for Food Aid |
| AIA | advance informed agreement |
| CAP | Common Agricultural Policy of the European Community |
| CCC | Commodity Credit Corporation |
| CCP | Committee on Commodity Problems of the Food and Agriculture Organization of the UN |
| CFA | Comprehensive Framework for Action of the UN High-Level Task Force |
| CFGB | Canadian Foodgrains Bank |
| CFS | Committee on World Food Security of the Food and Agriculture Organization |
| CIDA | Canadian International Development Agency |
| CIEC | Paris Conference on International Economic Cooperation |
| CIF | cost, insurance, and freight |
| COMESA | Common Market for Eastern and Southern Africa |
| CSSD | Consultative Subcommittee on Surplus Disposal for the Committee on Commodity Problems |
| CWB | Canadian Wheat Board |
| DAC | Development Assistance Committee of the Organisation for Economic Cooperation and Development |
| EC | European Community |
| ECHO | European Community Humanitarian Office |
| EU | European Union |
| FAC | Food Aid Convention |
| FACE | Food Aid Coordination and Evaluation Centre |
| FAO | Food and Agriculture Organization of the United Nations |
| FFP | food, feed, and processing |
| G-8 | Group of Eight |
| G-20 | Group of Twenty (leading economies) |
| G20-WTO | Group of Twenty (agricultural negotiating block at the WTO) |
| G33-WTO | Group of Thirty-three (agricultural negotiating block at the WTO) |
| GAFSP | Global Agriculture and Food Security Program |
| GAO | Government Accountability Office of the United States |

| | |
|---|---|
| GATT | General Agreement on Tariffs and Trade |
| GMO | genetically modified organisms |
| HLTF | United Nations High-Level Task Force on the Global Food Security Crisis |
| IFAD | International Fund for Agricultural Development |
| IFPRI | International Food Policy Research Institute |
| IGC | International Grains Council |
| JICA | Japan International Cooperation Agency |
| LDC | least developed countries |
| LRP | local and regional procurement |
| MSF | Médicins Sans Frontières (Doctors Without Borders) |
| NFIDC | net-food-importing developing countries |
| NGO | nongovernmental organization |
| NIEO | New International Economic Order |
| OAU | Organization of African Unity |
| ODA | official development assistance |
| OECD | Organisation for Economic Cooperation and Development |
| OMB | Office of Management and Budget |
| OPEC | Organization of Petroleum Exporting Countries |
| P4P | Purchase for Progress program (WFP) |
| PL 480 | Public Law 83-480 (U.S. Agricultural Trade Development and Assistance Act) |
| PVO | private voluntary organization |
| RUF | ready-to-use foods |
| SADC | Southern African Development Community |
| STE | state trading enterprise |
| TAFAD | Transatlantic Food Assistance Dialogue |
| TNC | transnational corporation |
| UMR | usual marketing requirements |
| UNCTAD | United Nations Conference on Trade and Development |
| UNICEF | United Nations Children's Fund |
| URAA | Uruguay Round Agreement on Agriculture |
| USAID | U.S. Agency for International Development |
| USDA | U.S. Department of Agriculture |
| WFP | World Food Programme |
| WTC | Wheat Trade Convention |
| WTO | World Trade Organization |

# FOOD AID POLITICS

## The Old and the New

More than 900 million people on the planet are undernourished. Food aid has long been one of many responses to global hunger. It is by no means the primary response or the best approach to ensuring food security. Nevertheless, some 150–200 million people depend on food aid every year. In situations of acute food shortages, particularly when crises hit people who are already suffering from chronic undernourishment, such aid can mean the difference between life and death. And food intervention in the first two years of a child's life can make enormous improvements in both long-term health and quality of life.

Food aid as a response to global hunger has been controversial ever since institutionalized food-aid programs began in donor countries in the 1950s and 1960s. In the early years, debates over food aid centered largely on the geopolitics of the Cold War and the trade and development impacts of surplus disposal of donor grains in poor countries. By the 1980s and 1990s, many felt that donors had moved beyond dumping unwanted grain and seeking political favors and had begun to use food aid as a development tool geared more toward recipient needs than those of the donor. In political terms, food aid moved to the back pages, and was assumed to have taken on a largely uncontroversial role. But in the last decade, it once again began to make front-page headlines, though not in the ways it had in the past. Although the debates and contexts were different, the level of passion about the issue ran just as high.

This book seeks to explain why food aid politics have become so heated in recent years. I argue that the renewed politicization of food aid is linked to two major developments. The first is the emergence of different, but strongly held, viewpoints among donors regarding the appropriateness of providing aid in its tied, commodity form—that is, food aid given in kind to the recipient country as a direct transfer of food sourced in the donor country. The second is that food aid has become increasingly linked to other international debates—over agricultural biotechnology, over international agricultural trade rules, and over the reorganization of global food security governance in the face of a new global food crisis. These debates have been particularly intense between the major food aid donors: the European Union (EU) and the United States. The fact that these two donors follow different policies with respect to tied food aid has only made these debates more heated.

What is the significance of these new debates? Although food aid as a development resource has shrunk significantly since its early days by comparison with other forms of assistance, the stakes are very high. The political controversies over food aid are important in determining whether it can play a helpful role in addressing world hunger. It is by no means clear that food aid will continue to play the role it has in the past. Its future will depend on the outcomes of debates over the most appropriate mode of delivery of food assistance and over the relationship of food aid to the other international debates noted above. And for the several hundred million people who at present have little choice but to rely on food aid for their daily survival, the outcome of these debates is crucial.

## Past Understandings of Food Aid Politics

A great deal of scholarly literature has looked at various aspects of food aid since it became a major component of international aid programs in the 1950s and 1960s. Since that time, food aid policies and practices have evolved. Economic studies have kept pace with these changes and provide a good picture of their economic implications, for both donor and recipient countries.[1] But there have been relatively few explicitly *political* analyses of food aid in recent decades, particularly with respect to the dynamics of donor country policymaking and its ramifications for international-level debates over food aid. At a time of intense debate over food aid, both at the international level and within certain donor countries, it is important to uncover the reasons that food aid has become so politicized.

Early studies on the politics of international food aid focused primarily on the interests of donor states. Realist approaches within the field of international

---

1. See, for example, Barrett and Maxwell 2005; Clay and Stokke 2000b.

relations focused on states' self-interest—both economic and political—as a key driver of policy. Realist scholars saw food aid as a classic example of donor self-interest. Food aid served both the domestic interest of donor states in supporting their farm sectors and their foreign policy interests. The former included a desire to remove surplus grain from markets in order to bolster farmers' incomes. The latter included the development of international markets for their surplus agricultural products and the use of food as a tool to influence policies of recipient states as part of their diplomatic and strategic efforts to gain political leverage during the Cold War.[2] Food aid was often used as both a carrot and a stick, particularly by the U.S. government, in the 1950s and 1960s with respect to these aims. These factors were widely recognized as the primary driving forces of food aid policy in its early years.

More radical scholars of international relations and development studies also emphasized the material self-interests within donor countries that drove policy decisions. Not unlike the realists, this literature focused on the ways in which donor states used food aid as a mercantilist tool to establish new commercial market outlets for their surplus.[3] For radicals, this practice transformed countries that were once self-sufficient into highly dependent recipients of food aid and commercial food imports.[4] Radical scholars also saw food aid as a means by which to bolster capitalist agribusiness interests within donor states, especially agricultural producer groups and the grain trading and processing firms that often supplied the food. Their critique, not unlike early economic critiques of food aid, also pointed to the potential distortions to farmer incentives in poor countries that surplus disposal by donor countries could create.[5]

Partially in response to a growing popular critique of the self-interested nature of donor food-aid policies, and partially as a product of changing circumstances, some changes in food aid policies were ushered in during the 1970s and 1980s.[6] The 1970s food crisis in particular brought attention to the donor-oriented and geopolitical nature of food aid, prompting increased allocation to more needy recipient countries. This shift occurred in the context of overall lower food aid donations in the 1970s and the unwinding of the Cold War by the late 1980s.

These modifications in the context and practice of food aid prompted some scholars to reinterpret donor motives in food-aid politics and policymaking.[7]

---

2. An examination of food aid policies along these lines is offered in Wallerstein 1980.

3. Friedmann 1982, 1993; Cohn 1990; Cathie 1982.

4. Friedmann 1982.

5. For an early economic analysis of potential disincentive effects of food aid, see Schultz 1960; on this debate, see also Isenman and Singer 1977.

6. On the popular critique, see Jackson 1982; George 1976.

7. Uvin 1992; Hopkins 1992.

Drawing on liberal institutionalist approaches to international relations, these thinkers argued that the interest-based approaches of the realists and the radicals were no longer as relevant as they had been previously. They contended that food aid was increasingly shaped by norms of international development cooperation promoted by international institutions such as the World Food Programme (WFP), the UN agency that provides a multilateral channel for food aid, rather than by donors seeking to dispose of donor surplus grain. Peter Uvin, for example, argued that after the mid-1970s a development-oriented international "regime" for food aid began to emerge that was geared toward recipient needs rather than donor self-interest.[8] As Uvin notes, "Food aid donation is increasingly governed by multilateral institutions, norms and procedures."[9]

This institutionalist interpretation of food aid policies was complemented by constructivist analyses that focused on norms and ideas as key factors in shaping donor policies. Raymond Hopkins, for example, highlighted the emergence and influence of an "epistemic community" of like-minded development experts who held shared notions of what constitutes appropriate food aid policies.[10] These food aid experts, Hopkins argued, identified improvements to make food aid policies more development-based and needs-oriented. They championed their ideas to improve the development effectiveness of food aid through international institutions such as the WFP, which subsequently filtered down to influence donor-state policies. Hopkins noted that the WFP had increased its role significantly by the late 1980s, and had "become the major arena in which new norms for all food aid were being articulated." The result, he argued, was incremental reform of food aid policies away from those that primarily serve donor self-interest and toward policies that better serve the poor.[11]

These new interpretations of food aid politics in the 1990s were important in opening up our understanding of the range of forces that influence donor policies. Beyond material interests, norms and ideas were increasingly seen to affect at least some aspects of donor policies that were in need of change. Most donors have reformed their food aid policies since the mid-1970s to reduce practices such as the allocation of aid to geopolitically important countries, rather than those most in need, and large-scale disposal of donor surpluses that result in gross distortions in agricultural trade and on local markets in recipient countries. Norms against these practices are now widely accepted.[12] Similarly, the WFP, as

8. Uvin 1992.
9. Ibid., 303.
10. Hopkins, 1992, 230; the concept of epistemic communities was first introduced by Haas 1992.
11. Hopkins 1992, 230.
12. Uvin 1992; Hopkins 1992.

the key institution for multilateral food aid, has taken a far greater role in the provision of food aid and has been important in shaping the food aid regime in practical terms.

The liberal institutionalist and constructivist contributions to the debate suggested that incremental reforms to food aid were well under way by the early 1990s and that donor self-interest had diminished significantly. Food aid was, as a result, largely considered by scholars in the field to be no longer driven by political and economic interests. Instead, it played a more functional role in fostering international development, shaped by an international regime that established the rules and norms for food aid and upheld by international institutions. But far from becoming depoliticized as these analyses suggested, food aid became highly political again by the early 2000s. Yet surprisingly, few studies have been published since the 1990s that address broad debates on the politics of food aid in the international context. It is again time to update our understandings of the politics of food aid.

## A New Politics of Food Aid

The international political clashes over food aid since the early 2000s have differed in some important ways from earlier politics surrounding this form of assistance. At the same time, some aspects of today's food aid politics are linked to long-standing issues, especially with respect to donors' economic interests. Old debates about the use of food aid to further foreign policy goals or dispose of grain surpluses have given way to debates over *how* food aid is given. In particular, the question of whether food aid is tied to food sourced in the donor country has generated heated exchanges between donors. As some donors began to untie their food aid, divisions among donors emerged. At the same time, and not entirely unrelated to the tying question, food aid has been launched into new political arenas where it has been fiercely debated in contexts that could not easily have been foreseen only a decade earlier.

### Tied Food Aid: A New Dividing Line between Donors

The earlier literature on the politics of food aid did not foresee the potential political divisions that would emerge over the practice of tying food aid. Tying was largely a given—an assumed feature of food aid. Donors gave what food they had available to give. Indeed, a key rationale for donor countries to give food aid in the first place was the fact that it could be tied to food procured within their borders as a means to dispose of surpluses. This rationale was especially prominent in the key grain-producing countries: the United States, Canada, and Australia. It also became important in Europe which had been a net food importer in the 1950s and 1960s but began to produce more food than it consumed by the 1970s. Indeed, most food aid was tied to donor-sourced food well into the 1990s, and the practice provoked little debate at the time. But food surpluses were no longer held by governments by the late 1980s and early 1990s as a result of restructuring of agricultural and farm policies within donor states. Food aid continued to be tied but under new circumstances, where donor governments procured food on open markets.

In these new circumstances, the European Union took steps to untie its food aid in the mid-1990s. A decade later, Australia and Canada followed suit. The United States, however, as the world's largest donor of food aid, continued with a nearly 100 percent tied food aid policy. Japan, which had previously sourced in other countries the food aid it provided, increasingly tied its aid starting in the 1990s after it was no longer itself dependent on food imports. The division that emerged between donors over whether food aid should or should not be tied sparked enormous controversy. Countries that untied their food aid accused those that did not of using food aid to support their own domestic agricultural sectors. The donors who untied their aid argued that procuring food assistance closer to the point of use was a more efficient, timely, and effective response, particularly because it provided incentives for farmers in developing countries to produce more food rather than rely on foreign-source food shipped in from afar.

The idea of untying food aid is not a new one. It had in fact been championed by development experts since at least the mid-1970s. The Paris Conference on International Economic Cooperation (CIEC), a meeting of twenty-seven governments representing industrialized, oil-producing, and developing countries held in 1975–77 as part of global negotiations on a New International Economic Order (NIEO), strongly promoted the idea in its final declaration. It noted that where appropriate, donor countries should try "to provide food aid through cash resources in the form of triangular arrangements between themselves, developing food exporting countries and recipient countries."[13] Although the untying of food aid was promoted by development experts alongside other proposed food aid reforms, the uptake of the idea was very slow and uneven among donors, and these differences resulted in political clashes between them.

As will be shown, the maintenance of policies that tied food aid to donor country sourcing until the mid-1990s (and in some cases even today) indicates that economic self-interest continued to influence donor policymaking well after

---

13. Quoted in Cohn 1979, 66.

other reforms to food aid had taken place. Despite the promotion of new norms at the international level with respect to untying food aid, economic interests of donor states and actors that operate within those states have had a key influence over the direction of policies in donor countries that tie their food aid. And even when we look more closely at those donors who have untied their food aid in recent decades, it becomes clear that economic interests played a role in their decision. The enduring role of economic self-interest in influencing donor policies shows that constructivist and institutionalist approaches to food aid politics, that focused on ideas and institutions as the key driving forces, cannot alone explain the evolution of the food aid regime. Indeed, to explain divergent donor policies vis-à-vis the tying of tied food aid, it is important to return to some of the concepts presented in the earlier literature on donor food aid policies that focused on the material interest of states in expanding export markets and the interests of agribusiness.

At the same time, however, the mix of actors with an economic interest in tied food aid today is more complex than in the past, especially in the United States. For example, it is not just agribusiness that has a stake in tied food aid. Nongovernmental organizations (NGOs) based in the United States that are charged with programming and delivering food aid also have a strong economic stake in the maintenance of tied food aid policies because their own organizations depend on it as a key source of revenue. These organizations have lobbied to maintain those policies and their voices have been influential. The shipping industry in the United States is also a keen supporter of in-kind food aid because it benefits directly from U.S. rules that require such aid to be transported on U.S.-flagged vessels.[14] Some economists had pointed to the significance of these actors in influencing U.S. food aid policy even as early as the mid-1990s, but few political scientists have picked up on this analysis to explain the repoliticization of food aid in a global context.[15]

The significance of these domestic interests in shaping the food aid policies of donor states highlights another weakness of the constructivist and institutionalist analyses of food aid. Although they correctly noted the emergence of new ideas and their promotion by international institutions, those studies tended to overplay the significance of the international institutional context in shaping donor policy. International institutions are certainly important in promoting new norms. But no matter how much those institutions push for the adoption of certain types of policies, donor countries are still the source of food aid and they are the ones that set the policies that govern their donations. Although an

---

14. Barrett and Maxwell 2005.
15. Ruttan 1993; Barrett and Maxwell 2005.

increasing share of international food aid is delivered via the WFP, for example, the agency still relies on donors for its funding and must abide by any restrictions they place on their donations. This reality points to the need to look more deeply into the domestic institutional and economic context of donor countries to understand how and why policies on tying have emerged in different ways.

The continued wide divergence of tied-aid policies among donors illustrates that the evolution of the food aid regime is far more complex than a gradual diffusion of new ideas promoted by international institutions. A deeper political understanding of when those ideas translate into actual policy change within donor states is necessary to fully comprehend why some countries have untied their food aid while others have not.

## New Political Debates over Food Aid

Early studies of the international politics of food aid focused on its linkage to the Cold War. By the time East-West tensions eased in late 1980s, food aid had largely become delinked from security issues. And with the end of grain surpluses in donor countries, as noted above, it was assumed that food aid had become detached from donors' broader economic interests as well. Although food aid is no longer associated with these particular dynamics, it has since become linked to new political interactions outside the immediate food aid regime. Since the late 1990s food aid has become entangled in international disputes over agricultural biotechnology, the setting of international agricultural trade rules, and discussions on reforming the architecture of global food security governance. These are very different from the past contexts within which food aid was debated. As the global economic and political context has changed, food aid debates have changed in response.[16]

### AGRICULTURAL BIOTECHNOLOGY
### AND INTERNATIONAL BIOSAFETY

The international debate over agricultural biotechnology intensified in the late 1990s and early 2000s.[17] Genetically modified crops were not grown commercially until the mid-1990s, and earlier writings did not foresee that food aid would become so tightly connected to this issue.[18] As the United States

---

16. Clay and Stokke 2000a noted this changed context early on and identified the shifting nature of food aid debates. Since that time, these debates have evolved further and have become highly politicized.

17. See, for example, Bernauer 2003.

18. Several studies were published on this theme at the time, however, such as Zerbe 2004 and Clapp 2005.

increasingly adopted agricultural biotechnology for key internationally traded grains, in particular corn and soy, tensions grew with other countries that had not approved those same organisms for either consumption or planting. From 1998 to 2003, the European Union had in place an effective moratorium on the approval of genetically modified organisms (GMOs), meaning that it refused to import genetically modified grains from the United States. This stance sparked a serious backlash, and a transatlantic war of words over the science and safety of GMOs erupted.[19]

International rules regarding the trade in genetically modified organisms were under discussion from 1996 to 2001 as part of the Cartagena Protocol on Biosafety. But in the late 1990s and early 2000s, prior to the ratification of that agreement, there was much uncertainty about how to handle this trade.[20] Many developing countries, lacking the scientific expertise to establish their own biosafety policies, began to follow the EU's lead regarding the import of GMOs. Because U.S. food aid is tied to U.S.-grown agricultural commodities, and because that country does not segregate GM from non-GM grains, it was inevitable that GMOs would end up in food aid shipped from the United States to countries that had not approved them. Incidents of GM food aid in southern Africa in the early 2000s fueled debates over GMOs and over the tying of food aid. Tensions between the United States and southern African countries were very high, with the United States accusing leaders in the region of turning their backs on hungry people. The incidents also sparked tensions between the United States and Europe, as Washington accused the EU of stoking fear of GMOs in developing countries.[21]

### AGRICULTURAL TRADE AT THE WTO

There have long been concerns that food aid has the potential to distort international agricultural trade as well as farmer incentives in developing countries.[22] Rules to ensure that commercial agricultural trade is not displaced by food aid have been in place under the United Nations Food and Agriculture Organization (FAO) since the 1950s. It was largely assumed that these rules were adequate to ensure that food aid did not distort international trade in agricultural commodities. Agricultural trade was not subject to international trade rules under the General Agreement on Tariffs and Trade (GATT) until the Uruguay Round of trade negotiations was completed in 1994, creating not only an agricultural

---

19. Prakash and Kollmann 2003; Bernauer and Meins 2003.
20. See, for example, Gupta 2000; Falkner 2007a.
21. See Paarlberg 2002.
22. On this question, see for example Schultz 1960; Isenman and Singer 1977; Maxwell and Singer 1979.

agreement but also the World Trade Organization (WTO).[23] The major trade players had resisted strict trade rules on agriculture until the mid-1980s, when agricultural protectionism became very costly to maintain. The Uruguay Round Agriculture Agreement (URAA) sought to bring levels of domestic agricultural support under control, reduce export subsidies, and improve market access by reducing tariff levels and other trade barriers. The URAA also contained wording that encouraged member countries not to use food aid as a way to circumvent their obligations to reduce export subsidies.[24] The agreement asked donor countries to meet minimum food aid commitments under the Food Aid Convention (FAC), an international agreement among donors that commits them to provide a certain amount of food aid each year, because of concern that agricultural trade reform might have negative implications for food security in developing countries.[25]

The URAA was widely seen as inadequate to the task of reducing distortions in international agricultural trade and as particularly detrimental to developing countries.[26] When the Doha Round of trade talks was launched in 2001, renegotiation of the URAA was a key priority. In the early stages of these talks, it became clear that the EU planned to press the rest of the WTO membership to adopt more stringent rules on tied food aid in return for concessions on the reduction of its own export subsidies. Food aid thus became wrapped up in the broader politics of agriculture trade rules, which pitted the United States against the EU.[27] The WTO, in turn, became yet another international political arena in which food aid was hotly debated.[28]

## GLOBAL FOOD SECURITY GOVERNANCE

Food prices have climbed markedly since 2006, exacerbated by rising volatility.[29] The food price spikes in 2007–8 sparked an international food crisis that pushed hundreds of millions of people into the category of "food insecure," that is, not having enough to eat to lead a healthy and productive life.[30] In this context, pressure mounted for reforms to the architecture of international food security

---

23. See Anderson and Martin 2005; Josling and Hathaway 2004.
24. Shaw and Singer 1996; Christiansen 2000.
25. Christensen 2000, 261.
26. Murphy, Lilliston, and Lake 2005.
27. Clapp 2006.
28. Konandreas 2007; Clay 2006; Barrett and Maxwell 2006.
29. Heady and Fan 2008; Clapp and Cohen 2009.
30. The FAO defined food security at the 1996 World Food Summit as follows: "Food security exists when all people, at all times, have physical and economic access to sufficient, safe and nutritious food that meets their dietary needs and food preferences for an active and healthy life." FAO 2006c.

governance.[31] Food aid is only one part of the broad constellation of governance mechanisms and institutions that touch on global food security, but it has been the focus of much discussion and debate. In the midst of the food price spikes, for example, the WFP was forced to make an emergency appeal to donors to drastically increase their donations because it could not meet its feeding targets with its existing budget. This appeal raised the issue of tied food aid, as the WFP asked specifically for cash funding to enable local and regional purchase.[32]

Calls have also been made to renew the Food Aid Convention.[33] The 1999 FAC formally expired in 2002, and the out-of-date agreement has been extended each year since in order to give time for the Doha Round of negotiations in the WTO to finish first. But with the WTO talks indefinitely stalled and with global hunger rising, talks began in mid-2010 to renegotiate the FAC. The form in which food aid should be pledged has been a sensitive topic within the FAC membership: some prefer a move to monetary value commitments, while others insist on maintaining commitments in tons of wheat or its equivalent. Another question up for debate is whether the FAC should remain a separate, donor-only agreement with its secretariat located in London under the International Grains Council (IGC) or whether the agreement should widen its membership and be placed within the constellation of broader food security mechanisms, including the WFP and FAO, which are housed in Rome. At the same time, it is unclear what level of overall commitment donors are willing to make to the FAC. Some donors, such as the United States, have signaled a desire to move away from food aid as a key response to global hunger, instead preferring to promote agricultural production with new technologies in developing countries. The EU, on the other hand, is pushing to make the FAC more of an emergency relief agreement rather than a broader food security mechanism.

The existing literature on the international politics of food aid has not fully examined these new contexts in which food aid has been politicized in recent years. Indeed, there have been relatively few studies emanating from the field of international relations on the topic since the 1990s. Similarly, the literature on agricultural biotechnology, international agricultural trade politics, and global food security governance have mentioned food aid but have not focused on it, primarily because it occupies a unique place within the broader debates in those fields. Given the recent changes in the international political arena, it is now important that we deepen our understanding of the current political dynamics of food aid.

---

31. See, for example, Oxfam International 2009.
32. WFP 2008b.
33. See Hoddinott, Cohen, and Barrett 2008.

## Outline of the Book

Chapter 2 sets the broader context for discussion and analysis by outlining past and current trends in international food assistance. It highlights the ways in which food aid has changed over the years in terms of its allocation, volume, and form. The chapter then examines the current debate over tied food aid. It maps out the critiques of tying that have been put forward and examines other forms of food assistance, such as the allocation of cash financial resources for local and regional purchase and the direct distribution of cash and vouchers to recipients along with their benefits and risks.

The next two chapters examine trends in the major donor countries with respect to the question of tying and untying food aid. Chapter 3 focuses on policy development in the European Union, Canada, and Australia as the major donors that have untied their food aid. It also looks at Japan as a donor whose policies have become more tied in recent decades. Chapter 4 then focuses in depth on food aid policy decision making in the United States, the largest donor of food aid. In each case, an examination of the interaction between ideas, the institutional policy-setting context, and material interests, particularly at the domestic level, helps to explain trends in donor food aid policy.

Chapter 5 examines the donor-recipient and donor-donor tensions that emerged in 2002 over the GMOs found in food aid delivered to southern Africa. The incident was widely publicized and generated enormous debate, not just with respect to the suitability of GMOs as food aid but also because it was a product of the U.S. policy of tied food aid. Different interpretations of scientific risk, unclear international rules, and economic interests in donor states all played into the political dynamics of this controversy.

Chapter 6 focuses on the way in which food aid once again became a hot political topic in the context of the ongoing WTO Doha Round of trade talks, launched in 2001. Tensions grew among donors in 2004–6 as the European Union made the case that in-kind, tied food aid is an unfair and market-distorting export subsidy to producers in donor countries, a claim that the United States strongly resisted. Despite this basic disagreement, WTO members agreed in principle that some restrictions should be placed on in-kind food aid to ensure that it was not market-distorting but maintained the acceptability of tied food aid in genuine emergencies. The Doha round has not yet reached a conclusion, however, and it remains to be seen whether these rules will be included in the final deal.

Chapter 7 looks at the way in which food aid became the subject of continued debate at the international institutional level in 2007–8, when world food prices rose dramatically and had a serious impact on the ability of the WFP to provide enough food to address the rise in hunger. The specter of food aid shortfalls prompted the WFP to ask donors to increase their aid commitments and in particular to make cash available as part of those donations. Long-distance shipments had become increasingly expensive as oil prices reached record high levels. In such a context, local purchases could have been much more efficient and effective than tied aid shipped over great distances. The situation also sparked a growing chorus of calls from international experts for reforms to the Food Aid Convention. In the context of these negotiations, differences emerged between the United States and the EU over how the role, form, and purpose of food aid should be articulated in the agreement.

Chapter 8 offers concluding analysis and examines new trends on the horizon of food aid politics.

## The Broader Implications of Food Aid Politics

Recipients of food aid in developing countries are profoundly affected by the international political dynamics around donor food aid policy. Yet while recipient country governments are acutely aware of the potential impacts of donor policies on their own food security situations, they have had only a marginal voice in most international forums over this issue.[34] Recipients are effectively shut out of domestic policymaking decisions in donor countries, and developing countries have been afforded only a small role in the broader international discussions. This is because the major donor countries, especially the United States and the EU, have dominated the debates. Further, some food aid recipient countries are not members of the WTO or the Cartagena Protocol, and none are members of the FAC, which means they are effectively excluded from international decision making in these forums.

Yet this debate is crucially important for the world's poorest and most vulnerable developing countries and their hungry citizens who have become reliant on food aid over the past fifty years. Food aid can make up a substantial portion of the budget in the least developed countries. Over the 1994–2003 period, for example, food aid accounted for between 15 and 20 percent of food imports in the least developed countries, many of which are in sub-Saharan Africa.[35] In some cases, the reliance on food aid is much more extreme. In 2001–3, for example, food aid made up 46 percent of Ethiopia's entire food supply, while it comprised at least 5 percent of the total food supply of nineteen other countries.[36] A large

---

34. Except for the WFP, where developing countries make up the majority of members of its governing executive board.
35. Clay 2006, 3.
36. FAO 2007, 4.

number of countries rely on food aid in emergency situations, which are difficult to predict in advance. However, as the number of emergencies has increased in recent decades, the share of food aid provided for emergency relief has risen. Today, over three-quarters of food aid is provided in response to emergencies, with sub-Saharan Africa experiencing a significant rise in food emergencies.[37]

The recent increase in food prices has raised the stakes on the debate over food aid for countries that count on food assistance to meet an important share of their food security needs. Reforms to food aid policies that reduce the amount of in-kind aid and increase cash funding for local purchase of food could stretch food aid dollars much further and reach more people in need, particularly in times of crisis. But such changes could also reduce political support for food aid in donor countries, in turn affecting the overall levels of aid provided. Any reforms that are undertaken will also need to be carefully coordinated with policies to boost domestic production in the world's poorest countries. Reaching the right balance with respect to reform of food aid policies will be difficult, to say the least. The current global food situation underlines the importance of understanding the forces behind recent political clashes over food aid, as well as the requirements for effective food aid policy reform.

------

37. FAO 2007.

# 2

# PAST AND PRESENT FOOD ASSISTANCE TRENDS

In order to fully grasp the current landscape of food aid politics, it is important to first look back briefly to its origins and to trace its evolution over the years.[1] The international political and economic context in which food aid operates today is very different from the context in which it first emerged as a form of international development assistance. In its early days, food aid policy was driven largely by forces no longer relevant in the current context: sizable grain surpluses needing to be disposed of, which determined the largest donors, and geopolitical considerations of the Cold War, which determined the most likely recipients. Humanitarian concerns always underlay food aid policies, but the economic and political considerations of donor countries typically dictated the terms. Starting in the mid-1970s, food aid became more oriented toward the needs of recipient countries, aiming to address their broader development goals. Today food aid is increasingly serving an important role as a resource in emergency situations—ranging from natural disasters to conflict—in developing countries.[2]

We now know a lot more today than we used to about the impact of food aid, especially in recipient countries. The problems associated with tied food aid in particular, as well as the unpredictable amounts allocated from year to year, have

---

1. Others have provided a comprehensive review of food aid's origins (e.g., Barrett and Maxwell 2005; Cathie 1982, 1997; Clay and Stokke 1991; Wallerstein 1980); this chapter will focus instead on trends in food aid policies.

2. These shifts in focus of the food aid regime from surplus disposal to development to humanitarian goals is outlined in Hopkins 2009 and Clay 2003.

presented challenges for countries that receive it. Because recipient countries lack a strong voice in international food aid policy formulation, there is little they can do to directly influence policy outcomes in donor countries. In some ways, international food aid policies have been adjusted over the years to adapt to the new political and economic context as well as our improved understanding of food aid impacts. Yet while the context has changed and we know much more, there are still remnants of the original policies in place in some donor countries, such as the tying of food aid to grain grown in donor countries, that critics say are leading to counterproductive and inefficient outcomes. This chapter outlines the broad trends in food aid over the years in terms of donor policy directions, food aid flows in practice, and our understanding of the impact of tied food aid and other forms of food assistance.

## Food Aid's Early Years

Regular programs of food assistance began to be adopted by donor countries starting in the 1950s. Prior to that time there were international transfers of food on a more ad hoc basis, responding to emergency situations, such as U.S. aid to Venezuela following an earthquake in 1812, aid to Ireland in the mid-1800s, and assistance to Europe and the Soviet Union during the First World War.[3] The more regularized food aid programs that came later were intimately tied with domestic agricultural support programs in donor countries. In the United States, agricultural price support policies practiced from the 1930s as part of the New Deal legislation were retained after the Second World War. Tight supply and higher food prices during the war prompted governments in grain-growing countries to build up additional stocks after the war had ended. By the early 1950s these surplus stocks were significant and began to pose problems for countries that held them.[4] Large grain-producing countries struggled to cover the cost of storing a growing mountain of food, and food prices began to plummet because the stocks were so large. At the same time, European countries devastated by the war, as well as several Asian countries, were in food deficit. This stark inequality in the global distribution of food was an early impetus for institutionalized global grain redistribution in the form of international food aid.[5]

In the early postwar years, various countries, including Canada, Australia, and the United States, experimented with transfers of food as a form of international

---

3. On this early history, see Ruttan 1993, 4–5.
4. Friedmann 1993.
5. See Hopkins 1992, 229–30.

assistance. In 1947 the United States launched the European Recovery Plan, also known as the Marshall Plan, to send aid to war-torn European countries. Although it was not initially intended as a mechanism to transfer food aid, in the five years that followed, 29 percent—worth approximately $4 billion—of the total aid sent by the United States through this program was in the form of food, feed and fertilizer.[6] Food aid was also directed to developing countries in this period. Canada and Australia began to provide food aid to Asian countries in the early 1950s when they became members of the Colombo Plan, an organization composed of Commonwealth countries that focused on development cooperation in South and Southeast Asia.[7] In 1954 the United States passed the Agricultural Trade Development and Assistance Act (Public Law 83-480, also known as PL 480 and Food for Peace), which set the parameters for U.S. food assistance to developing countries.

In the early days, as is still the case today, the United States was by far the largest donor of food aid. In the 1960s this dominance was overwhelming. In 1963, for example, the United States supplied 96 percent of all international food aid.[8] It sold food aid on terms that were easier than fully commercial sales to countries that were able to buy it and gave it away in grant form to those that were not, as well as in emergency situations. The sales, referred to as concessional sales, were still considered aid because they were sold at lower prices than those that prevail on international markets or on credit at below-market interest rates with long periods for repayment, or both. Unlike the United States, Canada and Australia supplied all of their food aid in grant form. The early food aid programs were driven by and served multiple objectives: economic, political, and humanitarian. Economically, food aid was attractive as a means by which to dispose of large grain surpluses. Farm support policies in the Unites States, for example, meant that the government acted as a buyer of last resort at a set price. This policy gave farmers stability and assurance that they would be able to sell their crops. But it also gave the government the problem of storing the stocks and managing them so as to prevent a collapse in prices on the open market. It was expensive for governments to store this grain, and its mere presence put downward pressure on prices. Disposing of excess grain in the form of food aid to food-deficit countries—especially developing countries—seemed to be an obvious answer to these problems. Although selling the grain abroad on a commercial basis would have been the first obvious choice, the food-deficit countries lacked hard currency with which to purchase it. The second-best option of giving the grain away—or in the

---

6. See Singer, Wood, and Jennings 1987, 20; Friedmann 1990, 13.
7. Barrett and Maxwell 2005, 51–52; Shaw and Clay 1993, 143.
8. IWC Secretariat 1991, 2.

U.S. case of selling it at a discount or on credit—was seen by donor countries as a promising path to eventually selling it at full price once recipient countries were able to purchase it on commercial terms. Some early recipients of food aid—such as South Korea, Indonesia, and the Philippines, for example—became important export markets for the United States.[9] Food aid policies in this era thus became important ingredients in the maintenance of nationally managed agricultural systems in donor countries. Some analysts, including Harriet Friedmann and Theodore Cohn, argue that food aid policies were part of a broader mercantile approach to agricultural policy, especially on the part of the United States.[10]

Because the initial economic rationale for food aid was to dispose of surpluses, in most cases it was explicitly tied to grain grown in the donor country. But as food aid programs were being established, other agricultural exporting countries besides the United States—whose program was by far the largest—became concerned that food aid could harm their own commercial exports to countries that received the aid. To address this issue, the Committee on Commodity Problems (CCP) of the FAO adopted the Principles of Surplus Disposal in 1954, the same year that the United States adopted PL 480, largely in response to complaints from other grain exporters that U.S. food aid programs were merely "dumping" under the guise of foreign assistance.[11] The Principles of Surplus Disposal are a nonbinding code of conduct that seeks to prevent the disposal of agricultural surpluses in the form of food aid from disrupting domestic production or displacing normal amounts of commercial imports in recipient countries. Keeping up levels of normal commercial trade also ensures that food assistance is additional consumption on the part of recipients and not merely the displacement of commercial sales.[12]

The CCP established the Consultative Subcommittee on Surplus Disposal (CSSD) in 1954 to monitor food aid transactions to ensure that they follow these principles. The CSSD membership is made up of both donors and recipients, and its secretariat is housed in Washington, D.C. Food aid donors were and still are required to report their transactions to the CSSD, which then reviews the market implications.[13] Donors reported regularly to the CSSD in its early days, although since 2000 reporting has dropped significantly.[14] The establishment of the CSSD was in many respects an open acknowledgment by donors from very early on of the potential for food aid to result in market distortions.

---

9. Mousseau 2005, 6.
10. Friedmann 1993; Cohn 1990.
11. Ruttan 1993, 16.
12. See FAO 2001, 3.
13. FAO 2007, 17–18.
14. See FAO Committee on Commodity Problems 2010.

In addition to serving the economic agenda of the donor countries, food aid policies also had political benefits. In the United States, food aid served as an important tool of its foreign policy, particularly during the Cold War.[15] As the U.S. senator Hubert Humphrey, one of the key proponents of the early U.S. food aid programs, notoriously declared in 1953, "We have got to look at America's food abundance, not as a liability, but as a real asset.... Wise statesmanship and real leadership can convert these surpluses into a great asset for checking communist aggression. Communism has no greater ally than hunger; and democracy and freedom no greater ally than an abundance of food."[16]

And the United States did use its food aid policies aggressively as a means by which to collect allies in the developing world during the this period. During the 1960s, for example, U.S. food aid went predominantly to Vietnam, South Korea, Cambodia, and Taiwan, all important U.S. allies that were embroiled in Cold War conflicts at the time.[17] The United States also refused food aid to certain countries on the basis of their political alliances during the Cold War. In 1973, for instance, despite severe food shortages and rising food prices, the United States withheld food aid shipments to Bangladesh because the country exported jute to Cuba. By the time Bangladesh agreed to the U.S. insistence that it stop the exports before food aid could be resumed, the country was ravaged by floods and famine.[18] For Canada, food aid was also allocated in ways that could be perceived as political, especially given that it focused the majority of its aid on just four countries—Bangladesh, India, Pakistan, and Sri Lanka—as a means by which to increase its presence in South Asia as part of its participation in the Colombo Plan.[19]

The economic and political motivations were important for these early food aid donors even as those donors highlighted humanitarian goals in the justification and promotion of their policies to a wider public. The idea of sharing the bounty with the developing world, particularly Cold War allies, was a large part of the public appeal of food aid. The United States, Canada, and Australia began broader programs of international development assistance in the 1950s, and food aid made up a significant part of those programs. In the 1960s and 1970s it made up approximately 20 to 25 percent of all official development assistance (ODA).[20]

---

15. See Uvin 1992; Hopkins 1993; Wallerstein 1980.
16. Quoted in Reutlinger 1999, 9.
17. See Uvin 1992, 297.
18. Sobhan, 1979.
19. Barrett and Maxwell 2005, 52.
20. Clay 2003, 698; Clay, Riley, and Urey 2006, 14.

## Sharing the Food Aid Burden

Food aid started out as a set of donor bilateral policies, but by the early 1960s donors had become interested in having the UN provide a multilateral institutional structure and common rules for food aid. This idea originated in a U.S. proposal in 1960, the start of the first UN development decade, and was promoted by President John F. Kennedy.[21] The United States wanted to share the burden of food aid, and a UN-based agency that could accept voluntary contributions from its grain-exporting member states as an additional source of multilateral assistance could help spread the responsibility for the redistribution of grain supplies among a wider group of potential donors. In 1961 the World Food Programme was established as a joint initiative of the UN and FAO as a UN specialized agency tasked with coordinating donations of food aid for both long-term development needs and emergencies. It began operations in 1963.

Based in Rome, along with other UN food-based organizations such as the FAO and International Fund for Agricultural Development (IFAD), the WFP accepts contributions from donor countries and provides a multilateral channel for food aid provision in recipient countries. The United States has long been the largest donor to the WFP and in many respects has used the organization as an extension of U.S. food aid policy. It also used the WFP to channel some of its aid that might be politically difficult to justify domestically because of Cold War tensions.[22] Initially, assistance channeled via the WFP constituted approximately 10 percent of total food aid delivery, but by 2009 this had grown to almost 70 percent.[23]

The idea of sharing food aid responsibilities among a broader range of donors was also on the table during the Kennedy Round of the GATT talks, which began in 1963. Grain-exporting countries began to discuss replacing the International Wheat Agreement, which, although periodically updated in the 1950s and early 1960s, had governed the global trade in grains since 1949.[24] This agreement sought to regulate global grain prices by instituting maximum and minimum prices in international wheat trade and also by requiring members to supply grain to other countries in cases of scarcity. In the early 1960s, grain stockpiles of the largest donors—the United States and Canada—were drawn down significantly after poor harvests in the Soviet Union and India. The two donors increasingly sought to share the task of providing bilateral food aid because they were

---

21. See Shaw 2001.
22. Ruttan 1993, 17–18.
23. IGC 2004; WFP 2010a.
24. International cooperation on wheat trade dates back to the 1930s. See IWC 1974. See also IGC 2009.

worried about the growing cost of providing this aid through their development assistance programs as more developing countries, particularly in sub-Saharan Africa, gained independence in the 1960s.[25]

An international food aid agreement that required a number of donors to make food aid commitments was very attractive to the United States and Canada. Having by this time largely recovered from the war, Western European countries and Japan were seen as obvious candidates to become donors of food aid. But these countries were concerned about the cost of participating in an international agreement, especially because they continued to be large importers of food. Several European countries and Japan finally did agree to provide food aid after negotiating concessions in a new Wheat Trade Convention (WTC).[26] The result was a close relationship between the WTC and the Food Aid Convention—which together compose the International Grains Agreement—secured as part of the Kennedy Round of the GATT negotiations, concluded in 1967. Both agreements are overseen by a single secretariat—the International Grains Council—which is based in London. The original signatories of the agreement were Argentina, Australia, Canada, Denmark, Finland, Japan, Norway, Sweden, Switzerland, the United Kingdom, the United States, and the European Economic Community and its then member states: Belgium, France, Germany, Italy, Netherlands and Luxembourg.[27]

The Food Aid Convention establishes minimum food aid commitments for donor countries in tonnes (a tonne is a metric ton of 1,000 kg) of wheat or its equivalent. The idea behind minimum commitments is to ensure predictability in donations across a range of donors, a feature that aimed to benefit both donors and recipients by enabling forward planning. The initial minimum tonnage level set by the agreement was approximately 4 million tonnes overall, with each donor taking a set portion of that amount. Donor commitments under the FAC are determined largely, although not entirely, on the basis of donors' levels of grain production and gross domestic product. From early on, grain-importing donor countries such as Japan and Great Britain were allowed to provide the cash equivalent of their minimum tonnage commitment. But they had to use that cash to buy their promised tonnage of wheat equivalent from other members of the convention. They were encouraged to purchase it from developing country members, which in effect meant Argentina, as it was the sole member in that category.[28] This arrangement effectively meant that grain was removed from world

---

25. IWC Secretariat 1991, 3.
26. Ibid.
27. Ibid.; Parotte 1983, 11.
28. IWC Secretariat 1991, 4.

markets for food aid at the expense of European countries, opening up commercial export opportunities for the United States.[29]

The FAC's governing body is the Food Aid Committee, which is made up of donor states.[30] Recipient countries have occasionally attended sessions as observers, but all decisions are made by the donors when the committee meets alongside meetings of the IGC. Civil society organizations have not typically been allowed to observe meetings of the Food Aid Committee. The committee has updated the FAC on a somewhat regular basis, typically renegotiating the commitment levels of donors and rules regarding what types of assistance count as wheat equivalents. The FAC was successfully renewed in 1971, 1980, 1986, 1995, and 1999.

With the establishment of the WFP and the FAC in the 1960s, the United States and Canada were effectively able to spread the responsibility for food aid to a broader base of donors. By 1969, grain surpluses were again evident on world markets, and export prices fell below the minimum levels outlined in the WTC. Along with these changed market conditions, a growing number of food aid transactions were in what are referred to as gray areas, i.e., food exports such as concessional sales that were somewhere between fully commercial sales and fully grant form. These developments prompted renewed concern about the impact of food aid on commercial trade in agricultural exporting countries.[31]

In response to these concerns, in 1970 the CSSD introduced new rules under the Principles of Surplus Disposal on what are referred to as usual marketing requirements (UMRs). UMRs are commitments by recipient countries, embodied in food aid transaction agreements, to maintain their "normal" level of commercial imports of that same commodity for a period of one year despite the influx of food aid on concessional terms during that time.[32] The United States had used the concept of UMRs in its own food aid transaction agreements prior to 1970, and the idea was seen to be one that other countries could accept as a way to ensure that commercial trade was not disrupted by food aid.[33] Under the Principles of Surplus Disposal, donors and third-party exporting states set UMRs in consultation with recipient countries according to historical patterns of commercial imports into those countries. As stated in the principles, the UMR "is not to be set at a level that would represent an undue burden and should take into account the economic, financial and developmental situation in the recipient country."[34] Some food aid transactions, such as aid delivered via the WFP and

---

29. Ruttan 1993, 17.
30. See Hoddinott, Cohen, and Barrett 2008, 284.
31. See FAO 2001; FAO 2007, 17–18.
32. See FAO 2007, 17.
33. Cathie 1982, 64.
34. FAO 2001, 7.

channeled via NGOs, and emergency food assistance, were exempt from meeting these UMR requirements.

## The 1970s Food Crisis and Policy Reform

When the Food Aid Convention was renewed in 1971, the overall commitment levels remained at 4 million tonnes, despite the fact that actual deliveries of food aid had been averaging well over 12 million tonnes in previous years. Agricultural surplus in donor countries, however, fluctuated, and although there was ample surplus in the late 1960s, by 1972–73 tight supplies sent food prices soaring. This dramatic change in international food market conditions had a serious effect on both food aid policy and practice. Food prices remained high throughout 1974 and 1975, reaching unprecedented levels during a period of economic turmoil that included currency instability, trade tensions, and a quadrupling of the price of oil.

Several factors contributed to the 1970s food crisis. Most analyses point to poor harvests in the Soviet Union in 1972–73, which led to large grain transactions on international markets that drew down grain stocks in exporting countries to very low levels. Poor weather conditions affecting production in Asia and in North America and the impact of higher oil prices were also cited as contributing factors.[35] More important than these, however, were specific U.S. policies, but they have been largely overlooked in most analyses despite the fact that they occurred *before* these other factors.[36] The United States, for example, instituted a deliberate policy starting in the late 1960s and early 1970s to draw down its grain stocks because it had grown increasingly unhappy with bearing the high cost of storage for global benefit, especially as the new European Common Agricultural Policy (CAP) sought to actively protect European markets.[37] Further, significant devaluation of the dollar in 1971 following U.S. trade deficits that began in the late 1960s led the United States to try to increase its commercial exports, including agricultural commodity exports. Indeed, U.S. commercial grain exports rose dramatically in 1972 and 1973.[38]

The result of this U.S. "bare-shelf" grain stock policy was serious downward pressure on food aid donations just as it pushed up grain prices.[39] Although

---

35. Allen 1976; Rothschild 1976.
36. Cathie 1982, 121–129.
37. Allen 1976; Rothschild 1976, 289–30.
38. Rothschild 1976, 230.
39. Cathie 1982, 126.

FAC commitments were maintained in this period at the minimum of 4 million tonnes per annum, deliveries fell markedly from their previously record high levels. Food aid deliveries to the world's poorest countries in 1973 and 1974, for example, were less than 20 percent of what they had received in the mid-1960s.[40] But because FAC commitments had been kept at low levels to begin with, donor countries were not in contravention of their agreed international food aid obligations.

The FAO convened a World Food Conference in 1974 to address the precarious global food situation. This conference marked an important moment for international food aid policy.[41] At this time, in the wake of widespread criticism, the donor countries began to reorient their food aid policies to be more focused on norms of development and the needs of the recipient rather than on the economic and political aims of the donor, which had driven these policies in the previous two decades. The conference raised awareness of the possible problems associated with food aid from the recipients' perspective, including dependence on it as a food source and its potential to act as a disincentive to domestic production. Resolution XVIII adopted at the conference, "An Improved Policy for Food Aid," called for better ways to deliver food aid that would avoid these potential problems. It specifically noted that the aid should be allocated primarily for emergency relief and the promotion of economic development in recipient countries rather than serving mainly as a way for donors to manage their own grain stocks. In light of the prevailing high food prices at the time, the resolution recommended an increase in the minimum tonnage commitments under the FAC to at least 10 million tonnes per year. It also called for more food aid to be given in grant form, for more aid to be directed through multilateral channels, and for greater predictability and continuity in food aid policies of donors.[42]

The 1974 World Food Conference also established two institutions that dealt directly with food aid policy development: the WFP Committee on Food Aid Policies and Programs and the FAO Committee on World Food Security (CFS). The former set out specifically to monitor donor food aid policies and to coordinate those policies, while the latter dealt with food security issues more broadly, including food aid.[43] Although these Rome-based institutions were established to help with the coordination of food aid policies and programs internationally, donor countries preferred to have food aid policy coordination made via the Food Aid Convention. Consequently, these new institutions did not play a

---

40. Rothschild 1976, 289.
41. Uvin 1992, 302.
42. Resolution XVIII, reprinted in Shaw and Clay 1993.
43. See Konandreas 2007, 323; Shaw 2001, 137–138.

significant role in the coordination of food aid, and by 1995 the Committee on Food Aid Policies and Programs ceased to exist and was replaced by the WFP Executive Board. The CFS, meanwhile, did not put much focus on food aid issues after its initial work in the 1970s.

The FAC was not renegotiated until 1980, and at that time it increased overall minimum commitments to only 7.6 million tonnes per annum, well below the 10 million tonnes recommended by the international community at the World Food Conference. Signatories, however, did indicate that 10 million tonnes was the goal that all donors, including both signatories to the FAC as well as other donors, aspired to deliver each year.[44] In the interim, food aid levels throughout the 1970s remained at much reduced levels compared with those of the 1960s.[45]

From the mid-1970s, food aid policy in the United States began to focus more on food security and development as it moved away from its earlier surplus-disposal aims.[46] Throughout the late 1970s and 1980s, the government passed a number of reforms that included measures to ensure that 75 percent of its food aid was directed to the poorest countries rather than being allocated according to geopolitical concerns.[47] It also added specific programs to direct food aid to development purposes that included more grant-based aid, especially for those countries most in need. It limited concessional sales of food aid to middle-income countries and took much more care to ensure that its food aid programs did not harm production or distort domestic food markets in recipient countries.[48] In 1990, the United States passed further reforms to its food aid programs, placing much more emphasis on food security, nutrition, and child survival.[49] According to Raymond Hopkins, an epistemic community of food aid experts played a key role in pushing these reforms toward a more development-oriented food aid regime based on widely understood development norms.[50]

Other donor countries also moved closer to development-oriented food aid programs at this time, though many had already moved further in that direction than the United States. In the early 1980s, the EU moved to exclusively grant-based food aid targeted to the world's poorest countries and allowed for cash aid for the purchase of local food as aid where appropriate.[51] More aid was also channeled through the WFP, which by the early 1990s was handling around

44. IWC 1991.
45. Hoddinott, Cohen, and Barrett 2008, 285; Parotte 1983, 13.
46. See Uvin 1992; Hopkins 1992; Ruttan 1993.
47. Singer, Wood, and Jennings 1987, 24; Uvin 1992.
48. Uvin 1992, 302.
49. Shaw and Clay 1993, 217–220.
50. Hopkins 1992.
51. Uvin 1992, 303; Hopkins 1992, 232.

one-quarter of all food aid donations. Further, much more multilateral coordination on food aid issues via the FAC and WFP took place from the mid-1970s onward. In the 1980s and 1990s donors and the WFP also began to rely more on NGOs to deliver food aid on the ground rather than through government distribution channels.[52]

With a growing reliance on NGOs as distributors of food aid, donors began to actively encourage the practice of food aid "monetization" in the 1990s. NGOs that deliver food aid monetize the aid by selling a portion of the donated grain (i.e., food aid in its commodity form that is shipped from the donor countries) for local currency in the recipient country as a means by which to raise funds to cover the cost of food distribution and to fund their other development projects in those countries.[53] This practice grew, and in fact monetization was required by donors such as the United States because it saved money in terms of allowing the commodity form of the aid to pay for its own distribution.

## Current Trends

Food aid has seen some important changes over the years that reflect shifts in the global political economy and specifically in the global food economy. First, overall amounts of food aid have fluctuated greatly and have been on the decline since 2000. In 2009, food aid deliveries hit their lowest level since 1961 (the first year for which we have reliable data). The overall amount given in 2009 was 5.7 million tonnes, a stark decline from the 15.9 million donated in 1999 (see figure 2.1).[54]

There have also been shifts in the proportion of food aid given by different donors. Although the United States remains the world's largest donor, its share of world food aid has declined significantly. In 1965 the U.S. share was 94 percent; by 1970 it had fallen to 70 percent, and in 2009 it was 51 percent (figure 2.2).[55] In 2009 the EU was the second-largest donor, followed by Japan, Canada, and other donors. As the proportion of aid supplied by different donors shifted and overall aid declined, the overall number of donors has risen, with fifty-five countries giving food aid in 2009 and sixty-two in 2010. There are now many more developing countries giving food aid than in the past. These new donors—for example, China, Saudi Arabia, South Korea, India, Brazil, and South Africa—are

---

52. Barrett and Maxwell, 2005, 43.
53. Barrett and Maxwell 2005; Oxfam International 2005, 23.
54. WFP 2010a, 10; WFP 2008a, 1.
55. Maxwell and Singer 1979, 226; WFP 2008a, 4; WFP 2010a, 12.

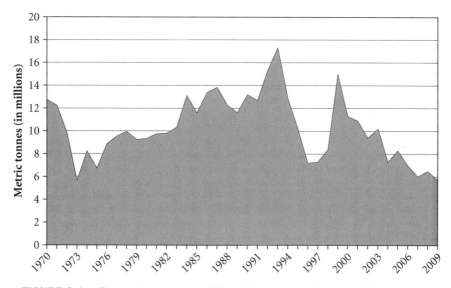

**FIGURE 2.1.**   Food aid deliveries, 1970–2009. Source: FAO and WFP Interfais.

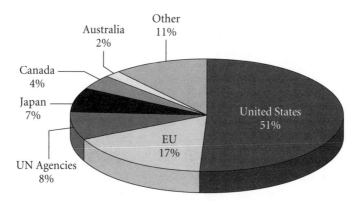

**FIGURE 2.2.**   Food aid deliveries by donor, 2009. Source: WFP Interfais.

not signatories to the FAC and have been somewhat erratic in the level of their donations from year to year.

The main recipients of food aid have also changed over the years, as shown in figure 2.3. Asian countries were the main recipients in the 1960s and 1970s, but since the 1990s there has been a gradual shift to sub-Saharan African countries as the main recipients. In 2009, sub-Saharan Africa received 63 percent of all food aid, Asia 25 percent, the Middle East and North Africa 5 percent, Latin America 5 percent, and Eastern Europe and the Commonwealth of Independent States

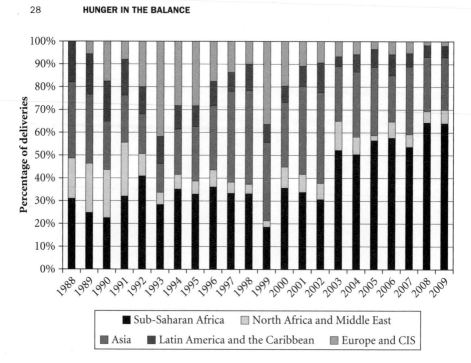

**FIGURE 2.3.**   Food aid deliveries by recipient region, 1988–2009. Source: WFP Interfais, Food Aid Flows 2009.

2 percent. The overall number of recipients has fallen—from 120 in the early 1990s to 89 countries in 2009.[56] With the drop in the number of recipients, food aid deliveries have also become highly concentrated in a few countries. In 2009, 55 percent of all food aid was directed to just 8 recipients: Ethiopia, Sudan, Somalia, Democratic People's Republic of Korea, Pakistan, Zimbabwe, and Afghanistan.[57] Most of this was emergency aid.

The delivery of food aid has also become more multilateral, with a growing proportion channeled via the WFP (which includes bilaterally donated aid delivered by the WFP). In the 1960s, less than 10 percent of food aid was channeled through multilateral institutions; by the late 1980s this figure was closer to 25 percent, and by 2009 it was 67 percent.[58] The vast majority of multilaterally delivered food aid is handled by the WFP and a small portion by other UN relief agencies. Today the bulk of this aid is directed to emergency relief, a shift from

---

56. See WFP 2010a, 8.
57. WFP 2010a, 44; WFP 2008a, 40.
58. WFP 2010a, 34. In 2007 the WFP delivered 55 percent of world food aid. See WFP 2008a, 9.

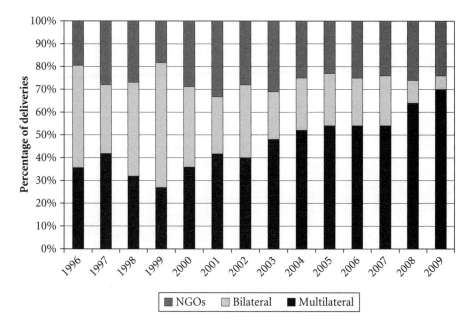

**FIGURE 2.4.** Global food aid deliveries by channel, 1996–2009. Source: WFP Interfais, Food Aid Flows 2009.

the focus of the 1970s through the 1980s on the use of food aid for longer-term development programs and projects. The greater reliance of donors on NGOs as delivery agents has also been apparent. Between 1990 and 1997, NGOs managed approximately 19 percent of all global food aid.[59] By 2009 they channeled around one-quarter (see figure 2.4).

In addition to the major shifts in terms of donors and channels through which food aid has been directed, the surplus disposal function of the aid has declined considerably. Food aid is now sourced mainly on open markets after donor countries reduced the amount of government-held stocks in favor of privately held stocks, which means that the opportunity cost of providing food aid is higher for donors today than it was in the past.[60] The tying of food aid to grain sourced in the donor country has also declined and in the case of some donors has been eliminated entirely (as will be discussed in chapter 3). In 2009, 50 percent of food aid was tied (as a direct transfer of food from the donor), which the WFP noted

59. Clay and Stokke 2000b, 274–75.
60. Barrett and Maxwell 2005, 88–89.

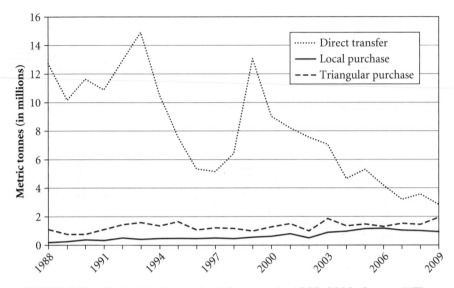

**FIGURE 2.5.** Food aid deliveries by delivery mode, 1988–2009. Source: WFP Interfais.

was an all-time low.[61] As tied aid has fallen, the amount that is untied and/or allocated in funds for local and regional purchase has risen, and together they make up the remaining 50 percent of food aid. Most of the drop in food aid deliveries since the late 1990s has resulted from a decline in tied, direct transfer aid, most of which had been provided bilaterally (see figure 2.5).

The proportion of food aid given in grant form has gone up since the 1990s. In 2008 and again in 2009, all food aid was provided in grant form.[62] This is up from its level in 2007, when 92 percent of food aid was given in grant form and 8 percent was delivered on concessional terms.[63] From the inception of the U.S. food aid program in the 1950s until the late 1970s, over 60 percent of food aid was sold to recipients on concessional terms.[64] These sales were significant, and food aid made up one-quarter to one-half of all U.S. agricultural exports in the late 1950s and early 1960s.[65] By 2006 the United States had phased out its food aid sales, and other countries had taken over as primary sellers of discount food as aid. Most of the aid from South Korea is sold to North Korea in this fashion. As a percentage of global grain trade, food aid has declined from 10 percent to around 2 percent in recent years. At the same time, this aid makes

---

61. WFP 2010a, 21 (in 2007 some 59 percent of food aid was direct transfer, WFP 2008a, 16).
62. WFP 2010a, 23.
63. WFP 2008a, 6.
64. Friedmann 1982, S262; see also Cathie 1982, 19.
65. See Barrett 2002, 8.

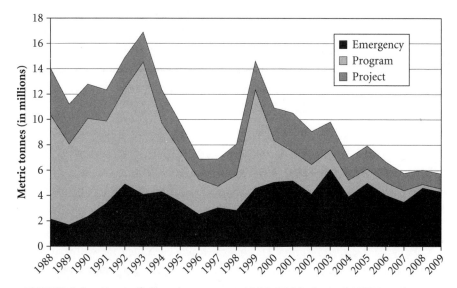

**FIGURE 2.6.**  Food aid flows by category, 1988–2009. Source: WFP Interfais, Food Aid Flows 2009.

up 5–10 percent of food imports in recipient countries.[66] Food aid as a proportion of overseas aid has declined markedly, to around 5 percent of ODA by 2005.[67]

Food aid is typically categorized today as being either project, program, or emergency in nature. Project aid supports projects that involve food—for example, school feeding, mother and child nutrition, and food-for-work projects. Program food aid refers to food sent over long time periods that is not tied to specific projects but is meant to support general development in the recipient country. Emergency food aid refers to food sent specifically to respond to humanitarian crises. In its early days, program aid was the dominant type of food aid. Today the proportion of food aid that goes to emergencies has risen sharply as project and program aid has fallen. In the 1960s emergency food aid made up only about 20 percent of food aid donations, and by 2009 it was over 76 percent.[68] Today most emergency food aid is directed to sub-Saharan Africa and Asia. In 2009, only 4 percent of food aid was allocated to long-term programs (down from 14 percent in 2007), while 20 percent went to project aid (see figure 2.6).

The United States has been largely responsible for the increased monetization of food aid since the 1990s. In the 1990s the United States lifted limits on the amount of food aid that could be sold on open markets in recipient countries

---

66. FAO 2007, 4, 10.
67. Clay, Riley, and Urey 2006, 14.
68. WFP 2010a, 26.

to raise funds.[69] U.S. NGOs monetized some 10 percent of the food aid they delivered in 1990, and this rose to over 60 percent by the early 2000s.[70] By 2009, 62 percent of all bilateral food aid globally was monetized, one-third of it by NGOs.[71] For all food aid (bilateral and multilateral combined) in 2009, however, only 8 percent was monetized, with the highest proportion ever, 92 percent, being freely distributed to beneficiaries.[72]

## The Impact of Tied Food Aid

As the form and significance of food aid have changed over the years, so has understanding of the impact of food aid both on recipient countries and with respect to global trade. The improved understanding of food aid impacts has in many ways shaped reforms. This has especially been the case with respect to the allocation of aid according to political allegiances. Throughout the 1960s and 1970s, geopolitically important countries such as Egypt, India, South Korea, South Vietnam, and Israel were among the top recipients of food aid, while many desperately poor food-insecure countries, particularly those in sub-Saharan Africa, received very little aid.[73] Increased awareness of past policies regarding allocation, as well as its stark impact on the world's poorest countries in the 1970s just as their ability to command food on international markets shriveled up, resulted in widespread outcry and critique by civil society groups and food aid experts. This critique prompted changes over the course of the 1970s–1990s by nearly all donors in the allocation of aid to the poorest and most food-deficient countries, as outlined above.

With respect to the market-distorting impacts of food aid, however, policies have not changed as uniformly across donors even with growing evidence of the impacts. Because its origins were so closely linked to the idea of surplus disposal, food aid was originally tied closely to the donation of food grown, processed, and sold in the donor country. It is doubtful that food aid would have made up as high a proportion of development assistance in the 1950s and 1960s had it not been tied to the disposal of surpluses. But from early on, researchers pointed out that tied food aid could be a disincentive to agricultural production in poor countries by outcompeting local production and could disrupt both local and

---

69. Barrett and Maxwell 2005, 43.
70. Clay, Riley, and Urey 2006, 46; see also Tschirley and Howard 2003, 9.
71. See WFP 2010a, 17.
72. WFP 2010a, 24.
73. See Barrett and Maxwell 2005, 11, 39.

international trade.[74] The surplus disposal function declined in importance in the 1970s, and food aid was increasingly procured on open markets rather than from government-held stocks. As this shift occurred, the rationale for maintaining tied food aid became subject to a great deal of study and debate.[75]

Some donors have moved to untie their food aid, often in step with a wider movement to untie all development assistance. Since at least the 1980s donors have considered whether aid tying should be reduced because of the inefficiencies associated with restrictions on where the goods or services provided by international aid could be sourced. In 1987 the Organisation for Economic Cooperation and Development (OECD) adopted a set of guiding principles for donors regarding aid tying, which articulated definitions of tied, untied, and partially tied aid.[76] In 2001 the OECD adopted a recommendation that its members untie most types of ODA to the least developed countries (LDCs), although food aid was specifically exempted from this recommendation, along with technical cooperation and donor administrative costs. Because food aid transactions were already being reported to the CSSD, it was assumed that screening them through this body would address any trade displacement concerns.

The untying recommendation was part of a larger move within the OECD to improve aid effectiveness, as reflected in the 2005 Paris Declaration on Aid Effectiveness.[77] The OECD aid-untying recommendation was updated in 2008, and although food aid was still exempt from the commitment to untie aid made by donors as part of the declaration, donors were encouraged at that time to untie their food aid as well.[78] After the OECD encouragement to untie aid, the level of untied ODA did rise from around 30 percent in the late 1980s to 56 percent in 2003–5. With respect to food aid, however, 58 percent of all aid in cereals was still firmly tied to donor-produced commodities in 2007, although this figure had been 90 percent in 2001.[79]

Numerous economic studies have examined the impact of tied, direct-transfer food aid in both local and global contexts. Within this literature, there has been a growing consensus that tied food aid can have market-distorting effects in recipient countries. It is also critiqued for inefficiencies that result in less food being provided than would be the case if financial resources were provided to purchase food locally in recipient countries. Further, tied food aid limits food choices for recipients. Various reports sponsored by international organizations,

---

74. Schultz 1960; Maxwell and Singer 1979, 226–27, outline problems with food aid.
75. Clay, Riley, and Urey 2006.
76. OECD 1987.
77. OECD 2005.
78. OECD 2008a.
79. Clay et al. 2008, 9, 14.

the U.S. government, and development and agriculture NGOs detail the effects of continued tying of food aid.[80] These critiques are briefly summarized below.

## Delays

There is typically a considerable time lag for deliveries of tied, direct transfers of food aid from donor countries, a factor that makes it difficult to rely on the aid in situations requiring an immediate response. On average it takes at least four to six months for a direct-transfer shipment to reach its destination once it has been approved. This delay is linked to the time required for the numerous steps involved in moving food grown in one part of the world to another. These steps include sourcing and purchasing the food in the donor country, bagging and/or processing it, taking bids and arranging transport contracts, transporting the food by ocean (which itself can take up to two months), clearing the food in recipient country ports, and transporting it within the recipient country by truck or train. In the case of the United States, 75 percent of its food aid must be shipped on U.S.-flagged vessels to meet cargo preference rules, which results in serious delays because there are relatively few carriers that meet this criterion.[81]

A further problem with tied food aid from the United States is that most of it is procured in August and September. This timing is in large part a product of the funding approval process, which can take six months, and it is also driven by the donor's needs rather than those of the recipient. Poor coordination between agencies involved within the donor country and between donors and recipients also contributes to delays.[82] The delays mean that direct-transfer food aid cannot be relied upon to reach emergency situations quickly and that lives are potentially endangered. The time it takes to reach its destination also makes it less reliable as a food source. There have been recent reports, for example, of food shipments that are spoiled or rotten by the time they arrive in the recipient country. A U.S. Government Accountability Office (GAO) report notes, for example, that in October 2006, some 1,925 tonnes of U.S. cornmeal food aid arrived in Durban, South Africa, heavily infested with both live and dead insects.[83]

---

80. E.g. Clay, Riley, and Urey 2006; GAO 2007; FAO 2007; Oxfam International 2005; Bread for the World Institute 2006.
81. Barrett and Maxwell 2005, 94; GAO 2007.
82. GAO 2007, 4–5.
83. Ibid., 32.

## Market Distortions

There is a significant body of literature that highlights the ways in which tied food aid can distort markets—both locally and globally. Although food aid today accounts for only around 2 percent of the global grain trade, it can result in serious distortions to local economies in recipient countries. For one thing, tied food aid tends to be procyclical with food availability (or countercyclical with respect to prices) such that the amount of food aid shipped varies according to both supply and price and is thus somewhat unpredictable for recipients. When food stocks are high and prices are low, more food aid is typically donated, but this is when it is less valuable as a resource for the recipient country because it is available and inexpensive to purchase commercially. But when stocks are low and prices high, food aid donations tend to fall (see figure 2.7).

These trends are unfortunate because when prices are high and supply is tight, food-deficit countries are most in need of aid because their ability to commercially purchase food on world markets is constrained by the higher prices. Exacerbating these trends are broader economic conditions that also dictate amounts

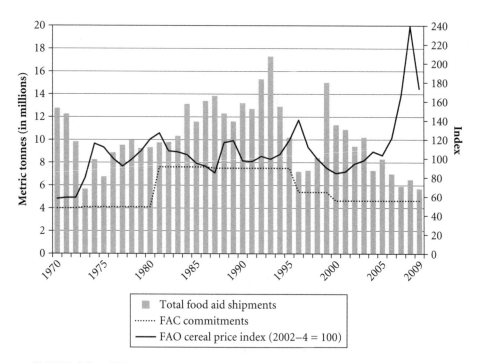

**FIGURE 2.7.** FAO cereal price index as compared with food aid deliveries and commitments under the Food Aid Convention, 1970–2009. Source: WFP Interfais, International Grains Council, FAO.

of aid available and the ability to obtain credit for commercial purchases in food-import-dependent countries. In a global economic downturn, as occurred in the 1970s and in 2008–10, food aid often dries up as a resource because donor countries tighten their aid budgets. At the same time, obtaining trade credit to import food also becomes more difficult for poor countries.

Fluctuating amounts of food aid can be very disruptive to local economies. As food stocks and prices are often linked to changes in economic policies in industrialized countries, the dramatic shifts in availability of food aid are a burden on recipient countries in that the availability of food changes not according to their own policies but according to economic policies of donors. Simply put, the amount of food aid they receive is largely out of their control. This variability in food aid supply increases uncertainty.[84] It is difficult for farmers to plan which crops and how much to plant and for traders to arrange shipments when they do not know how much or what kinds of foreign food will be entering their local market. If prices rise because of a decline in food aid, it is often difficult for farmers in developing countries to increase their supply immediately. Because low levels of agricultural investment in developing countries have been the typical pattern for most of the last thirty years, infrastructure and other supports for moving production to market are often missing.

Markets are often disrupted by food aid in other ways as well. Nonemergency program aid in particular can result in the displacement of commercial imports, which is distorting to global markets for grains.[85] Disruptions are felt locally as well from this type of food aid. It is extremely difficult for farmers to maintain sustainable livelihoods in situations where cheap imported grains are brought in over a long period of time and outcompete the locally grown products they are trying to sell on domestic markets. Even emergency aid can be quite disruptive to local economies. For example, after the Asian tsunami in late 2004, large amounts of food were shipped in to affected countries, in many cases beyond the amounts that were actually required. The Indian Nicobar Islands received so much food that it rotted in warehouses before it could be distributed.[86] Research has shown that local market prices for food tend to fall in recipient countries after the distribution of food aid.[87] Monetization also puts downward pressure on prices on local markets. When direct-transfer food aid is monetized, the portion that is sold is not usually targeted to those most in need (i.e., those who

---

84. Clay, Riley, and Urey 2006, 30; Bread for the World Institute 2006, 9; Murphy and McAfee 2005 point out, however, that not all food aid is procyclical; the WFP provision of aid tends to be countercyclical.

85. FAO 2007, 44; Oxfam International 2005, 18.

86. Singh 2009, 51.

87. FAO 2007, 38.

cannot afford to buy it). Rather, it is made available to those who already have resources to purchase food. These kinds of disruptions to local markets in recipient countries that result from monetization frustrate efforts to promote local economic development.[88]

Finally, the timing of food aid can also lead to market disruptions in recipient countries. Although aid is typically requested in times when local food supply is short, by the time the aid arrives at its destination, it can (and often does) coincide with local harvest times. This can result in oversupply and declining prices on local markets when the aid does arrive, which can be harmful to local farmer incentives to plant in the following season.[89] This happened in Guinea in 1988, [90] in Ethiopia and Somalia in 2000, [91] and in Mozambique in 1992–93.[92]

## Cost Inefficiency

On top of distorting markets, direct-transfer food aid is typically expensive to provide and thus translates into less food distributed. There is a wide consensus that in most circumstances cash aid to purchase food locally or regionally is more efficient.[93] OECD studies have shown that tied food aid costs on average 50 percent more than food purchased locally in the recipient country and on average one-third more than it would cost to buy food from a third country on the open market.[94] Often there is food available in the local market or in a nearby market at prices much lower than the cost of shipping aid halfway around the world, but people cannot afford to buy it. The local or regional purchase of food can be much more timely and cost-effective.

A closer look at the U.S. case reveals why direct-transfer food aid is so much more expensive. Higher costs there are the product of both a lack of competition among grain companies, which has driven up prices, and to shipping costs. The grain must be processed in the United States and shipped on carriers registered under the U.S. flag. According to the GAO, around 65 percent of U.S. food aid costs go toward transportation of the food, and these costs are particularly high. In 2006 the United States spent on average $171 per tonne for ocean freight; by contrast, the WFP spent just $100 per tonne to transport its food aid. The GAO estimates that each $10-per-tonne reduction in the cost of transporting food aid

---

88. Ibid.; Oxfam International 2005, 23.
89. GAO 2007, 72.
90. Clapp 1997.
91. Barrett and Maxwell 2005.
92. Tschirley, Donovan, and Weber 1996.
93. Clay, Riley, and Urey 2006, 46.
94. Ibid., 17.

could feed an additional 850,000 people in an average hungry season.[95] Part of the reason for these particularly high costs in the United States is that purchases of food for aid tend to be bunched in certain months, which can create bottlenecks that drive up logistical costs. According to the FAO, globally some $600 million annually is lost because of the costs associated with tied food aid.[96] In the U.S. case, the higher cost has translated into less food shipped overseas as food aid, with a 52 percent decline in average tonnage of food aid delivered over the 2002–7 period.[97]

## Limited Food Choices

Tied food aid has the potential to change food preferences in recipient countries, as was seen in a number of cases where wheat was introduced to areas where it is not normally grown and has resulted in dependencies.[98] From the 1960s to 1980s, when wheat composed by far the bulk of food aid commodities supplied to developing countries, there was a major shift in diets in developing countries away from traditional food crops and toward wheat.[99] A key problem was that wheat does not grow particularly well in some countries, as in West Africa, where it has become a major part of local diets. As a result these countries have become dependent on imported wheat, either bought commercially or obtained as food aid, to meet their demand.[100]

There are numerous other instances where countries have been given culturally inappropriate foods; for example, giving grains to pastoralists in the Horn of Africa caused them to shift from a meat- and dairy-based diet to one more reliant on Western grains such as maize.[101] It can also be problematic when foods that recipients view as undesirable, such as foods that are spoiled or considered inedible or environmentally harmful, are shipped against their wishes.[102] Examples of this are the genetically modified organisms in food aid maize shipped to southern Africa in 2002–3 and GMOs in food aid rice sent to West Africa in 2006 (these instances are discussed further in chapter 5). In cases where foods are undesirable because of their physical or cultural inappropriateness to the recipients, the result may be that those who are hungry choose not to eat the food

---

95. GAO 2007, 15–16.
96. FAO 2007.
97. GAO 2007, 1.
98. Clay, Riley, and Urey 2006, 42.
99. Byerlee 1987.
100. Delgado and Miller 1985.
101. Barrett and Maxwell 2005, 182.
102. Clay, Pillai, and Benson 1998, 49.

rather than to go against their beliefs or convictions, which defeats the point of the aid.[103]

These problems underscore the fact that introducing food from other contexts is not always the right response to hunger. The specific critiques of tied food aid have been discussed in the academic literature for decades, but policy, especially in the United States, has been very slow to adapt. Some change is evident among some donors. As mentioned above and as will be discussed in more detail in chapter 3, the European Union shifted toward cash-based food aid provision in the mid-1990s. Other countries have now begun to follow the EU lead. In 2004 Australia moved to untie up to two-thirds of its food aid. And in 2005 Canada untied up to 50 percent of its food aid and fully untied it in 2008.[104] But the United States, as the largest food aid donor, has not significantly altered its policy despite increasing pressure to do so. Although it has recently adopted several pilot projects to allow some local and third-country purchase of food aid, the vast majority of its food aid remains firmly tied to U.S. commodities.

## New Modes of Food Assistance

The WFP and other food aid-providing NGOs have practiced alternative modes of providing food as a form of aid, including the use of local and regional procurement (LRP) and cash and vouchers, for over thirty years. The use of new forms of food assistance has grown markedly in the past decade as the number of disasters requiring immediate response has risen and as donors have changed policies to untie their aid. The value of LRP transactions undertaken by the WFP, for example, grew fourfold from 1999 to 2005.[105] The WFP's purchases in developing countries are carried out mainly on large commodity exchanges in countries such as South Africa, Uganda, and Zimbabwe.[106] Over 55 percent of WFP procurement of food aid in 2007 was from LDCs or other low-income countries.[107] There has also been a growing interest in the use of cash and vouchers by the WFP, although to date experience with these instruments is more limited than that with LRP.[108] The increased use of these new tools has shifted the discourse away from "food aid" and toward "food assistance," the latter incorporating a broader range of ways to assist the hungry, including but not limited to direct

103. Renzaho 2002.
104. Clapp 2010.
105. Tschirley and del Castillo 2007, 1.
106. Interview with Allan Jury, director, WFP U.S. Relations Office, November 4, 2009.
107. USDA 2009, 16.
108. WFP 2008c.

transfers of food aid. It also includes mechanisms such as local and regional purchase, vouchers for food, and cash transfers directly to the hungry.[109]

## Local and Regional Purchase

The idea behind LRP is to source food assistance closer to where hunger occurs.
Often there is sufficient food available in a community experiencing hunger, but
the problem is one of access—people are hungry because they cannot afford to
purchase the food. This was a key point made by Nobel Prize-winning economist
Amartya Sen in his seminal work *Poverty and Famines.* Sen demonstrated that it
is people's ability to access food, rather than the general availability of food in a
country, that is the key to understanding hunger.[110] In some famines throughout
India's history, for example, food was available within the country, but people
starved to death because they were too poor to buy it. This situation continues to
this day in India. In 2010 the government held enormous stocks of grain that it
had been unable to sell on domestic markets because its people could not afford
it.[111] Drawing on Sen's ideas, LRP prioritizes access and at the same time avoids
some of the key problems associated with tied, direct transfer aid outlined above.

As noted, LRP food assistance tends to be much more efficient than tied food
aid in terms of costs. The overall lower costs of LRP food aid transactions enable
scarce food aid dollars to go further so that the assistance reaches more people.
LRP transactions are also more efficient than direct-transfer food aid because
they tend to reduce delivery times, often by a significant amount, since the travel
distance is much shorter and delays at the border (or indeed interception by
pirates) are less frequent. In comparing countries in sub-Saharan Africa that had
received both LRP and direct-transfer food aid, the GAO found that aid that was
tied to a direct transfer of food from the donor country took on average 147 days,
whereas local procurement averaged 35 days, and regionally procured food aid
took 41 days.[112] The shortened delivery times for LRP food aid transactions are
extremely important in that they enable food to reach those afflicted by hunger
much sooner, averting loss of lives, particularly those of children, due to pro-
longed undernutrition.

By recognizing that food is often available in a hunger-afflicted region, LRP
operations tend to improve rather than dampen local farmers' production incentives and provide incentives for investment by local traders. Incentives to improve

109. Harvey et al. 2010.
110. Sen 1981.
111. Kinetz 2010.
112. GAO 2009, 21.

production and trade of agricultural products in developing countries is key for breaking the cycle of dependency that is often associated with direct-transfer food aid. By stimulating demand for locally produced food, LRP operations provide local farmers and traders with secure markets. In Ethiopia and Uganda, for example, LRP has led to greater investment by some traders to improve practices in the local food aid supply channel, though the broader impacts on the grain market were unclear.[113] Over the medium and long term, such incentives foster greater self-reliance in food production in regions affected by poverty and hunger.[114] This type of economic stimulation for the agricultural sector has been identified as a key factor in overall development in poor countries.[115]

Sourcing food close to the source of hunger ensures that food made available through LRP transactions is culturally appropriate to the recipient, because the foods are familiar and fit with local traditions and diets.[116] Locally sourced foods are also more likely to be environmentally acceptable, particularly when local varieties of grain are provided as aid. The environmental appropriateness of aid is especially important in cases of grains that are in whole seed form, as in the case of maize, which can be planted. Grains that are also seeds can easily mix with local seed supplies, or if the grain, like maize, is an open-pollinating one, there is also a chance that grain varieties could mix. Some developing country governments are worried about such prospects, especially with the import of genetically modified grains from donor countries that may not be approved for planting in recipient countries.[117] Locally and regionally sourced grains tend to mitigate such worries.

Although it has many benefits over tied food aid, it is important to note that LRP food aid is not necessarily a silver-bullet solution in all circumstances. Although it is typically much less costly to provide than direct-transfer food aid, there may occasionally be cases where food from outside the region is equally or more efficient in terms of costs. In Latin America, for example, a GAO study found that LRP food aid cost approximately the same as providing food sourced in the US.[118]

There is also a risk that LRP transactions, by increasing demand for locally grown foods (especially if this occurs in scarce periods), may drive up food prices to levels that could have a negative impact on access to food within that

---

113. Coutler et al. 2007.
114. USDA 2009, 20.
115. World Bank 2007.
116. USDA 2009, 17; GAO 2009, 25–26.
117. USDA 2009, 17.
118. GAO 2009.

community.[119] Although in some instances local price spikes and price volatility have occurred with LRP purchases, they are not automatic. Prices did rise, however, in some cases, such as in Ethiopia and Uganda in 2003.[120] Because local procurements made by the WFP tend to make up only a small portion of local food markets in developing countries—typically less than 5 percent of production—the risk of price spikes is small. In analyzing WFP use of LRP over the 2001–5 period, David Tschirley and Anne Marie del Castillo found that in "most countries, in most years, pressure on local prices from LRP has likely been minimal," though they do note that further research on this issue is needed.[121]

To mitigate the risk of market disruptions due to LRP purchases, the WFP monitors local markets closely, checks local prices against international ones, puts out tenders for small amounts of food early in the season, and is careful not to purchase a large percentage of locally purchased food, especially in scarce periods. Such precautions help to ensure efficiency and to minimize the risk of harm from local purchases. Problems may still arise if there is a lack of reliable market data or where local markets function poorly, as is sometimes the case, though the WFP now has substantial experience and has built up its data collection capacities in most recipient countries.[122]

LRP food aid also involves other risks such as a potential lack of reliability of suppliers and traders of local foods and compromised food quality and safety. The failure of a local trader to supply the required amount of food could result in serious delays to the provision of food aid. Contracting a larger number of local suppliers can reduce the risk of delays from defaults, but it can also increase the cost of providing the aid, so a balance between these goals must be achieved. Although some traders have defaulted on contracts in practice, there has not been a consistent pattern of this occurring with WFP local procurements.[123] WFP mitigates this particular risk by prescreening traders and penalizing those that default.

There is also a risk that locally procured foods may not meet standards set by donor countries for food aid.[124] However, there is as yet very little evidence that LRP food aid performs any worse than internationally sourced food aid on this front. Food supplied and shipped by the United States is often spoiled by the

---

119. Ibid., 27–28; Tschirley and del Castillo 2007.
120. GAO 2009, 28.
121. Tschirley and del Castillo 2007, 2.
122. GAO 2009, 29–32.
123. Tschirley and del Castillo 2007, 3.
124. Interview with Patrick Webb, dean and professor, Friedman School of Nutrition Science and Policy and former chief of nutrition, WFP, November 13, 2007.

time it reaches its destination, as noted above. Similarly, Tschirley and del Castillo reported, "We know of no instances of food safety breaches in WFP procured food."[125] To mitigate this risk, the WFP and other food aid NGOs have put in place safeguards to ensure food safety and quality.[126] Recent studies on LRP food aid in practice have concluded that although these potential risks must be taken seriously, with careful planning and design, such operations can avoid these risks while greatly enhancing efficiency.[127]

## Cash and Vouchers

The use of vouchers and cash transfers represents another alternative to direct-transfer food aid. The WFP has experimented with these tools, sometimes combined with food-for-work projects, in various countries, including Bangladesh, Myanmar, Pakistan, and Malawi. Vouchers and cash go beyond the idea of a physical commodity transfer by instead providing purchasing power directly to beneficiaries. Because markets in many developing countries function better now than they did even twenty or thirty years ago, it has become much more feasible to allow beneficiaries to acquire food themselves with either cash or a voucher that can be traded in for a fixed amount or a fixed value of food in selected market outlets.

Like other forms of food assistance, these instruments carry both benefits and risks. Their use so far has been largely in pilot projects on a small scale in short-term emergency situations, and thus an evaluation of their pros and cons on a large scale is somewhat tentative. One of the key advantages of vouchers and cash transfers is that they are very flexible tools and can be distributed quickly, which can be particularly useful in emergency contexts. They enable beneficiaries to prioritize their own food needs by allowing for choice. The use of these tools can also enhance local economic opportunities by providing incentives to both farmers and traders to provide food for purchase in local markets. At the same time, there are some risks associated with these instruments. While vouchers can be targeted specifically to food purchases, the transfer of cash does not carry any guarantee that beneficiaries will actually spend the funds on food. However, research has shown that food purchases are typically made with at least some of the cash, and in this sense they can still be considered a food assistance tool. The use of cash transfers and vouchers also requires well-functioning markets,

---

125. Tschirley and del Castillo 2007, 3.
126. USDA 2009, 58.
127. GAO 2009; Tschirley and del Castillo 2007.

as well as high levels of government capacity to ensure that the program runs smoothly with a minimum of corruption and fraud. As is the case with LRP, cash transfers and voucher programs could feed into inflationary pressures on local food markets, and transferring them in a value amount passes the price risk onto beneficiaries if prices are rising.[128]

While the WFP and some donors and NGOs have endorsed the idea of using these new instruments such as LRP and cash and vouchers for food assistance, they have also faced a broader, more political, critique beyond whether they might work in the field. Some politicians and NGOs, particularly in the United States, have argued that donor support for food aid will be far weaker than support for tied-aid programs. The simple reason for this, as will be discussed in subsequent chapters, is that it is easier to get domestic support for food aid programs if it can be shown that the donor country also benefits from them. If domestic groups within donor countries do not gain from LRP or cash transactions, their overall support for food assistance may weaken. Further, food-aid-programming NGOs may not have the appropriate expertise to undertake LRP or cash and vouchers with the caution needed, which is part of the reason that some of these groups have resisted them.[129]

## Conclusion

In many ways food aid has evolved considerably from its origins as a surplus disposal mechanism and source of development assistance. Its significance as both an aid resource and a trade outlet has diminished to the point that it has become what some call a "marginal resource."[130] Today the food aid regime has evolved to become one largely based on the provision of humanitarian assistance in emergencies. As such, it remains a very important lifeline, albeit one that must be implemented very carefully. Although food aid has become less of a means for donors to offload surpluses and boost aid transfers to developing countries, it has retained some of its early characteristics in the case of some donors, especially with respect to the tying of food aid to domestically sourced food.

Today there is a greater understanding of the impact of food aid depending on whether it is provided in its commodity form, as a direct transfer, as a financial resource with which to purchase food locally or regionally, or in the form of cash

128. On the pros and cons of cash transfers and vouchers, see WFP 2008c; Harvey 2007; Gentilini 2007; Oxfam Great Britain 2006.
129. Webb interview, November 13, 2007.
130. Clay 2003, 298.

and vouchers. Most food aid analysts have come to conclusion that flexibility is the key in food assistance policy. Tied aid has become too inflexible to be used in every situation: it is highly inefficient and constrains the ability to respond appropriately in emergencies. LRP transactions, as well as cash and vouchers, can improve efficiency and effectiveness, but they may not be appropriate in all situations. In some cases where local food is not available or market situations are tight, food from outside the area in need and even from outside the region may be the most appropriate response. Flexibility would allow donors to choose the best form of food aid for each situation.

# 3

# DONOR POLICIES ON THE QUESTION OF TYING

The idea of untying food aid has been discussed by donor countries since at least the 1970s. It gained significant momentum in international policy circles starting in the mid-1990s, after the European Union adopted the policy in 1996. Agencies such as the FAO and the OECD have taken up the issue in extensive reports directed at their membership since 2005, and from 2007 the WFP began to strongly endorse the idea. Some donors, such as Canada and Australia, eventually followed the EU on this idea by untying their own food aid programs. Others, however, have not. Japan has moved in the opposite direction, with more of its food aid, rather than less, being tied since the early 2000s. The United States has struggled over the issue but has managed only to adopt a small pilot program to allow some partial untying on a scale that is tiny compared with the overall size of its food aid programs.

What explains why some countries have taken steps to untie their food aid while others have not? Is it simply that some countries have been convinced by the arguments in favor of the idea while others are more skeptical? In this chapter I argue that the explanation is not just that international norms and ideas have filtered down from international agencies to the level of donor governments. Examining a range of donors and their policies makes it clear that although changing ideas about the most appropriate forms of international aid are very important in shifting norms and behavior of donors, other factors are also integral to the story and interact with ideas in complex ways. The international institutional context is important in shaping new norms, as earlier international relations studies on the politics of food aid have shown. But when it comes to policies on tying and untying, the donor's own domestic institutional context is extremely important for understanding how new ideas filter into policy.

Within donor countries, economic interests have also continued to be important in the story of food aid tying and untying and have not lost their significance just because donors no longer use food aid as a surplus disposal mechanism. Moreover, it is not only state and commercial interests that have a potential stake in the question of aid tying; other actors do too, most prominently NGOs that program and deliver food aid. These various interests are not necessarily all uniformly in favor of tying, and clashes between them have been common. Because the interpretation and acceptance of new norms, the nature of interests with a stake in the policy outcome, and institutional context are unique for each donor, it is not surprising that donor policies regarding tied food aid have evolved in different ways in different countries.

## The European Union

As noted in chapter 2, Europe was initially a somewhat reluctant participant as a food aid donor. This was largely because at the time it was not a large food producer and was itself briefly a recipient of food aid after the Second World War. But the European Common Agricultural Policy adopted in the early 1960s eventually resulted in agricultural surpluses by the end of that decade. European food aid is made up of a Europe-wide program that began in 1968 (initially under the European Community [EC], and after 1993 under the European Union) plus individual national-level food aid policies of the European countries.[1] The Europe-wide program provides a significant amount of world food aid, typically averaging around 15–30 percent of all food aid since the program began. Europe fully untied its food aid in 1996 after taking initial steps in that direction in the 1980s.[2] Most of the individual member states' food aid programs were also untied around this time. Switzerland and Norway are not participants in the Europe-wide food aid program, and they both have their own largely untied food aid programs.[3]

---

1. On the early EC food aid program, see Clay 1983a; 1983b.

2. Some member states, however—namely, France and Italy—continued to tie their bilateral food aid for some years after this policy change. France untied its program in 2005. Interview with Marc Cohen, senior research fellow, International Food Policy Research Institute (IFPRI), October 17, 2007. Other European donor states who are not members of the European Union have also largely untied their food aid.

3. Switzerland and Norway are also members of the Food Aid Convention. Sweden and Finland were already moving toward untying their food aid when they joined the EU in 1995.

From its inception, the Europe-wide food aid program was managed primarily by the Agriculture Directorate of the European Commission (the administrative body of the European Economic Community, and later the European
Union), which organized the procurement of that aid within Europe (via national
intervention boards in the member states) and was responsible for its delivery.
Although the Agriculture Directorate procured and delivered it, the Development Directorate of the Commission was responsible for programming the aid.
This division of responsibilities reflected European policymakers' acceptance
from early on that development aims should play a large role in its food aid
program. The Europe-wide food aid program was not established primarily as a
mechanism by which to dispose of agricultural surplus.[4] However, some linkage
of food aid policy with surpluses had emerged by the 1970s. At that time, food aid
became more tightly linked to production patterns in member states, indicating
an important role played by economic interests in shaping policy. In practice, the
institutional setup that involved both the Agriculture Directorate and the Development Directorate in food aid policy was cumbersome and inefficient.

From early on there were differences among member states regarding the
direction of food aid policy, particularly after the first enlargement of the European Community in 1973 to include the UK, Ireland, and Denmark in addition to the original six members (Belgium, France, Germany, Italy, Netherlands,
and Luxembourg). In the mid-1970s, for example, there was a divergence among
members regarding in-kind, commodity-form aid versus financial assistance and
the extent to which food aid should or should not be used as surplus disposal. In
particular, the fact that some members, such as the UK, were net food importers
led them to advocate financial rather than in-kind assistance, and this started
the debate among donors in the Europe-wide program on the issue of tied versus untied food aid.[5] Although each member also had its own bilateral food aid
program, overall only a small proportion of the nine member states' aid budgets
were made up of food aid, while about half of Europe's food aid was channeled
through the collective program.[6]

Changing ideas were a large part of the impetus for initiating a gradual reform
of European food aid away from tied, in-kind requirements. Several academic
and policy studies undertaken in the 1970s and early 1980s highlighted serious
problems associated with food aid from Europe. Shortly after the Europe-wide
program first started, European countries experienced dairy surpluses, which
were then shifted into the collective program as a way to dispose of them. By the

---

4. Cathie 1997, 63.
5. Von Helldorf et al. 1979, 253.
6. Ibid., 239.

1970s, dairy products made up a significant portion of the Europe-wide program.[7] In 1974, a period of rising food prices internationally, the European Commission published a memo on food aid policy that acknowledged the potential market disruptions and disincentive effects of its food aid but also pointed out the potential benefits of that aid if it was managed carefully.[8]

By the late 1970s and early 1980s, annual reports by the European Court of Auditors regarding the Europe-wide food aid program revealed very poor performance resulting in serious delays in delivery (up to two years from commitment to delivery), delivery of poor-quality aid, and gross inefficiencies, particularly with respect to the delivery of dairy products as opposed to grains.[9] In addition to these audits, there were two independent evaluations of European food aid. The first, carried out in 1981–82, showed that there were serious cost inefficiencies associated with the program, especially with the donation of dairy products.[10] The second evaluation focused on the development effectiveness of European food aid. This study identified many weaknesses in program design and implementation and made recommendations to refocus European food aid in support of food security and national food strategies in recipient countries.[11]

These harsh criticisms of the European food aid program prompted a restructuring of the Europe-wide food aid administration and also marked the beginning of the process of untying that aid. In response to proposals from the European Parliament, funding for cereals food aid was increased and that for dairy aid was decreased. Regulatory changes within the European Community in the mid-1980s, including a reorganization of the different directorates and more streamlined requirements for tendering food aid contracts, allowed for more flexible arrangements, including the use of financial resources for procurement of food aid in developing countries. In the mid-1980s the European Commission argued for a break between the CAP and food aid management in Europe, and food surpluses were increasingly addressed with export subsidies rather than food aid.[12] A 1984 regulation passed by the Council of Ministers, the political leaders of the member states, allowed for the substitution of financial and technical aid on a grant basis for all or part of food aid allocated to a certain country when it was deemed that commodity food aid could disrupt local markets and

---

7. Clay and Mitchell 1983.

8. Cathie 1997, 70–71.

9. Interview with Edward Clay, senior research associate, Overseas Development Institute, UK, December 17, 2007; Cathie 1997, 81.

10. IDS/CEAS 1982. See also Clay and Mitchell 1983.

11. Maxwell 1982.

12. Cohen interview, October 17, 2007.

farmer incentives.[13] This regulation allowed for "triangular" transactions of food aid, sourced from a third country.[14]

These regulatory changes dovetailed with a shift in norms regarding the use of food aid in Europe in the 1980s. With a growing number of emergency situations arising around the world, including a general increase in food insecurity in Africa and particularly the Ethiopian famine in 1984–85, the European Commission began to view food aid as more of a humanitarian emergency response tool than a development instrument.[15] The idea of shifting European food aid to focus on humanitarian emergencies was expressed as early as 1981 by a member of the European Parliament, Katharina Focke, who noted that European food aid was "an inefficient way of distributing European surplus production to the poor countries, associated with high costs, countless mishaps, delays, wrangling over responsibility and bureaucratic obstacles; there is scarcely any control over how it works and what effects it achieves....Any attempt to hold it up to scrutiny leads to a radically different suggestion: confine food aid to emergency aid and otherwise replace it with financial assistance."[16]

The European Council Regulation on Food Aid Policy and Management (3972/86) was adopted in 1986. This regulation outlined the aims of the Europe-wide food aid program and explicitly incorporated food security, enhancement of nutrition, emergency assistance, and improved food production within recipient countries as key objectives.[17] Several member states were undertaking similar reforms at the domestic level in the 1980s to untie their food aid and were keen to see the Europe-wide program also take such steps.[18] Other European countries outside of the collective program, including Switzerland and Norway, were moving in a similar direction.

Institutional shifts that occurred within the European Commission also shaped policy in practice and interacted with the new norms in ways that facilitated change. After the adoption of the 1986 regulation, the Commission transferred the overall management of food aid from the Agriculture Directorate to the Development Directorate in 1987.[19] As John Shaw and Edward Clay note, "The management, procurement and delivery of EC food aid was separated from the management of the Community's Common Agricultural Policy under the

---

13. Shaw and Clay 1993, 166.
14. Clay and Benson 1990.
15. Clay interview, December 17, 2007.
16. Quoted in Jackson 1983, 53.
17. Cathie 1997, 77. See also Clay, Pilliai, and Benson 1998; Belfrage 2006.
18. Clay interview, December 17, 2007.
19. Shaw and Clay 1993, 167; Clay 2004.

1986 regulation."[20] An important aspect of this institutional restructuring was the fact that responsibility for managing food aid was taken away from the national agricultural ministries that had influenced it when it was under the direction of the Agriculture Directorate. The institutional restructuring of Europe's collective food aid program opened it more to the ideas that were being promoted to improve the overall efficiency and effectiveness of food aid. As Edward Clay has noted, this restructuring was "fundamental," altering the balance of influence in the development of European food aid policy that then enabled subsequent reforms to take place.[21]

There was some resistance at the time from national agricultural trade interests in the member states to this institutional restructuring as well as to the new norms governing food aid policy, but those interests were not able to halt the reform, which was by this time widely seen to be necessary to address gross inefficiencies in the program. Since each member state involved in the program at that time wanted to benefit in terms of obtaining contracts to provide the aid, there was no single unified lobby of these interests that was able to influence this outcome.[22] The Agriculture Directorate still maintained a small role in procurement, but it was the Development Directorate that was now responsible for the programming and most logistical details with respect to delivery. From 1993, rapid-onset and conflict-related emergency food aid from Europe was handled by a new agency, the European Community Humanitarian Office (ECHO), while slow-onset natural disaster and longer-term food aid was handled by the Food Security and Food Aid Service within the Development Directorate.[23]

The institutional shifts and new ideas within Europe were then diffused outward into international institutions. European policymakers, for example, pushed for allowing local and regional purchase of food aid to count toward their commitments under the Food Aid Convention when it was renegotiated in 1986. The United States was at the time bitterly opposed to the idea but was ultimately outnumbered as the Nordic country members and the European Commission were in favor of amending the FAC along these lines.[24] This change at the international institutional level opened space for European food aid to move more in the direction of triangular food aid transactions, which expanded in the late 1980s.[25]

By the early 1990s the Development Directorate and ECHO had much more control over the European food aid program than the Agriculture Directorate,

20. Shaw and Clay 1993, 166.
21. Clay interview, December 17, 2007.
22. Ibid.
23. See Clay, Dhiri, and Benson 1996, 11.
24. Clay interview, December 17, 2007.
25. Clay and Benson 1990, 32.

and European triangular food aid transactions were rising. Food surpluses had disappeared, and Europe was moving toward a single market with the passage of the Single European Act in 1986, which called for the full implementation of a single European market by 1992. This was an important moment in that the act required Europe-wide tendering of food aid procurement contracts under the single market. This applied to food aid contracts for both the Europe-wide program and the bilateral food aid given by individual member states of the European Union.[26] According to Edward Clay, this change "severely constrained the possibilities for national governments to tie food aid procurement to domestic sources."[27]

The implementation of the Single European Act, combined with the management of food aid under the Development Directorate, markedly reduced the ability of commercial agricultural trade interests to influence which foods were sourced as food aid[28] from what was already a weak position.[29] It had at that point become politically and administratively easier to justify and make use of financial instruments approved in the 1980s to procure food aid, including in developing countries. The use of financial resources to procure food aid either in recipient countries or through third-party countries further increased in the early 1990s, to account for roughly one-third of the Europe-wide food aid program by 1996, up from 11 percent in 1990.[30]

In 1992 the EU Council of Ministers requested an external evaluation of the European nonemergency (or program) food aid.[31] This report was a key factor behind a further overhaul in 1996 of nonemergency food aid in EU regulation 1292/96. This replaced previous food aid regulations and integrated European food aid policy under a broader food security strategy framework.[32] It required a focus on the countries most in need and also included as one of its objectives the reduction of recipient dependency on food aid. Toward this aim, it promoted the use of local and regional purchase. The regulation stated that whatever form it took, food aid should not disturb local markets in recipient countries. In addition to food aid, instruments available in this regulation included broader financial support for food security measures such as funding for seeds, tools, and storage schemes. This regulation has been seen as a watershed in finally achieving a European break from tied food aid and facilitating the use of untied

26. Clay and Stokke 2000a, 36; Clay 2004, 2.
27. Clay 2003, 705.
28. Clay and Stokke 2000a, 36; Clay 2004, 4.
29. Cathie 1990, 460.
30. Clay 2004; see also Thirion 2000, 278. See also Clay, Pillai, and Benson, 1998.
31. Clay, Dhiri, and Benson, 1996.
32. Madrid 2004, 18.

food assistance instead.[33] Because earlier reforms in Europe's collective food aid program had insulated the administrative and institutional oversight of its food aid from agricultural trade interests, there was little resistance from that quarter, while development agencies of member governments were strongly in favor of the policy, especially because it brought cost savings. The European Commission consulted with European NGOs that delivered food aid who had some input into the 1996 regulation, and thus they largely supported its provisions.[34]

Over a period of twenty years European food aid, including both the collective program and most individual European country programs, shifted away from tied and longer-term program food aid and toward the use of financial assistance for local and regional food purchases and a focus on the provision of emergency food assistance. In some ways, this shift appears to fit the earlier analysis of institutionalists and constructivists on the evolution of the food aid regime. Experts contributed to institutional restructuring by offering ideas for a more efficient and effective food aid policy. Once the control of food aid policy and management was largely out of the hands of the Agriculture Directorate and under the control of the Development Directorate, the European food aid program could be reformed along the lines of development and food security. This occurred within a broader context of untying other aspects of development aid, which proceeded much more quickly in Europe than in other donor countries.

But the embrace of the new norm of untying food aid differed in some important ways from the earlier institutional and constructivist analyses of food aid policy change. The new ideas regarding food aid untying were not pressed on Europe from international institutions. Rather, the policy change was a product of internal institutional restructuring, and it was Europe that pushed the idea outward into international institutional settings such as the Food Aid Convention. Economic interests were also not absent in the untying of European food aid. In this case, the donor's economic interest began to shift toward cost-saving efficiency in its development assistance programs and away from supporting national and private agricultural trade interests. This shift in part was a product of institutional restructuring that strengthened the Development Directorate vis-à-vis the Agriculture Directorate while also diffusing the power of private commercial economic interests. Moreover, NGOs that were important in food aid delivery were also in favor of untying and thus did not resist but rather supported the policy shift. The policy change to untie food aid, then, was not just one of a new norm being championed by a restructured European institutional

---

33. Barrett and Maxwell 2005.
34. See Thirion 2000.

context. Rather, a shifting balance among different economic interests also helps to explain the outcome.[35]

The European-wide food aid budget line was transferred to ECHO in 2007, signaling a further shift in European food aid toward primarily humanitarian purposes. The budget line accounts for about one-third of the EU's overall humanitarian budget.[36] The EU has increasingly moved to expand the use of its food aid budget lines to cover other forms of humanitarian and food assistance expenditures, including cash transfers and vouchers, especially after 2000.

## Canada

Historically Canada has been an important provider of food aid, typically being one of the top three or four international donors in terms of volume since its program began in 1951. Originally fully tied to homegrown commodities, Canadian food aid was partially untied by the government as far back as the early 1980s. At that time, Canada began to allow a small percentage of its food aid budget, ranging between 5 and 20 percent at different times, to be spent on local and regional purchase within developing countries.[37] The aid was largely tied in 2005, when the government began to allow up to 50 percent to be spent on procuring food in developing countries. Three years later, at the height of the 2008 food price spikes, Canada announced that it would allow up to 100 percent of its food aid to be sourced from developing countries. When announcing these policy changes in both 2005 and 2008, the government cited efficiency and effectiveness as key reasons for them, arguments frequently used to promote untying food aid. But, as in the case of the European Union, the full explanation for the untying policy is more complex than just the embrace of a new norm. The full story also involves shifting economic interests and the unique institutional context within which Canadian food aid policy is made.

Canadian food aid is primarily overseen by the Canadian International Development Agency (CIDA), which is under the Ministry of International Cooperation although in consultation with the ministries of trade and agriculture. Canada's food aid program originated in the early 1950s, just a few years before the U.S. program began. But it differs from the U.S. program in that the policy

35. Falkner 2007b notes a similar dynamic with respect to EU agricultural biotechnology policy. Whereas it appeared that the EU was championing a precautionary norm, domestic interests also helped to explain the policy outcome.

36. Grünewald, Kauffmann, and Sokpoh 2009.

37. Charlton 1992, 107.

is not set out in separate legislation and was always part of the country's over-all international development assistance program.[38] Canada's food aid has also been almost entirely in grant form. Food aid has consistently made up less than 4 percent of Canada's exports, and the proportion of all farm income devoted to such aid has historically been very small.[39] In 1986, for example, gross food aid expenditures were only 1.6 percent of net farm incomes.[40] Although it composed only a small percentage of Canada's exports, surplus disposal played a large role in the country's food aid policy. According to Mark Charlton, food aid provided an "escape valve" for the Canadian Wheat Board's (CWB's) management of its surplus stocks in the 1950s and 1960s.[41] In these early years, Canada's food aid policy was largely ad hoc in response to the need to address surplus stocks. After the 1970s food crisis, however, when the Canadian government reviewed its food aid policies, reforms resulted in a more integrated food aid program with more oversight by CIDA, although still in collaboration with the ministries of trade and agriculture.[42] This closer link to international development policy was insti-tutionalized with the establishment of the Food Aid Coordination and Evaluation Centre (FACE) within CIDA in 1978.[43] From that time Canadian food aid was increasingly channeled through multilateral organizations, primarily the WFP.

Food aid policy had come more fully under the development policy branch of the Canadian government by the late 1970s, but the procurement of food aid, handled by CIDA, was subject to rules set out by the federal government. Wheat, for example, had to be obtained through the CWB. The CWB, which purchases and markets most wheat grown in the Canadian west, dates back to the 1930s. At that time Canada opted for a marketing board as a less expensive option than the subsidies and production controls that the United States had begun to pursue as a way to assist the farming sector and facilitate exports.[44] The price for wheat purchased from the CWB for food aid was to be set at the "card price," which, according to Christopher Barrett and Daniel Maxwell, was almost always higher than prevailing international market prices.[45] Other commodities were to be pur-chased via other state and provincial marketing boards, at market prices.[46]

---

38. Shaw and Clay 1993, 157.
39. Barrett and Maxwell, 2005, 52.
40. Charlton 1992, 42.
41. Ibid., 18.
42. See Charlton 1992.
43. Shaw and Clay 1993, 157–58.
44. Charlton 1992, 17.
45. Barrett and Maxwell 2005, 54.
46. In the past, however, there have been cases where prices far above the prevailing market price have been paid by the government for food aid commodities—see Cohn 1979.

Most Canadian food aid has been provided directly by the government. But from the early 1980s a small but growing amount has been shipped via nongovernmental organizations typically under the umbrella of the Canadian Foodgrains Bank (CFGB). The CFGB was established in 1983 and is a partnership of Canadian faith-based organizations that work collectively to combat hunger in developing countries. The bank accepts donations of grain and funds to be provided as food aid and receives a four-to-one match from CIDA to support its food aid operations. However, it must abide by the Canadian government's rules regarding the tying level of food aid.

From the mid-1970s, as CIDA took a greater role in food aid policy, it concentrated on making the policy more coherent. This effort resulted in a new development strategy aimed at improving effectiveness and efficiency,[47] partly by untying a portion of its food aid. CIDA's strategy for 1975–80, for example, included a commitment to allow local purchases for up to 20 percent of its food aid, although it never came close to meeting that goal.[48] A parliamentary task force reviewed Canadian aid policy in 1980 and recommended that "every effort be made to supply food-deficit developing countries with food aid purchased by Canada from neighbouring food surplus developing countries." The Canadian government, however, reduced CIDA's untying authority to just 5 percent of its food aid in 1984, and this was to be allowed only in emergency situations that met certain criteria and only as a one-time response.[49] In 1987 a further review of Canadian aid policy was undertaken by the House of Commons Committee on External Affairs and International Trade. Its report, known as the Winegard Report, recommended the untying of food aid. The government did not take up this suggestion, however, and food aid was kept tied at 95 percent.[50] Charlton suggests that this adherence to a strictly tied policy may have been due to pressure from commodity producer organizations, who had long lobbied for increases in Canadian food aid.[51]

It was not just private economic interests that influenced the process, however. The government's own budget considerations were also important. The Canadian food aid program suffered deep cuts in the 1990s when the government scaled back its overall international aid program because of budget constraints. CIDA's expenditures on food aid fell from C$390 million to C$218 million between 1993 and 1997.[52] This was a time of relatively high grain prices, and in 1995

---

47. Charlton 1992, 5.
48. Ibid., 106–7.
49. Ibid., 107; Gillies 1994, 189.
50. Gillies 1994, 190–91.
51. See Charlton 1994, 77.
52. http://www.acdi-cida.gc.ca/acdi-cida/acdi-cida.nsf/eng/EMA-218132558-PNV.

Canada reduced its commitment to the FAC from 600,000 to 400,000 tonnes annually. Canada began to allow up to 10 percent of its food aid budget to be spent on local and regional purchases in developing countries at this time. CIDA had handled both procurement and delivery of that aid up until the late 1990s, when it handed those tasks to the WFP. The latter, however, still had to follow Canada's rules, which stipulated that 90 percent of its food aid donations had to be procured within Canada.

The tied nature of Canada's food aid did not seriously shift until Canadian NGOs became engaged with the issue in the late 1990s. The idea was originally floated by the Canadian Foodgrains Bank.[53] In 1999 the CFGB initiated the creation of the Canadian Food Security Policy Group, composed of NGOs working on food issues across Canada.[54] These groups, including Oxfam Canada and World Vision Canada, sought to convince the Canadian government to allow more local purchase of commodities in developing countries to give as food aid. These groups had been frustrated by their inability to respond quickly to emergency situations as a result of the 90 percent tying rule.[55]

The Canadian Food Security Policy Group carefully thought through how to present the idea of untying food aid as one that would provide more flexibility in terms of food needs and be more efficient in terms of cost-effectiveness and timing—broad goals it was aware that CIDA itself was trying to reach. The group was concerned, however, that certain interests, including those who benefited economically from supplying Canadian-grown food aid commodities, would resist the idea of untying aid. According to Oxfam representative Mark Fried, "People were easily convinced by the logic of the arguments—the challenge was motivating politicians and farm organizations to take the risk of alienating their constituents." Similarly, Stuart Clark of the Canadian Foodgrains Bank noted "We had a sound argument…but it was not sufficient. Without political support it wasn't going anywhere."[56] The NGOs first sought grassroots support from farmers and from their church base. They explained why untying food aid was beneficial for developing world farmers because it reduced distortions to markets that could hurt their incomes. They also aimed to show that Canadian farmers would not see their own incomes drop by any significant amount by untying food aid because less than 1 percent of Canada's production of any major food commodity went for food aid.[57] Canadian farmers were receptive to these ideas.

---

53. Interview with Stuart Clark, senior policy advisor, Canadian Foodgrains Bank, and chair, Transatlantic Food Assistance Dialogue, November 2007.

54. Carty 2006.

55. Clark interview, November 2007.

56. Both quotes in Carty, 2006, 50.

57. Ibid.

They understood the problems associated with foreign competition and wanted to help, not hurt, farmers in the developing world.

The next groups to convince were the agricultural lobbies—large farmer organizations like the National Farmers' Union and the Canadian Wheat Board. These organizations wanted assurance that the beneficiaries of untying policies would be farmers in the developing world, not those in other industrialized countries who might be producing food more cheaply because they were supported by hefty farm subsidies. Because the proposal was to allow untying only for the purpose of local purchase from developing countries, and not from other industrialized countries, these groups gave their support. Other farmer groups, including the Canadian Federation of Agriculture, the Western Wheat Growers Association and the Western Canadian Barley Growers Association, also came on board.[58]

Gaining the support of these groups was made easier by the fact that food aid had sustained such serious cuts in the 1990s that the economic stake that these groups had in the food aid program was at this point very small.[59] Moreover, food aid had become politicized on the WTO negotiation agenda, and Canada, like the EU and Australia (discussed below), were keen to push the United States to reduce its domestic subsidies, including what were seen to be unfair practices in its food aid policies (the politics around food aid in the WTO context will be discussed in detail in chapter 6). Making a bold move to untie a significant portion of its food aid would give Canada leverage in the WTO talks.[60] Gaining bargaining power in this context was a more important goal at that time for these groups than their desire to maintain rules on food aid tying.

Around the same time that Canadian NGOs began to campaign on the issue and the WTO talks had pushed it along, there was also a broad shift in policy away from longer-term development aid that had dominated the 1990s and more toward emergency and humanitarian aid. This change closely tracked a similar trend with the WFP, which began to see more of its aid directed toward emergency aid in the face of a rising number of humanitarian crises induced by both conflict and natural disasters. The Asian tsunami at the end of 2004 was an important moment for CIDA, which realized that the 90 percent tying rule imposed a serious barrier to responding to the crisis swiftly.

Although CIDA had come to agree with the idea of untying its food aid, it needed interministerial approval for a change in policy. Also influencing the context was the fact that Canada had fallen behind on its FAC commitments for much of the 2000–2005 period; its tight budget and rising grain prices made it

---

58. Ibid, 51.
59. Barrett and Maxwell 2005, 54.
60. Margulis 2005.

increasingly difficult to make up the backlog.[61] The cost savings from untying began to look attractive to the government, including the foreign affairs and agriculture departments, both of which also played a role along with CIDA in overseeing Canada's implementation of the FAC. After consultations, the Canadian government announced in September 2005 that up to 50 percent of its food aid budget could be used for local purchases in developing countries. The rationale given by the minister of international cooperation at the time of the announcement noted the importance of efficiency:

> This new policy gives us the ability to respond more quickly and with greater flexibility to disasters world-wide, buying more food and feeding a greater number of people in need.... It will help lower transportation costs, provide more culturally appropriate food, and allow Canada's aid dollars to go further while supporting local farmers in developing countries.[62]

The groups pushing for this change both inside and outside Canada were pleased.[63] Although they had wanted Canada's food aid to be fully untied, they were willing to live with 50 percent.[64] But just two and a half years later, in spring 2008 at the height of food price spikes, Canada announced that it was taking the step to fully untie its food aid. This time the policy change was not the result of an intense grassroots campaign, nor had it been especially politicized in the government. The announcement was made alongside the government's response to the World Food Programme's plea for additional funding in the midst of the food price crisis.

One of the key motivating factors for the 100 percent untying at this particular time was the high price of grain and fuel in the spring of 2008. The rules of procedure of the Food Aid Convention stipulate that financial contributions can be converted to wheat equivalents based on the previous year's average price of wheat. At the time, the conversion price of financial resources to wheat was roughly half the going market price. In effect, untying at that particular moment gave Canada a two-for-one deal if it untied its aid and provided financial resources instead of food in its commodity form. This would enable it to meet its FAC commitments at a much lower cost than providing actual grain, although the gain from the conversion formula was a one-time benefit.[65] Rising fuel prices

---

61. Clark 2002.
62. Quoted in CIDA 2005.
63. Canadian Foodgrains Bank 2005.
64. Carty 2006, 51.
65. E-mail communication from Stuart Clark, October 2009.

were also important, as even shipping 50 percent of its food aid from Canada had become very costly.

An additional push came from several reports from both outside and within the government that encouraged the policy change to 100 percent untying. Reports from several conservative think tanks argued that the change would improve both the efficiency and effectiveness of Canadian aid.[66] Under a conservative government at the time, these reports had significant influence. The OECD's Development Assistance Committee (DAC) also released a peer review of Canada in 2007 that encouraged the government to consider fully untying its food aid.[67] A further government review of aid to sub-Saharan Africa in 2007 also made this suggestion.[68]

In the Canadian case, the shift toward untying food aid was not just the product of a gradual uptake of new ideas for more effective food aid policy that came from international institutions. Although the idea had been around since the 1980s, the eventual policy change took place rapidly and decisively. Like in the case of the European-wide food aid program, shifts in both the domestic institutional aid context and in the economic interests of the government, agribusiness, and NGOs all played a role, although in somewhat different ways from the European case. Canadian NGOs played a central role in putting the issue on the agenda and championing the ideas. The increased interest in efficiency and cost-savings on the part of the government, combined with a weakened stake in tied food aid on the part of agribusiness interests and the prospect of using untying to increase Canada's leverage in agricultural trade talks, brought about a new balance of economic interests in favor of untying. As Stuart Clark of the CFGB noted, the 2008 untying was "90 percent pragmatic, 10 percent idealism."[69]

## Australia

Australia has been a regular donor of food aid since the 1950s. It was the third largest donor after the United States and Canada for much of the 1950s and 1960s, before Europe and Japan became donors. In recent years, it has typically maintained its role as the fifth largest donor, just behind Canada. In its early days Australian food aid was largely tied to domestic production of food commodities. Australia did experiment with local and regional purchases, particularly when it

---

66. Goldfarb and Tapp 2006; Harris and Manning 2007.
67. OECD 2007.
68. Parliament of Canada 2007.
69. Interview with Stuart Clark, December 2008.

was unable to provide domestic commodities. The country partially untied its food aid in 2004 and fully untied it in early 2006 as part of a larger policy decision to untie all its foreign aid. As in the case of the EU and Canada, a number of factors played into this policy change.

For most of its history, Australian food aid has been overseen by the country's overseas aid program, the Australian Agency for International Development (AusAID), which was initially established in the mid-1970s. This aid, unlike that of Canada and the United States, was never meant to act primarily as a surplus disposal mechanism. The country does not provide large subsidies for its producers, nor did it hold major stockpiles of food, as it typically clears its stocks of wheat and rice at the end of each season. Food aid has historically been only a small proportion of Australia's foreign aid budget, and it accounts for only a small percentage of domestic production and food exports.[70]

Australia's food aid before its untying was typically composed of domestic commodities, mainly wheat and rice. These products were purchased commercially at international market prices from the Australian Wheat Board and the Ricegrowers' Association. AusAID purchased wheat at the card price, equivalent to the Chicago futures price in U.S. dollars. For rice the price was agreed on ahead of time and was based on international price forecasts. Because the prices paid by AusAID were set in U.S. dollars, the aid agency took on the currency exchange rate risk. Although there have been claims that AusAID typically paid premium prices for the commodities it supplied as food aid, this claim has been contested by the Wheat Board and the Ricegrowers' Association.[71] Once it reached its destination, nearly all Australian food aid was monetized.[72]

Although most of its aid has long been tied to Australian products, the country has a history of allowing purchases of non-Australian commodities when required to meet its obligations under the Food Aid Convention. In the early 1980s, for example, when Australia itself was facing lower production due to drought, it purchased food from other countries in order to meet its FAC obligations. There was also a special provision in the aid budget allowing for local and regional purchase of food aid in emergencies.[73]

Because it makes up a relatively small part of Australia's exports and production, food aid has not been a major means by which to promote the country's domestic agricultural interests. Of more concern to the agricultural lobby has been the agricultural trade practices of its competitors. Although there was some

---

70. Clay and Shaw 1993, 143.
71. AusAID 1997, 90, 91–92.
72. See Shaw and Clay 1993.
73. Clay and Shaw 1993, 144, 151.

pressure in the early 1990s to ensure that Australian commodities were used as food aid,[74] more recently that lobby has had a greater interest in seeing other donors reduce those practices as a means by which to level the playing field. Australia has long been concerned about the potential trade distortions of food aid that could harm grain-exporting countries such as itself, and this concern was key in its push for the establishment of rules on surplus disposal.[75]

A major review of the Australian food aid program was undertaken by AusAID in 1997. Much of the report focused on the problems of tied food aid, and one of the key recommendations was greater focus on emergency relief through financial contributions for local and regional purchase and use of Australian commodities only where they were cost-effective. The report noted that such a focus would be consistent with the existing procurement policies of the Australian government, which called for the best value for the money.[76] A further recommendation of the report was to channel most of Australia's food aid through the World Food Programme in order to improve timeliness and efficiency of food assistance. The report also recommended reducing Australia's commitment under the FAC because of budgetary constraints. While untying was not immediately implemented, the government of Australia did reduce its FAC commitment from 250,000 tonnes to 150,000 tonnes in 1999.

Australia partially untied its food aid in 2004, continued its policy of sourcing the most cost-effective commodities, and also began to move away from monetization of food aid. By 2006 the majority of the aid was delivered via the WFP.[77] In early 2006 Australia announced that all its overseas aid, including food aid, would be fully untied. This was a bold step to take, as the recommendations from the OECD regarding aid untying specifically excluded food aid.

By contrast with the Canadian case, the move to fully untie Australian food aid was not the result of a specific campaign regarding tied food aid but rather was part of a broader move to untie aid, in a context where it was not required to include food aid as part of its untying commitments. Although food aid appears to have been thrown in for good measure as part of the larger aid-untying process, there were in fact several forces responsible for its inclusion. First, the ideas were important, at least in justifying the move. The earlier 1997 report that made the untying recommendation argued that untied aid was a superior way to provide assistance because it was more flexible and allowed more timely deliveries

---

74. Ibid., 152.
75. AusAID 1997, 15.
76. Ibid., xii, 66–68.
77. AusAID 2006, 3.

of food with the least amount of market distortion for both recipients and other agricultural exporters.[78]

The ideas, however, are difficult to fully disentangle from the interests. A large part of the reason that the idea of untied food aid was attractive was the cost savings. Australia had already reduced its commitments to the FAC in 1999 because it had experienced trouble meeting its obligations. In a background brief on the untying, AusAID noted the cost savings that could be expected, which were up to 50 percent for food aid.[79] With international food and fuel prices beginning to rise in 2005, untying aid at this time was seen as a way to make scarce aid dollars go further. It had become much more cost-effective to rely on the WFP's world-wide tender system to provide locally available food commodities in developing countries than to ship Australian rice over long distances.[80]

In addition to basic cost savings, there was also the issue of availability of domestic commodities. Australia had also been the victim of recurring and more frequent drought, which had hindered its overall food production, reducing the availability of domestic commodities to be donated as food aid. Agricultural interests, in other words, were not in need of drumming up additional demand for their products from AusAID because of their limited supply. Given how the deals with AusAID were made when the aid was tied, rice producers in particular could obtain better prices for their product on world markets.[81] For this reason the untying of Australian food aid did not encounter much resistance from the agricultural lobby, despite its earlier efforts in the 1980s to ensure that food aid was composed of Australian-grown commodities. At the same time, the agricultural lobby had an interest in ensuring that unfair trade practices would not be tolerated as part of the ongoing WTO negotiations. As a leading player in the Cairns Group, Australia and its agriculture lobby had long fought against what it considered to be unfair levels of farm protection in the United States.[82]

Although it had only recently ended food aid tying and monetization itself, Australia almost immediately took up the mantle of denouncing these practices in the context of the WTO negotiations. The Australian government commissioned a report in 2007 on food aid and agricultural trade reform, looking specifically at food aid as an export subsidy. The report provided a stinging critique of tied food aid and monetization.[83] It barely mentioned Australia's past food aid

---

78. AusAID 1997.
79. AusAid 2006.
80. Interview with Jayne Bates, food assistance coordinator, Humanitarian Policy Section, AusAID, August 19, 2008.
81. Ibid.
82. Ibid.; Harris 2007.
83. Harris 2007.

practices and targeted the United States and Japan in particular as undertaking trade-distorting food aid programs. The Department of Agriculture, Fisheries and Forests also published a fact sheet online in 2007, pointing out why tied food aid distorted markets and harmed Australian agricultural commodity exporters.[84] Such moves helped the government to get the agricultural lobby's support for its own untying policy and also put Australia in a stronger position in the WTO agriculture negotiations.

The policy shift in Australia toward untying its food aid was fairly swift and uncontroversial. But like the European and Canadian cases, it was more complex than just new ideas gradually filtering down to the domestic level from international institutions. Although the OECD promoted idea of aid untying generally did play a role in Australia, the domestic institutional context and the shifting balance of economic interests also help to explain the outcome. With AusAID as the sole administrative unit for food aid, the domestic institutional context was not terribly complex, and it was open to new ideas to improve the effectiveness and efficiency of its food aid programs. The economic interests of the state and the agricultural lobby also became closely aligned in favor of untying food aid, which brought both cost-savings and increased bargaining power for Australia at the WTO.

## Japan

Japan has followed almost the opposite trend from that of the countries discussed above in that its food aid has become more tied in recent years. Most of its contributions in the decade before 1995 were in the form of financial resources and supported local and triangular food aid purchases. Since the mid 1990s, its practices shifted dramatically toward direct-transfer, tied food aid. The reasons for this policy change have more to do with Japan's international trade agreement obligations than with a conviction that direct-transfer food aid is superior to other forms of food assistance.

Japan was in fact a large recipient of food aid itself after the Second World War. Although it had been a net-food-importing country, it began to give food aid after being pressured to join the FAC in 1967. Most of its donations then were in the form of financial resources because it did not have significant surplus food stocks to draw on, as did other donors. By the early 1970s and 1980s, Japan had built up fairly significant stocks of rice, which had an impact on its food aid donations. From the mid-1980s to the mid-1990s, its stocks dropped as a result of the

---

84. http://www.daff.gov.au/agriculture-food/wheat-sugar-crops/crops/market_access/misuse.

government policy of restricting production through farm support programs that encouraged crop diversification.[85] Today Japan is the fourth-largest donor of food aid after the United States, the European Union and Canada, though in recent years it has sometimes given more than Canada.

Japan's food aid is administered by the Japan International Cooperation Agency (JICA). Its annual commitment to the FAC is 300,000 tonnes, an amount it has exceeded, sometimes by over twice as much, in recent years. Roughly half of Japan's food aid is channeled through the WFP, while the other half is bilateral. Its contributions to the WFP have increased markedly since the late 1980s. In its early days Japan also gave loans for the purchase of food aid, a practice it ended in the early 1980s.[86]

From the mid-1980s to the mid-1990s, most of Japan's food aid was spent on triangular and local purchase of commodities, with very small amounts of direct-transfer aid from its own food stocks. But from 1996 onward as stocks began to grow significantly, the policy shifted. Most of its food aid is now tied direct transfer aid with smaller amounts given as triangular and local purchase.[87] This increase in direct-transfer aid indicates the rising level of tied aid from Japan. Its financial donations to the WFP, for example, have come with a condition that a portion is spent on procuring the commodity from Japan. In 2009, 62 percent of Japan's food aid was direct transfer, i.e., food (mainly rice) procured in Japan, which accounted for 9 percent of all direct-transfer food aid.[88]

This change in the form of Japan's food aid is linked to both its own domestic support programs for its rice farmers and its obligations under the WTO Uruguay Round Agreement on Agriculture (URAA), which came into effect in 1995. To support the domestic market, the government purchases surpluses of domestic rice, which have emerged despite the incentives put in place to reduce rice production.[89] These support policies mean that Japanese consumers pay three to five times the prevailing international price for domestic rice.

Combined with the domestic purchasing of rice, the URAA rules require WTO members to import tariff-free at least 5 percent of their domestic consumption of food commodities as part of the minimum-access provisions of the agreement. For Japan, this means importing some 770,000 tonnes of rice per year, mostly from the United States, Thailand, and Vietnam. Because it protects the market for domestic rice, the Japanese government prefers to stockpile the

---

85. Shaw and Clay 1993, 202.
86. Ibid., 201.
87. WFP data, available from WFP Food Aid Information System (http://www.wfp.org/fais/).
88. WFP 2010a, 22.
89. Harris 2007, 28.

imported rice rather than release it on its home market, which would defeat the purpose of its support program. This practice is justified on the grounds that Japanese people prefer domestic over imported rice because the former is seen to be of much higher quality.[90]

As a result of these practices, Japan has accumulated huge stockpiles of rice, including both domestic rice and foreign-origin rice (also called "minimum access rice"). These stockpiles have often reached over 2 million tonnes (and the imported portion often over 1 million) resulting in significant storage costs for the Japanese government. To reduce these costs while also minimizing disruption to the domestic rice market, some of this surplus is donated as food aid, some is sold as animal feed, and some is used in processed foods. According to David Harris, "Food aid has been the only option for generating an external outflow to relieve the supply pressures".[91] WTO rules prevent countries from commercially reexporting food imported under the minimum-access rules unless explicit permission is given from the country it is imported from, but these restrictions do not apply equally to food aid.[92] If the food is given in relatively small quantities, as a grant, such permission is not required.[93] During the food price crisis in early 2008, Japan released some of this stockpiled rice as food aid.[94]

The idea of untying food aid has not had much influence on policy in Japan. Its earlier policy of donating financial resources for local and triangular purchases instead of commodity aid was not based on the belief that this method was superior. The policy arose simply because the country is a net food importer and did not have any surplus to donate. But when Japan did become a holder of significant rice stocks, it changed its policy based on the government's and domestic rice producers' economic interests. The international institutional context of the WTO trade rules, as well as domestic institutional pressure to support Japanese rice producers, created an economic incentive for the country to dispose of rice surpluses in order to save on the high costs of storage.

## The United States

Since its food aid program began in 1954, the United States has maintained a nearly fully tied food aid policy. Although many studies have pointed out the

---

90. Ministry of Foreign Affairs of Japan 2007; see also Alpha et al. 2006, 7.
91. Harris 2007, 28.
92. Ibid., 29.
93. Slayton and Timmer 2008, 2.
94. Hall 2008.

inefficiencies and distorting effects of this policy, and vocal academics and policy administrators as well as activists have called for reform toward greater food aid untying, change has been only minimal. This is in large part due to the domestic institutional context within which policy on food aid is made in the United States, as well as to powerful economic interests, including not just commercial enterprises but also NGOs, which have easy access to policymakers. As a result, the debate in the United States has been particularly heated.

Because the United States is the world's largest donor of food aid and has played a prominent role in international debates over food aid policy, the debate over U.S. food aid tying is especially important for understanding debates over food aid in the global context. This subject is therefore covered in more depth in chapter 4.

## Other Donors

The countries discussed above are the main donors of food aid, but other countries have also taken on a growing role. Some of these donors provide their aid in tied form, while others do not. Several, including South Korea and China, have increasingly provided food aid to North Korea, in particular since the mid-2000s. Aid from both South Korea and China is typically tied, in commodity form. In the case of South Korea, it is provided in the form of a concessional loan rather than a grant.[95] During the 2008 food price crisis, as will be discussed in chapter 7, Saudi Arabia, which to that time had not been a major donor of food aid, stepped forward with an untied $500 million cash gift to the WFP. Aid from others donors who are not members of the FAC has been erratic, however. China, for example, was the third-largest donor to the WFP in 2005, providing nearly 500,000 tonnes of food, but in 2008 it provided only about 50,000.[96] Even some FAC members, such as Argentina, have not provided any food aid for years.

## Conclusion

The idea of untying food aid has been a powerful one. It appeals to ideals of economic efficiency and effectiveness. But despite international expert promotion of the idea, its uptake within donor countries has been uneven over the years. This indicates that more than just ideas promoted internationally are at play

---

95. Clay, Riley, and Urey 2006.
96. WFP data, available from WFP Food Aid Information System (http://www.wfp.org/fais/).

in shaping their food aid policies. As this chapter's review of the major donor countries shows, the process of untying food aid was different in the EU, Canada, and Australia. The domestic institutional context was different in each case, and it was this context, more than the international one, that particularly influenced how the new ideas were received by the three donors. Interests were also important in the policy process. For the donors that untied their food aid, private economic interests that had previously benefited from a tied food aid program either were already weakened to the point that they no longer had a large impact on policy processes or, as in the case of Canada and Australia, realized that the untying of food aid would serve larger trade interests at the WTO. At the same time, state interests had shifted in favor of untying food aid, either as a result of shifts in focus toward humanitarian aid—where untying was more efficient and timely—or because of budget constraints, or both. In the countries that untied, state interests eventually became strong enough to trump the private interests, allowing for a shift in policy.

In countries that maintained largely tied food aid policies, the patterns were also different. Japan is an unusual case in that it went from being primarily a donor of untied financial assistance for food aid to a tied food aid provider. In this case, the interests of the state in disposing of food that it was required to import as part of its WTO obligations and in protecting the livelihoods of Japanese farmers prevailed in determining policy. Efficiency and effectiveness were not predominant reasons for Japan's original untied food aid policy, and its interest in protecting its own agricultural sector, especially its rice growers, dictated the policy toward greater tying. In the United States, private interests with a stake in food aid—including in this case both commercial and NGO actors—combined with a unique institutional setting, were able to keep the aid largely tied, despite uptake of the idea of food aid untying at high levels of the government's administration.

4

# U.S. DEBATES ON TIED FOOD AID

The United States has maintained a nearly 100 percent tied food aid policy for most of the history of its food aid programs. It was not until 2008 that U.S. legislation even opened the door, however slightly, to the possibility of allocating a very small portion of the aid in the form of cash for local and regional purchases in developing countries. The United States is an important case to examine in some depth because the debate over the tying of food aid and food aid monetization practices became especially politicized at the domestic level in 2005–8.

This chapter shows that the debate was strongly shaped by the economic interests of key players, including the agricultural lobby, the shipping lobby, and food-aid-delivery NGOs. These groups were able to exert influence over a powerful part of the domestic institutional setting where important decisions regarding food aid policy are made: the U.S. Congress. Through extensive lobbying they fought hard to maintain existing policies, even in the face of proposals emanating from the very highest levels of government to untie a portion of the food aid and curb the practice of monetization. The result was that the country's policies remained largely intact. Under the 2008 U.S. Farm Bill, some small changes were made, including a pilot project providing cash for local and regional purchase, but that came only after extensive debate, and it was minuscule compared with the overall food aid program. Further changes were made in the wake of the food price crisis of 2008, although these were outside the regular channels in which food aid policy is made in the United States.

# The Institutional Setting

United States food aid policy is governed by a variety of legislative acts, including most prominently the Farm Bill. The country funds a variety of food aid programs authorized under Title III (Trade) of the U.S. Farm Bills, each with specific goals, requirements, and funding mechanisms. The Farm Bill, renegotiated every five years, is the main piece of legislation that sets out the basic rules regarding various agricultural support programs, such as commodity subsidies, rural development, international food aid, and programs to combat domestic hunger. The Farm Bills typically outline a minimum amount of tonnage to be donated under various food aid programs and can stipulate percentages that are to go to emergency and nonemergency uses, as well as proposed funding levels.[1] Food aid normally accounts for around $2 billion out of a total $60 billion authorized by the bill.[2] The actual funding for the programs, however, is approved annually as part of the federal budget process.

The Food for Peace program (PL 480) is the largest U.S. food aid program, accounting for 50–90 percent of the U.S. Department of Agriculture's (USDA's) food aid budget over the past decade.[3] The program has three titles under which it can fund food aid. Title I, Trade and Economic Development Assistance, is managed by the USDA and provides loans to both governments and private firms in developing countries for the purchase of food on concessional terms. Food aid provided under this title is typically not targeted and has historically been sold on local markets.

Title II, Emergency and Development Assistance, is managed by the U.S. Agency for International Development (USAID) and provides grant aid to countries in food deficit for both emergencies and nonemergencies. Title II aid is provided mainly through U.S.-based NGOs and the World Food Programme. Some of the aid under this title, especially that channeled through NGOs, is monetized in the recipient country to raise funds for transportation of the aid and other development activities.

Title III, Food for Development, is managed by USAID and provides funding for government-to-government grants to the least developed countries to support long-term development. Title III was added to PL 480 in the 1970s and provided government-owned surpluses of grain as food aid on credit terms for countries that promoted private-sector development. At that time it was managed by the USDA. Title III was changed in the 1990s to provide food aid on a

---

1. E.g., Hanrahan 2008, 2.
2. See Kripke 2009, 119.
3. Ho and Hanrahan 2010, 2.

grant basis and is now managed by USAID. Food aid under this title is also monetized, or sold on local markets in an untargeted fashion, and the funds raised are to be used to support long-term economic development and food security programs in recipient countries.[4]

Although the Food for Peace program has been by far the largest channel through which U.S. food aid flows, the significance of the various titles within the program has changed over the years. Before 1980, the vast bulk of aid was channeled through Title I, which meant that most of it was sold on concessional terms to poor countries and was in turn sold on local markets in an untargeted fashion. The primary purpose of this program was to develop export markets for U.S. grains. After the 1970s food crisis, Title I food aid diminished, and starting in the 1980s most of the aid was channeled through Title II. Title I and Title III food aid are now largely inactive. No budget appropriations have been requested for Title III aid since 2001 and none for Title I aid since 2006.[5]

Other U.S. food aid programs include Food for Progress, which provides food aid commodities for either donation or sale on credit to developing countries that are committed to promoting private enterprise development in the agricultural sector. Section 416(b) of the Agricultural Act of 1949 provides for the donation of surplus commodities to foreign countries or food-aid-delivery NGOs. The USDA manages this program and can use these surpluses to carry out the objectives of Food for Peace.[6] Because it is dependent on surplus commodities, which are currently nonexistent, this program is currently inactive. The McGovern-Dole International Food for Education and Child Nutrition Program, also managed by the USDA, was adopted as part of the 2002 Farm Bill. It provides food commodities by donation to NGOs, governments, and intergovernmental organizations for school feeding programs.

The commodities donated through Food for Peace are procured by the USDA through its Commodity Credit Corporation (CCC), operated by the USDA's Farm Service Agency.[7] The CCC, incorporated in 1933 and part of the USDA since 1939, provides financing for domestic income and price support programs in the United States, as well as for its export promotion programs, and is permanently authorized to borrow up to $30 billion from the U.S. Treasury.[8] It obtains grain stocks either through the price support programs or from purchases from

---

4. For more detail on each of these programs, see Ho and Hanrahan 2010.
5. Barrett and Maxwell 2005, 23; Ho and Hanrahan 2010.
6. GAO 2002, 4.
7. Barrett and Maxwell 2005, 23.
8. USDA Farm Service Agency 1999.

private stocks, and because it supports export promotion, it has long been involved in food aid programs.[9]

Funding for U.S. food aid has averaged around $2 billion per year over the past decade. The vast majority of this funding has gone to the Food for Peace program, with Food for Progress and the McGovern-Dole programs accounting for approximately $200 million and $100 million per year, respectively.[10] However, the allocation of funding for the bulk of the food aid programs, particularly Food for Peace and McGovern-Dole, is discretionary through annual agricultural appropriations acts. This means that each year funding for these programs must be approved by Congress.[11] Supplemental appropriations that fund these and other food aid programs are also approved by Congress as part of the president's annual budget. Funding for other programs is provided by the borrowing authority of the CCC.[12]

Budget requests and the Farm Bills are not the only measures governing food aid. The Cargo Preference Act of 1954 also affects food aid policy by setting out rules regarding the transportation of U.S. commodities under PL 480. The act as amended in the 1985 Farm Bill stipulates that 75 percent of PL480 food aid must be shipped on U.S.-flagged ships. The purpose is to keep U.S. ships in business so that a merchant marine will be available for national security purposes.[13]

By setting out food aid policies within specific pieces of legislation that it must approve annually, Congress plays a strong role in determining the direction of these policies. Any proposed changes must be approved by both houses of Congress. As a result, food aid programs have been the subject of numerous reports as well as congressional hearings, since each year the members of that body must update themselves on current policies and new proposals. This procedure differs from that in other donor countries, outlined in chapter 3, where policies are set largely within the agencies that administer food aid programs or by decree at higher levels.

## The Role of Domestic Interests

Domestic interest groups have played a strong role in determining the direction of U.S. food aid policy over the past decade. A high percentage of the food

---

9. See Barrett 2007; Cardwell 2007.
10. Ho and Hanrahan 2010, 10.
11. Abbott 2007.
12. Ho and Hanrahan 2010, 9–10.
13. See Hanrahan 2008, 7; Bageant, Barrett, and Lentz 2010.

aid budget is spent within the United States, which helps to explain the strong interest in the program among domestic actors who benefit from it. In 2004, for example, it was estimated that some 90 percent of the aid budget was spent inside the country.[14] The main domestic beneficiaries are agribusiness firms, the maritime industry, and food-aid-delivery NGOs (also referred to in the United States as private voluntary organizations [PVOs]). Each of these groups has organized into broader lobbies seeking to influence congressional decisions regarding food aid. Food aid experts have referred to this constellation of interest groups as the iron triangle because together their efforts to influence food aid policy have been very effective and difficult to break.[15]

## Agribusiness Firms

Domestic agricultural producers and processors have a strong interest in rules that tie food aid donations to U.S.-sourced commodities—which by law must be not only grown in the United States but also processed and packaged on U.S. soil. There is significant corporate concentration in the global grain industry, and the United States is important for them both as a site of production and as a market. Just four firms—Archer Daniels Midland, Bunge, Cargill, and Louis Dreyfus (referred to in the business as the ABCD firms)—control the vast bulk of the global grain trade.[16] All four have significant operations in the United States.

Given their importance in the U.S. and global grain markets, these companies are key players in current U.S. food aid operations. With most aid now purchased on open markets by the CCC rather than out of government-held surpluses, there are more direct benefits of tied aid for private grain-handling and -processing companies.[17] The fact that the aid must be sourced domestically means that there are a limited number of potential providers bidding on contracts. According to Celia Dugger, in the 2004–7 period, more than half of food aid in the Food for Peace program was purchased from just four large transnational agrifood companies and their subsidiaries: ADM, Cargill, Bunge, and Cal Western Packaging.[18] Just one of those firms, Cargill, is reported to have sold $1.09 billion in grain to the U.S. government for food aid between 1995 and 2005.[19]

Because of the limited competition among the grain companies, prices are often above market rates. When added to the inefficiencies in the procurement

---

14. Tarnoff and Nowels 2005, 19.
15. Barrett and Maxwell 2005.
16. ActionAid International 2005, 12.
17. Barrett and Maxwell 2005, 89.
18. Dugger 2007c.
19. Thurow and Kilman 2005.

process in the United States, the result is a significant price premium for food aid. These premiums, calculated by Barrett and Maxwell, range from approximately 3.2 percent above market rates for wheat to more than 70 percent for maize. As those authors note, domestically sourced food aid costs the U.S. government on average 11 percent more than market prices.[20]

Food aid is important for the wheat industry. For example, 23 percent of all hard white wheat exports for 2001–2 and 17 percent of hard red wheat exports in 2002–3 were sold to the government for food aid programs. The U.S. Wheat Associates, a lobby group for the wheat industry, made clear the importance of food aid by stating, "Losing in-kind donations and monetization would be a difficult blow for the U.S. wheat industry."[21] Food aid is also important to the rice industry, accounting for around 10–20 percent of all U.S. rice exports.[22]

## Shipping Companies

The shipping industry has a strong interest in U.S. food aid programs, having earned some $1.3 billion in contracts to ship food aid around the world over the 2003–6 period.[23] The voice of the shipping lobby is powerful in U.S. politics, as these companies donate significant sums to political campaigns.[24] Like the grain industry, the shipping industry is controlled by only a few companies. This is illustrated by the fact that just five firms were awarded contracts for over half of the $300 million spent on shipping food aid in 2004.[25] This concentration in food aid shipment is in large part a product of the policy requiring in-kind aid to be shipped on U.S.-flagged ships. In the 1990s there were only eighteen shipping companies that were qualified to bid on food aid contracts, and by the early 2000s this number had dropped to just thirteen.[26]

Corporate concentration is even more pronounced for the "freight forwarders," the firms that coordinate international transportation of food aid channeled through NGOs. According to Barrett and Maxwell, four freight forwarders handled 84 percent of the food aid shipped through the Food for Progress program in 2001.[27] This lack of competition at the shipping and freight end of food aid has led to inflated prices for transportation. When these premiums are combined

---

20. Barrett and Maxwell 2005, 91–92.
21. USWA 2007; on the historical significance of food aid to commodity producer groups, see Diven 2001
22. Oxfam America 2005, 58.
23. Dugger 2007c.
24. Interview with Marc Cohen, senior research fellow, IFPRI, October 17, 2007.
25. Dugger 2005.
26. Barrett and Maxwell 2005, 94.
27. Ibid.

with rising costs of fuel, it is not surprising that transportation now constitutes more than half the cost of providing U.S. in-kind food aid.[28]

Although the contracts to transport food aid are not essential for the viability of the U.S. shipping industry as a whole, several freight lines do profit enormously from it. For a few key shipping lines, such as Waterman Steamship Corporation and Liberty Maritime, food aid contracts are by far their main source of income.[29] As reported in an article posted on the American Shipper website: "[F]or U.S.-flag vessel operators, their bread and butter remains in the transportation of food aid."[30]

## Food-Aid-Delivery NGOs

NGOs based in the United States who are involved in food aid delivery have a strong economic interest in maintaining in-kind food aid and the practice of monetization. Most USAID Title II nonemergency food aid is allocated to NGOs, who are contracted to deliver it. As indicated in table 4.1, between 2006 and 2009, 100 percent of nonemergency and between 15 and 22 percent of emergency Title II food aid was channeled through NGOs. Allocations from USAID account for a substantial portion of the income of these NGOs. Each has received tens of millions of dollars' worth of in-kind food aid through the Food for Peace program each year over the past decade, and for some agencies in some years, that sum has been worth over $100 million.[31] Barrett and Maxwell have shown, for example, that food aid delivered by the top eight NGOs accounted for 30 percent of the weighted average of their gross revenues for 2001; some relied on U.S. food aid for up to 50 percent of their budget.[32]

Monetization of in-kind, commodity food aid helps these organizations raise funds for other non-food-related projects that might not otherwise attract funds.[33] Monetization was first introduced in U.S. food aid programs under the Food Security Act of 1985. The idea was to sell a small portion of in-kind food aid on the open market in recipient countries as a means by which to raise funds to pay for the administrative and distribution costs of the aid. At that time, NGOs were required to monetize a minimum of 5 percent of the in-kind aid they received under Title II and section 416(b). This was expanded to 10 percent in 1988, and the use of the proceeds was extended to include development projects with broader

---

28. GAO 2007, 1.
29. Barrett and Maxwell 2005, 96; Loewenberg 2008.
30. Gillis 2004a.
31. See USAID 2006, 2007, 2008 and 2009.
32. Barrett and Maxwell 2005, 98.
33. Barrett and Maxwell 2005, 98–100; see also Simmons 2009.

**TABLE 4.1** Percentage of U.S. food aid handled through WFP and NGOs

| YEAR | TOTAL* VALUE | WFP VALUE | WFP % OF TOTAL | PVOs (NGOs) VALUE | PVOs (NGOs) % OF TOTAL |
|---|---|---|---|---|---|
| | | TITLE II EMERGENCY ACTIVITIES | | | |
| 2006 | 1,157,970.2 | 907,817.5 | 78 | 250,152.7 | 22 |
| 2007 | 1,175,265 | 951,378.2 | 81 | 223,886.8 | 19 |
| 2008 | 1,965,076.6 | 1,531,761.1 | 78 | 433,315.5 | 22 |
| 2009 | 1,832,415.8 | 1,543,926 | 84 | 288,489.8 | 16 |
| | | TITLE II NONEMERGENCY ACTIVITIES | | | |
| 2006 | 341,128.1 | 0 | 0 | 341,128.1 | 100 |
| 2007 | 348,500 | 0 | 0 | 348,500 | 100 |
| 2008 | 354,288.3 | 0 | 0 | 354,288.3 | 100 |
| 2009 | 377,537.2 | 0 | 0 | 377,537.2 | 100 |
| | | TITLE II OVERALL ACTIVITIES (EMERGENCY AND NONEMERGENCY) | | | |
| 2006 | 1,499,098.3 | 907,817.5 | 61 | 591,280.8 | 39 |
| 2007 | 1,523,765 | 951,378.2 | 62 | 572,386.8 | 38 |
| 2008 | 2,319,364.9 | 1,531,761.1 | 66 | 787,603.8 | 34 |
| 2009 | 2,209,953 | 1,543,926 | 70 | 666,027 | 30 |

Source: USAID Annual Reports 2006–9, http://www.usaid.gov/our_work/humanitarian_assistance/ffp/annrep.html.

*Emergency totals do not include unallocated funds, pending funds, or funding adjustments.

objectives beyond just the delivery of food aid. The minimum amount was further increased to 15 percent in the 1996 Farm Bill.

The practice of monetization of in-kind food aid by NGOs quickly grew in the 1990s and 2000s. In 1996 the share of nonemergency Title II aid monetized by NGOs was 28 percent, and by 2001 the share had increased to 70 percent.[34] For some food aid operations, NGOs monetized the entire amount, as it is a major source of their development finance. Monetization of Title II food aid in recent years has remained high, as shown in table 4.2, ranging from 58 to 74 percent over the 2006–9 period.[35] In practice food aid became an important vehicle by which some NGOs could fund a variety of development projects. It is for this reason that Barrett and Maxwell refer to in-kind food aid as "merely bulky cash"

---

34. Simmons 2009, 6.
35. USAID 2006, 2007, 2008 and 2009.

**TABLE 4.2** Title II food aid: monetization rates

| YEAR* | PERCENTAGE MONETIZED |
|---|---|
| 2009 | 69 |
| 2008 | 74 |
| 2007 | 66 |
| 2006 | 58 |

Source: USAID Annual Reports 2006–9, http://www.usaid.gov/
our_work/humanitarian_assistance/ffp/annrep.html.
*Data represent percentages available as of fall of each year.

for these NGOs.[36] It is very attractive as a funding mechanism, even though it was often difficult to coordinate resource requirements with resource availability using this practice, and it brings some financial risk because of the requirement that the local sale price be at least 80 percent of the CIF (cost, insurance, and freight) price.[37]

The similarity of the NGOs' position on monetization and in-kind food aid to that of the industry groups gave a degree of legitimacy to the latter's position, and together they formed a powerful bloc fighting against food aid reform.

## The Role of Ideas: Proposals for Reform

The idea of reforming food aid away from 100 percent tied in-kind aid emanated from a variety of quarters, including the very highest levels of government. Since the early 2000s political support for reform has been put forward in several contexts, including the president's management agenda and annual budget requests throughout much of 2002–8, the WTO negotiations of 2005–6 (see chapter 6), the reformulation of the U.S. Farm Bill over the course of 2007–8, and the food crisis of 2007–8. Key studies were also published in this period, and the issue became a hot topic in the mainstream media. These ideas, supported by some politicians, NGOs, and scholars, met with controversy and debate from those interests opposed to change.

The 2002 Farm Bill was negotiated in 2001 and approved in 2002. The bill extended authority for PL 480 and other food aid programs through 2007. It increased the minimum amount of commodities to be provided and uncapped

36. Barrett and Maxwell 2005, 101.

37. Interview with Daniel Maxwell, professor, Department of Food and Nutrition Policy, Friedman School of Nutrition Science and Policy, Tufts University, and former CARE international deputy regional director, November 20, 2007.

the previous $1 billion spending limit on annual Title II costs. At the same time that this bill was under negotiation, however, President George W. Bush highlighted food aid in his "President's Management Agenda" of 2002 as one of fourteen areas of government policy that required significant reform.[38] The report acknowledged some key problems with existing food aid programs. These included the confusing bureaucratic and administrative structures under which aid was given, as well as rising costs and inefficiencies associated with it that had led to "waste and questionable spending." It also acknowledged that in-kind aid and monetization could harm incentives for local farmers in recipient countries, as well as displace commercial exports from the United States and other grain-exporting countries.

The president's agenda stated its primary goal as direct feeding of genuinely hungry people. To achieve this, it called for the establishment of more reliable levels of food aid, with the proportion of the U.S. programs that relied on unpredictable surpluses not to exceed 10 percent. It also called for better-focused programs, improved safeguards to avoid commercial displacement, and overall improved transparency and efficiency.[39] President Bush did not request any funding for Title III of PL 480, a program that promotes the monetization of aid in an untargeted way, after 2001.

In addition to executive-level support for reform of food aid policy, there was a push for reforms from USAID. Andrew Natsios, administrator of the agency from 2001 to 2005, was strongly in favor of rationalizing food aid policy. He advocated giving USAID increased flexibility to use cash for local and regional purchases in emergency situations since this would speed up the delivery of assistance at lower cost. He was also influenced by his own personal experience as director of the Office of Foreign Disaster Assistance and the Bureau for Food and Humanitarian Assistance (now the Bureau of Democracy, Conflict, and Humanitarian Assistance) within USAID in the late 1980s and early 1990s and as vice president of World Vision in the mid-1990s.[40] In 2002, for example, Natsios tried to secure permission to use PL 480 funds to undertake a local and regional purchase operation in Afghanistan because the country had been experiencing surpluses as a result of a U.S.-funded agricultural assistance program. He was unable to make this happen, and in the end the United States shipped in 300,000 tonnes of U.S.-grown wheat, contributing to a collapse in wheat prices for local farmers and pushing them the following year to invest in growing poppies for

---

38. Executive Office of the President 2002.
39. Ibid., 65–68.
40. On Natsios's background, see http://www.usaid.gov/about_usaid/bios/bio_asn.html.

heroin production instead. This episode only reinforced in his mind the need for greater flexibility in food aid programming.[41]

Academic studies were also influential in shaping Natsios's views on the topic. In a 2005 speech explaining his rationale, he cited several academic studies, including the work of Amartya Sen, on the question of hunger and famine. These works stressed that often it is not a lack of food in the economy that results in hunger but rather a lack of access.[42] For Natsios it only made sense to allow some cash for local and regional purchase: "I've seen children starve to death when there was a surplus of food in their local markets, but there was no one to buy the food because we didn't have the money to do that, so people died."[43]

As early as 2003, Natsios proposed to President Bush reforming food aid policy to allow up to one-quarter of the food aid budget to be allocated as cash for local and regional purchase in recipient countries.[44] Natsios described his encounter with the president in a 2005 speech on food aid at the time he announced his departure from USAID: "I went to the President and to the OMB [Office of Management and Budget] and the President's staff and I said we have a problem here. We need more tools because people die in famines who don't need to. The President told OMB, Who is going to be annoyed by this? I said you're going to annoy almost everybody. But it's the right thing to do ethically, and the President told OMB to go ahead and put it in the budget. It's the right thing to do."[45]

The combination of administrative inefficiency of the prevailing food aid programs and the moral drive to save lives was a powerful combination in the Bush administration. Despite knowing that there were strong interests against a change in policy, the administration took on the issue, driven by a core belief that it was doing what was right.[46] In early 2005, just as the food aid issue was heating up at the WTO, President Bush included in his 2006 budget proposal a request for authority to allow 25 percent of the food aid budget for that year to be provided in the form of cash for local and regional purchase. Natsios openly promoted the idea and made it the centerpiece of his speech at the annual USDA and USAID International Food Aid Conference in Kansas City in the spring of 2005.[47] Despite active campaigning by Bush and Natsios, Congress defeated that aspect of the proposal in the 2006 budget, which sparked considerable debate.

---

41. See *Religion and Ethics News Weekly* 2010.
42. Natsios 2005b.
43. *Religion and Ethics News Weekly* 2010.
44. See *Religion and Ethics News Weekly* 2010.
45. Natsios 2005b.
46. Interview with Christopher Barrett, professor, Dyson School of Applied Economics and Management, Cornell University, October 11, 2007.
47. See Natsios 2005c.

President Bush tried again in the 2007, 2008, and 2009 budgets to include the authority for USAID to untie one-quarter of its emergency food aid budget for local and regional purchases, but the idea was rejected by Congress every time, as will be explained in more detail below. This did not deter the president from repeatedly trying, however. Bush's budget proposals from 2006–9 also did not include any funding for Title I of PL 480. This may have been in response to the international pressures during negotiations at the WTO for the United States to end its sales of food aid, which were seen to be trade-distorting. Congress did not insist on funding for Title I, and the program has effectively gone unfunded since 2006.

During the same time period that the administration was attempting to untie a portion of USAID's food aid budget, Congress was gearing up to negotiate a new Farm Bill. The bill of 2002 was due to be replaced in 2007 with new legislation. The administration's proposal for the new Farm Bill, put forward by the USDA in May 2007, requested authority to use up to 25 percent of the PL 480 Title II funds in the form of cash for local and regional purchase of food aid.[48] The idea was to increase the speed and efficiency of the U.S. response to emergencies, as such a measure was intended to be used when it would cut delivery times and save on transportation costs. The proposal made clear that there was no intention of completely replacing U.S.-grown commodities with foreign food:

> The principal reason for the proposal is to save lives.... The Administration expects food would be purchased from developing countries, as defined by the OECD Development Assistance Committee list of ODA recipients.... We do not anticipate procuring commodities in one region of the world and shipping them to another distant region because commodities can likely be shipped from the United States just as quickly. We would not procure food from developed countries.[49]

The administration's Farm Bill proposal was bolstered by several studies published in the mid-2000s. Christopher Barrett, an agricultural economist, and Daniel Maxwell, then international deputy regional director of CARE, published a key book in 2005—*Food Aid after 50 Years: Recasting Its Role*. It argued that the current system for U.S. food aid was antiquated and inefficient and that it was time to reform the policy to be more flexible by including some cash for local and regional purchases.[50] At the same time that this book was being widely read in food aid policy circles, the OECD published a key report on the impact of

---

48. USDA 2007; for analysis of food aid and the farm bill debates, see Simmons 2007
49. Ibid., 82.
50. Barrett and Maxwell 2005.

tied food aid whose lead author was Edward Clay, a development economist and food aid expert at the UK Overseas Development Institute.[51] The report included analysis showing that food aid given in its in-kind, commodity form was both more costly and more time-consuming to provide than local and regional purchase. These critiques were hard-hitting and prompted further review within the U.S. government.

A key report on the performance of U.S. food aid programs was published by the GAO in April 2007. The report was prepared at the request of the Senate Agriculture Committee to inform Congress regarding the efficiency and effectiveness of food aid programs as it prepared to reauthorize the applicable provisions of the new Farm Bill. The report's findings indicated that there were challenges facing the food aid programs that hampered both effectiveness and efficiency. These included rules requiring the aid to be provided in kind and transported on U.S.-flagged ships, which was both costly and time-consuming, with shipments taking typically four to six months to reach their destination. The practice of monetization and the lack of proper targeting of monetized aid to the hungriest segments of society in recipient countries were also highlighted. The report found that 65 percent of total emergency food aid funding was eaten up by administrative and transport costs, leading to a 52 percent drop in average tonnage actually delivered in the five-year period since 2002.[52] This dramatic drop was exacerbated after 2006 by rising food and fuel costs, which had not previously been major concerns of the food aid program.[53]

The recommendations of the GAO report were that USAID and the secretaries of agriculture and transportation should reduce those inefficiencies by improving logistics, including transportation rules and procurement practices. Although it did not openly advocate a move to cash for local and regional purchase of food aid, it did recommend examination of ways to provide adequate "nonfood resources in situations where there is sufficient evidence that such assistance will enhance the effectiveness of food aid."[54]

Together, the presidential budget requests, the administration's Farm Bill proposal, and the 2007 GAO report presented new ideas on food aid that sparked debate over its reform. These ideas highlighted the inefficiencies of the current policies and practices and recommended ways to address them through revisions to existing policies. Although such changes were supported at the executive level of the government, bringing them about proved extremely difficult in the face of

51. Clay, Riley, and Urey 2006.
52. GAO 2007.
53. Cohen interview, October 17, 2007.
54. GAO 2007, 62.

resistance from key domestic interests. The institutional context, which required congressional approval of any change, proved receptive to the lobbying of these interests.

## Political Push-Back from Domestic Interests

Food-aid-delivery NGOs, agricultural processing and producer groups, and the shipping lobby teamed up and pushed back against plans to reform U.S. food aid in the context of the WTO negotiations, the president's budget proposals, and the Farm Bill, all of which overlapped with one another in 2004–8. In these various contexts, these groups attempted to shape public discourse by posting news items and press releases on their websites and testifying at numerous congressional hearings that touched on food aid. They traveled to Geneva to lobby trade negotiators not just from the United States but from other countries as well.[55] These different interest groups were opposed to untying, and each highlighted their specific concerns, some of which overlapped. At the same time, they also worked together through various coalitions.

Grain companies are represented by several industry groups who lobby on matters relating to food aid.[56] The U.S. Wheat Associates launched a public campaign in 2006 to "Keep the Food in Food Aid," while other grain associations and millers' lobby groups, including the National Association of Wheat Growers and the North American Millers Association, have also stressed the need to keep current food aid programs intact.[57] Similarly, the shipping industry, represented by organizations such as the American Maritime Congress, the American Maritime Officers, and the Maritimes Trades department of AFL-CIO, has actively lobbied Congress regarding food aid and cargo preference rules. Some individual companies, such as Maersk, have occasionally made public statements about food aid policies.

Some NGOs also work together as a coalition to press for policies that secure high levels of U.S. food aid and continuation of the practice of monetization, as well as for WTO rules that enable these programs to continue. The Coalition for Food Aid was an umbrella group representing over fifteen food aid NGOs, including World Vision, Mercy Corps, Catholic Relief Services, Save the Children, and

---

55. Kripke 2009, 119.
56. See Clapp 2009a.
57. See, for example, WETEC, NAWG, and USWA 2006.

CARE, from 1985 to 2006, that lobbied the Congress on food aid issues.[58] In 2006 this group disbanded and reemerged as the Alliance for Food Aid with somewhat different membership (discussed in more detail below), and in 2009 it reinvented itself yet again as the Alliance for Global Food Security.[59] The group employs a lobbyist, the lawyer Ellen Levinson—who is widely regarded as a very powerful figure in Washington—to make its case to lawmakers in Washington, D.C.

These groups explicitly planned to work together to lobby Congress to maintain high levels of funding for U.S. food aid programs.[60] They also formed additional coalitions that brought together groups within a single industry, as well as across industries and sometimes including NGOs, to add additional voice to their lobbying. For example, the Agricultural Food Aid Coalition emerged in 2007 specifically to lobby on the Farm Bill. Its members were primarily a range of milling and grain associations.[61] USA Maritime Coalition is a lobby group whose members are other shipping associations as well as individual corporations who have a specific interest in food aid and cargo preference.[62] Another coalition that spans the shipping, grain, and sometimes NGO sectors is the Ad Hoc Coalition in Support of Sustained Funding for U.S. Food Aid, which has submitted pleas to Congress to increase food aid funding levels.

Working through the various lobby groups, these domestic interests fought hard against the administration's various reform plans and any concessions that the United States might entertain with respect to the WTO trade negotiations and were very effective in their campaigns.[63] In resisting the idea of untying food aid, these groups put forward various arguments to defend current policies and practices. The most prominent of these is that untying food aid will lead to a drop in support for food aid programs, ultimately harming those who need the aid most. Rebecca Coleman from the U.S. Wheat Associates argued, "Converting to cash-only endangers agricultural support for food aid and creates a situation where food aid funding may be reappropriated elsewhere in accordance with priorities."[64] Lobby groups pointed to the European Union's move to cash-only food aid programs, which had resulted in a significant drop in aid. Domestic

---

58. The members of the Coalition for Food Aid included Adventist Development and Relief Agency International, ACDI/VOCA, Africare, American Red Cross, CARE, Catholic Relief Services, Counterpart International, Food for the Hungry International, International Orthodox Christian Charities, International Relief and Development, Land O'Lakes, Mercy Corps, OIC International, Project Concern International, Save the Children, and World Vision.

59. See the group's website, at: http://www.globalfoodsecurity.info.

60. Gillis 2004b.

61. Agricultural Food Aid Coalition 2007.

62. See USA Maritime's website at: http://www.usamaritime.org.

63. Barrett interview, October 11, 2007.

64. See, for example, Coleman 2006.

interests have also warned that support for food aid programs among their domestic constituents would evaporate, leading to significant cuts in funding. The Ad Hoc Coalition in Support of Sustained Funding for Food Aid stressed that "the proposal to buy commodities overseas, instead of from American farmers and processors, threatens to undermine the broad-based political and support framework that has made Title II a success over the last half century. Indeed, Europe's conversion to cash-based aid resulted in a dramatic drop in aid levels."[65] This sentiment was echoed by the Alliance for Food Aid as well as the shipping lobby.[66] Gloria Tosi, a key lobbyist for the shipping industry, put it bluntly: "There's no constituency for cash."[67]

Further arguments were put forward against the proposals. NGOs, through the Coalition for Food Aid, focused their interventions on the implications of the proposed reforms for developing countries. Early on they were unified in arguing that in-kind food aid and monetization did not disrupt either international or local markets. In 2006, however, several prominent food-aid-delivery NGOs—including CARE, Catholic Relief Services, and Save the Children—began to distance themselves from the coalition's stance on monetization.[68] These three NGOs, later joined by Mercy Corps, began to endorse the idea of local and regional purchases in emergencies, effectively lending support to the administration's proposal to allow for some untied aid.[69] While CARE openly denounced the practice of monetization, the other groups did not actively advocate against the practice, although they did continue to support the use of local and regional purchase.

With a difference of views between NGOs emerging on the use of financial resources for LRP, the Coalition for Food Aid dissolved in April 2006. After a meeting of the group to which CARE was not invited, there was a decision to dissolve the group and form a new organization.[70] Save the Children, Catholic Relief Services, and Mercy Corps chose not to take a strong stand on monetization. Given that they had already supported LRP, these groups, along with CARE, did not become part of the new organization that emerged several months later, the Alliance for Food Aid (AFA). The AFA bolstered its continued support of monetization with studies by its members concluding that monetization had more benefits than costs. One NGO study, for example, argued that the amount

65. Ad Hoc Coalition in Support of Sustained Funding for Food Aid 2007.

66. Evans 2007.

67. Cited in Dugger 2007d.

68. Interview with Gawain Kripke, director of policy and research, Oxfam America, October 15, 2007.

69. See, for example, CARE 2006; CRS 2007.

70. Maxwell interview, November 20, 2007.

of monetized food aid was tiny, composing less than a quarter of one percent of world trade in equivalent agricultural commodities; thus it was highly unlikely to have any impact on world trade.[71] The study acknowledged that some commercial displacement might take place but it claimed that it would be minor. In addition, it argued that there was no evidence of disincentive effects in developing countries as a result of monetization. The study instead made the case that monetized food aid, rather than disrupting world trade or local markets, actually contributed to food security in recipient countries and led to a savings of $160 million on imports for LDC recipient countries that would otherwise find it difficult to access credit for commercial imports of food.[72]

The Alliance for Food Aid actively promoted these arguments on monetization in its testimony in Congress and on its website. It added that monetization not only raised funds for valuable development projects but also acted to bolster market skills for local traders who purchased the food in monetization transactions.[73] At the same time, the alliance warned of hidden costs associated with local purchase transactions, including food safety concerns and potential negative market impacts from those purchases. But while the AFA was cautious with respect to changes to rules regarding monetization and cash aid to be covered out of the Title II budget, it endorsed the idea of a pilot program for local and regional purchases, provided this was carried out with additional rather than existing funds.[74]

The split among the NGOs was made even more pronounced when in August 2007 CARE announced its earlier (2005) decision to refuse to accept in-kind aid from USAID on the grounds that it was withdrawing support for the practice of monetization (which it pledged to phase out by 2009).[75] The other three NGOs that broke from the Alliance for Food Aid have also criticized monetization but continued to practice it while trying to sort out ways to phase it out or at least make it less distorting for local markets in recipient countries. This change in direction kept the debate over untying alive during the talks on the 2008 Farm Bill.

The farming and shipping lobbies also put forward additional arguments against the idea of allowing some cash food aid. For these industry groups, one of the more prominent reasons to keep in-kind food aid is that it has economic benefits for the United States, particularly in developing export markets. Indeed,

---

71. See Shaw and MacKay 2006. It should be noted that Save the Children was a sponsor of this report, even though it had distanced itself from the AFA. It continued to be less definitive in its position about monetization while it did support the move toward local and regional purchase.

72. Shaw and MacKay 2006

73. See Alliance for Food Aid 2007.

74. Levinson 2007.

75. Dugger 2007a; 2007b.

establishing export markets for U.S.-grown agricultural commodities was an early justification for the development of PL 480 food aid programs. Even though trade negotiators and some NGOs have argued that in-kind, commodity-form food aid does not affect global trade by displacing commercial exports from other exporting countries, the agricultural lobby has emphasized its importance in this regard, with some referring to food aid recipients as "future customers."[76] The Ad Hoc Coalition in Support of Sustained Funding for Food Aid, for example, has stressed that it opposes the proposal for local and regional purchase, which would "divert U.S. tax dollars to foreign producers."[77]

The domestic benefits of the aid programs were also highlighted by the grain- and food-processing lobbies, with frequent references to benefits that flow to American farmers and firms by providing jobs and income.[78] A representative of the Agricultural Food Aid Coalition stressed this link, emphasizing that $1 billion in grain sales in the United States generates some $2.7 billion in economic activity: "If you take that same billion overseas, there is no economic impact to the U.S."[79] Similarly, the shipping lobby has focused much of its efforts on stressing the importance of Cargo Preference rules for maintaining the strength of the shipping industry and providing jobs for mariners.[80]

The shipping and agricultural interests also argue that maintaining in-kind food aid programs is important for national security. They cite several reasons for this. First, the grain industry has stressed not only that U.S. grains are essential to provide food for the poor, who might otherwise be tempted to join groups hostile to the United States, but also that the U.S. label on the bags of grain provides a powerful symbol of American goodwill, promoting a positive attitude toward the United States abroad. According to Jim Madich of the North American Millers Association, "We are essentially reducing the pool of hopeless and disenfranchised people from whom our adversaries draw."[81] The shipping industry also points out that the cargo preference regulations are in place largely to ensure the economic viability of the shipping industry so that American ships are available if necessary in national security emergencies.[82]

Additional arguments against proposals for cash for local and regional purchase were also made by industry groups. Such a move, they argue, would fuel corruption in developing countries. Tom Mick of the U.S. Wheat Associates emphasized this

---

76. Ruth 2005, 30.
77. Ad Hoc Coalition in Support of Sustained Funding for Food Aid 2007.
78. Ibid.
79. John Gillcrest, quoted in Hedges 2007.
80. Promar International 2010; *American Maritime Officer* 2006.
81. Madich 2005, 27.
82. *American Maritime Officer* 2006.

point in a media interview: "[C]ash has a tendency to disappear in a lot of third world countries. But when you have 35,000 tons of grain coming in, it's kind of hard to steal that."[83] In addition to stemming corruption, maintenance of in-kind food aid programs, according to industry groups, ensured better-quality food for recipients because in their view U.S. food grains are more nutritious. Industry groups have supported more long-term, nonemergency aid that is required to be bagged and fortified before being shipped because a stable and reliable source of supplemental food is seen to be crucial in the fight against AIDS in Africa.[84]

The main objective of the interest groups' lobbying was to maintain in-kind, monetized food aid and increase funding for these activities. The Agricultural Food Aid Coalition stressed that its members not only favored maintaining high levels of funding for Title II food aid but also wanted to see Title I funding reinstated, as ending it only undermined the U.S. negotiating position at the WTO, and countries who could afford to buy food on concessional terms were being denied that opportunity.[85] Regarding the critiques of in-kind and monetized food aid, industry groups suggested that there were other ways to improve economic and delivery inefficiencies and supported the idea of prepositioning food aid in stockpiles closer to regions that received it.

The Coalition for Food Aid—and later its successor, the Alliance for Food Aid—lobbied hard for an increase in Title II nonemergency food aid, rather than Title I, with which they were not involved. They called for a "safe box" for the nonemergency aid of no less than $600 million or 1.2 million tonnes per year. This proposal would have safeguarded the amount of long-term aid devoted to development from waivers that had increased emergency funding and in effect lowered amounts for development. Throughout the debate over the Farm Bill, the AFA began to soften its stance regarding the cash option, stating that its members were not opposed to all LRP transactions but that they wanted them to add to, rather than subtract from, the in-kind programs. They began to call for a pilot program to test the idea.[86]

## The Outcome

These various arguments put forward by domestic interest groups operating against the Bush administration proposals to convert a portion of PL 480 Title II

---

83. Quoted in Pratt 2006; see also Ruth 2005, 29.

84. Madich 2005, 27.

85. See Agricultural Food Aid Coalition 2007; see also US Wheat Associates newsletters (http://www.uswheat.org/newsEvents/wheatLetter/archive) and the Ad Hoc Coalition in Support of Sustained Funding for Food Aid 2007.

86. Sandefur 2007; Levinson 2007.

funds to cash for local and regional purchase convinced Congress not to support the move in the 2006, 2007, 2008, and 2009 budget requests. Some influential senators initially endorsed the idea in 2005 but then backed down under severe lobby pressure.[87] According to Peter Timmer, previous administrations had not dared to confront this powerful lobby, and thus it was remarkable that the Bush administration even tried.[88] The shipping lobby was perhaps the most formidable of these groups. In a television interview in 2005, for example, Republican senator Charles Grassley lamented, "It's too bad we can't reform Cargo Preference but the maritime union and industry is so powerful in Congress that I usually get about 40 votes for doing that. I've tried several times."[89] Democratic representative Tom Lantos, chair of the House Foreign Relations Committee, warned in 2006 that separating food aid from the shipping and agribusiness lobby was "beyond insane," claiming that it would cause support for those programs to "vanish overnight."[90]

The first time Congress rejected the proposal in the 2006 budget request, its report stated that the "conferees...admonish the Executive Branch to refrain from proposals which place at risk a carefully balanced coalition of interests which have served the interests of international food assistance programs well for more than fifty years."[91] But the administration was not deterred. As Natsios, who chastised the arguments against the proposal as "morally indefensible,"[92] noted regarding the defeat of the measure in the 2006 budget, "[A]nybody who thinks the debate is over because we didn't win this year, let me tell you something, the debate is not over....We are going to eventually have the change. We can do it cooperatively, thoughtfully and intelligently, or we can have a big fight over it."[93]

Many thought Natsios mishandled the administration's interactions with the interest groups early on by pushing the ideas too forcefully and trying to do too much at once.[94] There was not much consultation with stakeholders before putting the proposal forward.[95] As a World Vision representative remarked of Natsios after his speech promoting the idea at the annual Kansas City food aid

---

87. Haider 2006.

88. Timmer 2005, 1.

89. Quoted in Nichols 2005.

90. Cited in Dugger 2007b.

91. Cited in Hanrahan 2006.

92. Cited in Thurow and Kilman 2005.

93. Cited in Timmer 2005.

94. Interview with Mary Chambliss, board member, Partnership to Cut Hunger and Poverty in Africa, and former USDA foreign agricultural service deputy administrator for export credits, October 15, 2007.

95. Interview with Emmy Simmons, independent consultant and former USAID assistant administrator for economic growth, agriculture, and trade, May 18, 2007.

conference in 2005, "He didn't make friends."[96] Natsios left USAID in late 2005, but the Bush administration continued to push the idea in its budget proposals and in the Farm Bill debates, as noted above. The issue remained controversial even among various departments within the government, and according to one media account, the day that Natsios left USAID, the USDA and Commerce Department approached the Office of Management and Budget to demand that the 25 percent cash proposal be removed from the president's budget request.[97]

Although the food producers and processors, along with the shipping lobby and an alliance of NGOs, resisted the various reform proposals, the debate continued to be heated because the Farm Bill was slated for renewal in 2007 and because of the split among groups in the NGO community.

The outcome of the Farm Bill was a less definitive reaction of Congress to the idea of cash for local and regional purchase than was the case with the budget proposals, in that some moves toward reform, albeit small in the larger context, were incorporated into the bill. Gawain Kripke of Oxfam suggests that its reaction was influenced by the fact that the Farm Bill was not finalized until the middle of a food crisis in mid-2008.[98] Indeed, food prices began to climb sharply just as Congress began to seriously deliberate on the bill in mid-2007, and the situation escalated when prices climbed by an average of 43 percent from March 2007 to March 2008 as the two houses of Congress were attempting to reconcile the two versions of the bill. After two years of intense debate, the bill was finally enacted in mid-2008. Congress overrode a veto from President Bush, who had considered that the deal incorporated subsidy levels that were too high, particularly in times of high food prices, and ran counter to American ideals of freer trade in agriculture.[99]

The main innovation regarding food aid in the final 2008 Farm Bill was the incorporation of a small pilot project for LRP. What was approved was much smaller than the original administration proposal of up to 25 percent of Title II funding in cash for LRP. The approved pilot project provides $60 million over four years, which is additional to PL 480 appropriations. The bill calls for a study of the pilot to evaluate its effectiveness. The small size and separate funding of the project reflect the intense debate over the issue. The original bill presented by the House of Representatives, for example, did not include any provisions for local and regional purchase. The Senate's version included the pilot project, which at one point appeared in danger of being dropped but eventually made

---

96. Thurow and Kilman 2005.
97. Lillis 2008.
98. See Kripke 2009.
99. Abbott 2010.

it into the final reconciled bill.[100] The response of Natsios to the final outcome was not enthusiastic: "I was upset that they did that in the middle of a crisis like this.... [W]e don't need a pilot like this. It works. We know it works."[101]

The Farm Bill also increased annual funding for food aid, with the Title II funding authorization increasing from $2 billion to $2.5 billion annually. It also included a minimum 2.5 million tonnes to be donated through Title II each year, the same as in the 2002 bill. Those lobbying in favor of keeping tied food aid and monetization, however, were able to secure 1.875 million of that tonnage for nonemergency aid, though this provision often was waived to reallocate funds toward emergency operations. At the same time, though, the NGO proposal for a safe box for development aid was adopted. The Bush administration had objected to the idea because it denied USAID the flexibility to respond to emergencies. The safe box was set at $375 million in 2009, climbing to $450 million by 2012. These amounts can still be waived under some circumstances, including in situations of extraordinary food emergency. Several other provisions under the bill affect food aid policy. Regarding monetization, the 2008 Farm Bill required that no less than 15 percent of Title II nonemergency aid be monetized.

Further, the Cargo Preference rules were left unchanged. The title of the overall food aid legislation was changed from the Agricultural Trade and Development Assistance Act to the Food for Peace Act, reflecting the move away from promotion of Title I food aid sales and toward almost exclusively grant aid. Title I of the act was reauthorized, under a new name, Economic Assistance and Food Security. The title removed reference to recipient countries as potential commercial markets and eliminated the requirement that organizations seeking funding of this title prepare and submit agricultural market development plans. But the commitment to providing substantial amounts of in-kind aid, even for emergencies, remained intact. Reflecting this but also seeking to demonstrate an effort to improve efficiency, the bill also increased funding for prepositioning of food aid from $2 million to $10 million annually, in order to reach crisis hot spots more quickly with in-kind aid.

Changes to food aid policy under the 2008 Farm Bill were important in that they opened the door to local and regional purchase, albeit slightly. Perhaps more significant were appropriations for food aid during and immediately following the food crisis of 2007–8, which provided further funding for local and regional purchase operations as part of the response to the crisis. In mid-2008, Congress approved $50 million in supplemental funding to USAID for LRP operations as

---

100. Hanrahan 2008; Partnership to Cut Poverty and Hunger in Africa 2008; Kripke 2009.
101. Quoted in Salzman 2008.

part of a larger package of $770 million in funding for the president's Food Security Response Initiative—funding that was completely unrelated to the Farm Bill.

The U.S. leadership transition in early 2009 brought a continued push for provision of cash for local and regional purchase, though in a somewhat different form. In early 2009, the new Congress under President Obama approved a further $75 million for USAID as part of the Development Appropriation Act for Food Security. The act was intended to support global food security and included funding for up to $20 million in LRP operations.[102] In addition, the new Obama administration allocated $75 million to USAID for LRP food aid through international disaster assistance funding.

These additional appropriations were approved relatively swiftly without much debate, largely because they did not involve a reduction in the provision of U.S.-grown food aid under the Farm Bill in order to fund LRP, as had been proposed by Bush, and did not threaten the existing food aid budget.[103] For this reason, it was much easier to gain the approval of Congress after the 2008 Farm Bill had already become law because the safe box that the NGOs and agricultural and shipping lobbies had demanded was already securely in place. Although these new funds for LRP marked an important opening, through a different institutional channel that enabled Congress to approve them without intense lobbying from the interest groups, the GAO notes that there may be some constraints on actual use of LRP because of lack of clarity on how to implement cargo preference rules.[104]

## Conclusion

Despite the penetration of ideas regarding reform of U.S. food aid programs, in particular the proposal to allow more local and regional purchase of food aid with cash, achieving change along these lines has been fraught with resistance and debate. President Bush had tried consistently to allow up to 25 percent of USAID Title II funds to be allocated for LRP operations in order to achieve efficiencies in food aid provision without increasing the budget for it. But the institutional channels through which this reform attempt was made required congressional approval for reallocation of existing funds in a period when the U.S. Farm Bill was under renegotiation. Lobby groups with an economic interest in the issue, including NGOs, agribusiness, and shipping, fought hard to resist

---

102. USAID 2010.
103. See Ho and Hanrahan 2010; GAO 2009.
104. GAO 2009.

the idea of local and regional purchase and to keep in-kind food aid as a requirement of PL 480 and other existing food aid programs. The pilot project that was eventually approved under the 2008 Farm Bill was very small by comparison and was undertaken with funds that were additional to the PL 480 funds.

There was much more success in gaining the approval of Congress for cash funding for LRP under a different strategy, which involved additional funding through other channels rather than a reallocation of existing funding.[105] These approvals also came directly after passage of the 2008 Farm Bill, under which interest groups won hard-fought changes, including the safe box for long-term development aid and maintenance of monetization of in-kind food aid. The new funding for LRP also came in the midst of an international food price crisis in a context of rising hunger. Thus there was little resistance from the food aid interest groups. This signaled that the initial push-back on LRP was not so much about LRP as a practice as about securing and indeed increasing the existing allocation of resources for tied food aid. The outcome was greater use of financial resources for LRP but at the same time guaranteed long-term development food aid with monetization and all the issues that come with it. The prospect that the United States will ever untie a significant portion of PL 480 aid remains dim. According to the food aid expert Emmy Simmons, "there are a lot of reasons why that won't happen."[106]

The U.S. case is a clear illustration that the filtration of new ideas regarding food aid policies is mediated by both interests and institutions at the domestic level within the donor country, and this helps to explain the divergence among donors on the question of tying and untying. In the United States, a range of domestic interests, including not just commercial players but also NGOs, lobbied hard to keep food aid programs tied to domestically grown, packaged, and transported food because they had strong economic reasons to do so. At the same time, the domestic institutional setting was unique and especially open to being influenced by these interests. Thus the private interests were able to trump the government's economic interest in making efficiencies in its own budget. The U.S. case thus differed significantly from that of Europe, Canada, and Australia, discussed in chapter 3, which saw the balance of economic interests shift toward the government's desire to make cost savings in its aid programs. Incremental changes, however, have been possible in U.S. food aid policies through new institutional channels—outside the Farm Bill process, for example—with the support of new interests, including some advocacy NGOs that broke ranks with other

---

105. Indeed, as Mary Chambliss noted in 2007, cash for LRP could easily have come from some other account, just not PL 480. Chambliss interview, October 15, 2007.

106. Simmons interview, May 18, 2007.

food aid NGOs and allied with scholars and other organizations pushing for some food aid untying.

The importance of the domestic institutional context was not highlighted in earlier institutionalist and constructivist international relations studies of food aid, which instead focused on the power of ideas and norms promoted by international institutions. Further, they did not examine the role of nonstate actors with material interests or the competition between state and private interests in formulating policies. All these factors were important in the United States and determined the way in which new ideas about untying food aid were received.

The differences in policy on the question of tying between the United States—as the world's largest donor of food aid—and other donors has fueled political debate and tension among donors on the international stage. Food aid has become politicized in contexts that the earlier international relations literature did not foresee. As the next three chapters illustrate, these differences have led to heated debate over food aid in the context of international rules on trade in agricultural biotechnology, the WTO agricultural trade talks, and in the midst of rising food insecurity resulting from the extreme food price volatility after 2006.

# 5

# THE GMO CONTROVERSY

Differences between donor countries regarding tying and untying of food aid that emerged starting in the mid-1990s have resulted in renewed tensions at the international level. Heated political debates erupted in several new arenas in which food aid had not previously been so politicized. The first of these new clashes occurred in 2002–3, when food aid became caught up in the wider international debate over the trade in genetically modified organisms. U.S.-sourced food aid containing GMOs that was sent to southern Africa in the context of drought and looming famine was an initial catalyst to a wider debate over the issue that continued in subsequent years. There have been major disagreements between both recipients and donors, as well as between donors, over the acceptability of sending genetically modified food aid into a crisis situation.

This chapter examines the politics of GMO food aid at the international level. It highlights the ways in which policy divergence regarding both tied aid and GMOs between recipients and donors, as well as among donors, was at the root of this political conflict. The tying of food aid is vital to understanding why GMOs were sent in the first place. They would probably not have been sent if the aid had not been tied to the domestic production of major donors such as the United States. The differences in policy among donors with respect to tied food aid were compounded by the dramatically changed agricultural landscape after the introduction of genetically modified crops in the mid-1990s. The broader debate over GMOs has been especially heated between the United States and the EU, and it reached a near boiling point at the time of the 2002–3 GMO food aid incident. Because these debates have not been fully resolved, the international rules regarding the trade in genetically modified organisms remain unclear, and this affects food aid deliveries. Further, economic factors have shaped the political responses of the various actors involved. Although there has been much analysis of the trade in GMOs,[1] the literature on food aid has not kept up with these new developments and did not foresee the way in which GMOs, combined with the issue of tying, would repoliticize food aid.

## GMOs in Food Aid

GMOs have been present in food aid since genetically modified soy and maize were initially approved for production in the United States in the mid-1990s but had not received much international attention until the southern African crisis. The fact that the United States tied its aid predominantly to domestic grain and food products meant that it was highly likely that its GMO grains (including soy and maize) would eventually end up in its food aid donations, including those channeled through the WFP. By the early 2000s the United States was by far the largest producer of GM crops, accounting for over 60 percent of the global acreage planted. Between 1996 and 2003 the area planted with GM crops increased by fortyfold, in 2003 covering some 67.7 million hectares.[2] In 2002 some three-quarters of the soy and over a third of the maize grown in the United States were GM varieties.[3] Because there was not a segregated system for GM and non-GM crops, commingling of the two in the food system was widespread.

The potential for such commingling was highlighted by the StarLink incident in the United States in 2000. StarLink is a genetically modified variety of corn that was approved as animal feed in 1998. It was not approved for human consumption because of concerns over the potential for humans to be allergic to the proteins it contained.[4] Approval for one use but not another was referred to as a split registration, and strict procedures were to be followed to ensure that StarLink would be used only as animal feed or in nonfood industrial uses. Despite regulations on planting and segregation of the StarLink corn to ensure that it did not enter the human food supply, the genetically modified variety managed to do just that. It was present in around 10 percent of the U.S. corn crop and had been exported in both bulk maize shipments and processed foods to several countries around the world where it did not have approval. The wide and rapid

---

1. See, for example, Falkner 2000; Newell and Mackenzie 2000; Bail, Falkner, and Marquard 2002.
2. James 2003.
3. See USAID 2003.
4. For an overview of this incident, see Clapp 2008.

spread of GMOs through the United States had important implications for food aid, because in the early 2000s the United States alone accounted for 60 percent of all international food aid donations. When it was revealed that the DNA from StarLink corn had made its way into the human food supply, there were massive recalls in the United States of food products that contained this corn.[5] Relatively little was done, however, to notify other countries that had obtained the corn through either international trade or food aid.

Negotiations had begun in 1995 on a protocol on biosafety under the Convention on Biodiversity to address the safety issues related to trade in GMOs, but little attention was paid to their presence in food aid transactions in the 1990s. Both USAID and the WFP had sent shipments of food aid containing GMOs, amounting to some 3.5 million tonnes per year, for several years.[6] Indeed, as James Morris, the head of the WFP from 2002 to 2007, stated at the time of the southern African crisis, "The World Food Program has been distributing food with some biotech content in Africa and around the world for seven years." Such shipments were often in contravention of the national regulations in the recipient country. But as Morris noted at the time, "[A]ll our food is certified as fit for human consumption in the donor country—so the food our beneficiaries eat in Africa is the very same food eaten daily in cities like New York and Toronto."[7]

Ecuador was the first developing country known to have received food aid containing GMOs in a shipment of soy sent from the United States and channeled through the WFP. The aid was eventually destroyed after complaints by the government of Ecuador.[8] GMOs were also sent in food aid shipments to Sudan and India in 2000. In 2001 GMO soy was found in shipments sent to Columbia and Uganda. Food aid maize from the United States containing GMOs was also reportedly sent to Bolivia in 2002, despite the fact that the country had a moratorium in place on the import of GMO crops. The GMOs found in the Bolivian aid contained StarLink corn. NGOs claim that when StarLink was found in the U.S. food supply, it was immediately removed from the market but that the United States did not act to remove the maize from Bolivia. In 2002 Nicaragua and Guatemala were also sent GM corn seed as food aid from the WFP. This caused a stir in Nicaragua in particular, as that country is a center of origin for corn.[9]

By mid-2002, there were enough incidents of GMO food aid and accompanying NGO and government complaints to have made international donors fully

---

5. Segarra and Rawson 2001.
6. Lean 2000; Pearce 2003, 5.
7. Morris 2002.
8. Friends of the Earth International 2003, 5.
9. Ibid., 6–7; ACDI/VOCA 2003.

aware of concerns about the issue in recipient countries. Those countries were worried about the potential health and environmental impacts of GMOs, including allergenicity and outcrossing of GMOs with wild relatives (which can occur if whole-kernel forms of grains are planted rather than eaten). There was concern that the commingling of genetic material could reduce biodiversity by contaminating and driving out local varieties. Once GMOs are released live into an environment, they are difficult, if not impossible, to remove. Food aid in whole grain form is often planted by local farmers—who may already have eaten their own seed supply, as frequently happens in crisis situations.[10] The fact that many GM crops had not been approved at the time in many countries, including the European Union—which had a de facto moratorium on the imports and new approvals of such crops from 1998 to 2003—generated additional economic concerns, especially for countries that had export markets in the EU.

Until mid-2002 the food aid shipments identified as containing GMOs were mainly to areas that, while in food deficit, were not facing acute shortages. In those instances, returning the aid or destroying it did not have immediate and severe food security implications. This changed in mid-2002 with the threat of famine in southern Africa. Some fourteen million people in six countries faced imminent severe food shortages resulting from several factors. Drought and floods were identified as one of the immediate causes. However, underlying factors were just as important. These included the impacts of trade liberalization under structural adjustment in some countries in the region, weak investment in the agricultural sector, and the high prevalence of HIV/AIDS, as well as conflict in Angola (and refugees from Angola in neighboring countries).[11] It was the worst food shortage faced by the region in fifty years.

The food crisis in southern Africa prompted the WFP to call for donors to pledge aid to address the situation. It specifically asked for financial donations, which would give it the most flexibility. While most donors did send untied funds, the United States sent in-kind, commodity-form aid, as it traditionally had done. It sent around 500,000 tonnes of maize to the region in the summer and fall of 2002. It was estimated by the WFP that around three-quarters of the food aid shipped to the region at that time contained GMOs, but the recipients were not warned of this beforehand.[12] The countries that received the shipments were Zambia, Zimbabwe, Malawi, Swaziland, Mozambique, and Lesotho. The aid was channeled through the WFP as well as NGOs.

---

10. GRAIN 2002.

11. For a more detailed explanation of each of these factors, see Oxfam International 2002, 2002a, 6.

12. WFP 2003, 4–5.

# Heated Exchanges in Southern Africa

When the aid arrived in southern Africa, many of the countries began to question whether they should accept it. They were put in a particularly difficult position because the food security of large numbers of people was threatened by the food shortages. Recipient countries were worried about the health impacts of a diet of mainly genetically modified corn, especially in a population with a high prevalence of HIV/AIDS which results in a suppressed immune system. They also had concerns about the potential contamination of their own varieties of maize if the whole-kernel food aid were planted. Zimbabwe and Zambia at first said they would not accept the food aid at all, while Mozambique, Swaziland, and Lesotho said they would accept it if it was milled first to prevent it from being planted. Malawi accepted it with strict monitoring to ensure that its farmers did not plant it and asked that it be milled before distribution during the planting season. Zimbabwe eventually said it would accept it if milled first. In late August 2002 a coalition of 126 nongovernmental groups from around the world issued a statement of solidarity with the southern African nations to raise awareness of the issue during the World Summit on Sustainable Development, which was being held in Johannesburg at that time.[13]

Under pressure from the U.S. government and the WFP, other countries in the region began to soften their stance by accepting milled food aid. Zambia, however, stood firm in not accepting any GMO food aid for its own people and rejected the shipments from the United States as well as from Canada.[14] It did eventually accept it in milled form, but that aid was only for distribution to the 130,000 Angolan refugees in camps within its borders.[15] The Zambian government expressed its concern that any health problems that might arise from eating GMOs would be too costly for the country to address. Since the Zambian diet consists of far more maize than the diets of North American consumers, such health problems might not be foreseen. Moreover, Zambia does export some maize to Europe, and contamination of its maize with GMOs could affect those exports.[16] The WFP scrambled to find non-GMO aid for Zambia, which had some three million people at risk of starvation.

---

13. This statement is posted at Norfolk Genetic Information Network, http://ngin.tripod.com/230802c.htm.

14. See report at http://www.science-metrix.com/pdf/SM_2005_001_NRC_Biotechnology_Developing_Countries.pdf.

15. Bennett 2003, 29.

16. The value of Zambia's exports of maize in 2002 was $ 2.23 million, according to the FAO. FAO Statistical Database, http://faostat.fao.org.

The WFP found it difficult to mobilize non-GMO food aid quickly enough. A UN statement was released at the height of the crisis that spelled out WFP policy on the issue. It stated that the WFP distributes only food that meets the food safety standards of both the donor and recipient country, as well as any international safety standards. The statement also stressed the safety of the GMO food aid, noting that "[b]ased on national information from a variety of sources and current scientific knowledge, FAO, WHO and WFP hold the view that the consumption of foods containing GMOs now being provided as food aid in southern Africa is not likely to present human health risk. Therefore, these foods may be eaten."[17] The statement made clear that the UN bodies respected the right of the countries to refuse to accept the aid, but it did call on southern African governments to carefully consider the consequences of limiting access to it.

The executive director of the WFP at the time, James Morris, took a stronger stand, defending the delivery of in-kind food aid containing GMOs and stressing that external food aid was required in this situation. As he noted in an op-ed published in the *International Herald Tribune,*

> External food aid simply must be part of the solution because stocks in southern Africa are very low and heavy buying would drive up food prices, bringing added misery to the lives of the poor people throughout the region....If the World Food Program cannot give biotech food to countries in southern Africa, it will have substantially less to offer in the weeks ahead and we are running out of time to appeal for more funds from donors.[18]

In a speech to the governing council of the International Fund for Agricultural Development in early 2003, Morris noted that the UN statement was vital in getting the message out to recipient countries that GM food was safe to eat.[19]

The presence of GMOs in food aid certainly complicates the WFP's work. In 2002 it did what it could to organize the milling of the maize for those countries that would accept it in that form and to source non-GMO aid for Zambia. The WFP had to quickly arrange local milling, and in the case of Zambia, it had to remove shipments that had already been delivered. The milling did, however, enable the WFP to fortify the grain to raise its micronutrient content, which was seen as an unexpected benefit.[20] Further, the WFP did manage to solicit donations

---

17. United Nations 2002.
18. Morris 2002.
19. Morris 2003.
20. Interview with Patrick Webb, dean and professor, Friedman School of Nutrition Science and Policy, and former chief of nutrition, WFP, November 13, 2007.

from nontraditional donors of aid for food, including a number of developing countries.[21] Some donors, such as Japan, the Netherlands, and the EU, stipulated that they wished their pledges of food aid to be spent on non-GMO food.[22]

As the principal donor of the GM food aid, the U.S. government took a defensive position. It initially refused to send non-GM varieties of maize to the region and refused to mill the grain. Its position was spelled out clearly in a "Questions and Answers" document posted on the USAID website.[23] On the question of why it did not give financial resources for LRP instead of in-kind food aid, it did not get into details of the debate over tied food aid. Instead, it simply noted that the United States is a large agricultural exporter and that its policy is to supply U.S.-grown food as aid, as it has done for nearly fifty years. It did note later on in the document, however, that local purchases would not be feasible in this particular case because they would drive up prices in the region and cause further food insecurity. The statement did not address the possibility of sending non-GMO food aid to the region. It stated that because U.S. farmers had widely adopted bioengineered crops, U.S. food aid likely contained GMOs.

The United States justified not offering to mill the grain on the grounds that it would be costly (typically milled grain is twice as expensive as whole grain) and cause delays. It noted that "[a]ny milling supported with U.S. food aid funds must be conducted in the United States" and would then have to be shipped at additional cost. But the United States did not object to other donors' paying for the milling. It stressed that it would respect the wishes of the countries that did not want GMO food aid sent to them. At first it said it would be impossible to source non-GM aid. But it did eventually give Zambia a donation of GM-free maize of some 30,000 tonnes, after heavy international pressure to do so.[24]

A striking aspect of the U.S. response to the crisis was the blame it placed on others for the controversy. Its principal target was Europe, because of its de facto moratorium on approvals of new GMO crops. But criticism was also directed at the recipient governments. Republican senator Charles Grassley from Iowa, for example, was blunt in his assessment of who was to blame:

> It is shameful to me that the leaders of some southern African countries, who are apparently well-fed, would rather see their populations go hungry than eat the same food we consume daily in the United States.... The European Union is partly to blame for the situation in Africa.... I am particularly troubled by reports that some EU member

---

21. Bennett 2003, 29.
22. Third World Network 2002; EU 2003a.
23. USAID 2003.
24. Mellen 2003.

states have warned that their relations with poorer countries, including those in Africa, could be harmed if those countries accept U.S. biotech food aid. Any such threats are unacceptable. Food aid should not be used as a bargaining chip.[25]

In the midst of the African crisis the United States seriously considered launching a formal complaint at the WTO over the EU's moratorium on GMOs, claiming that it was in contravention of WTO rules. WTO rules do allow countries to ban imports of a product on food safety concerns while the country seeks further scientific evidence, but the United States argued that five years was plenty of time and that no such evidence had been gathered. There was growing concern among policymakers that the EU's position was influencing too many countries, including those in Africa.[26] This view was bolstered by the work of some academics who argued that not only the EU but also environmental NGOs were having an inordinate amount of influence on African countries' responses to the crisis. As Robert Paarlberg notes, "In fact, Africa's rejection of genetically engineered crops today is far more western than it is African."[27]

Throughout the fall of 2002 and early in 2003 the United States put heavy pressure on Europe to remove its moratorium. In May 2003, joined by Canada and Argentina, it finally launched the formal complaint against the EU at the WTO.[28] At the time President Bush stated, "European governments should join—not hinder—the great cause of ending hunger in Africa."[29] Egypt was initially listed as a co-complainant, but it withdrew. Although Egypt does have an active agricultural biotechnology research program, it stepped away from the dispute because Europe is a very important market for its exports of fresh fruits and vegetables. The United States had hoped that having Egypt on board would help it drive home the point that GM crops are beneficial to Africa. It retaliated against Egypt by pulling out of talks on a free trade agreement with that country.[30]

When the United States launched the dispute, the European Union issued a press release stating its regret over the U.S. decision to take action on this case. It criticized the United States for using the African countries' refusal of GM food aid to pressure the EU: "A number of developing countries, including a large number of African countries suffering a shortage of food have requested main

---

25. Grassley 2003.

26. Borlaug 2003.

27. Paarlberg 2008, 16.

28. For an overview of the technical issues involved in the dispute, see Brack, Falkner, and Goll 2003.

29. Quoted in Denny and Elliott 2003.

30. Alden 2002.

donors of food aid to avoid providing GMO food. The European Commission finds it unacceptable that such legitimate concerns are used by the US against the EU policy on GMOs." The EU then stressed that its own policy of sourcing food locally and regionally was one that would have avoided such a problem in the first place.[31]

## More GMO Food Aid Incidents

The southern African crisis is the best-known case of GMOs in food aid. The scale of the crisis made it a powerful example of the problems not only of tied food aid but also of GMOs. There have been further incidents, however, which while they have been less prominent in the media, have sparked ongoing political debate over the issue. Shortly after the initial flurry over the southern African crisis, another dispute emerged over GMOs in food aid, this time in Sudan. The conflict in western Darfur in the early 2000s had resulted in millions of displaced people, many of whom were living in refugee camps and in were desperate need of food aid. In one of its largest operations, the WFP had been feeding some 2.4 million people who had fled from the conflict. Sudan was pressured by the United States to accept GM food aid, despite the fact that it had passed legislation requiring such aid to be certified GMO-free. In response to heavy U.S. pressure, Sudan issued a temporary six-month waiver to its legislation in order to give the United States more time to source GMO-free food aid. In March 2004, however, the United States threatened to cut the aid completely.[32] This action prompted Sudan to extend the waiver to early 2005 in order not to disrupt the flow of food aid.

According to some accounts, the eastern part of Sudan had good harvests in 2000–2004, but it was difficult to move grain west into Darfur.[33] Instead of relying on the local foods, the country brought in aid from abroad, and this required it to relax its own GMO legislation. The WFP began to ask the United States to supply sorghum rather than corn-soy blend for its program in Sudan because sorghum is an indigenous crop in Sudan and GM varieties of it are not yet widespread in the United States. This strategy appears to have smoothed out the relationship between the United States and Sudan over GM food aid, but not entirely. The Sudanese government lifted its waiver on GM imports in early 2007 and at the same time acquired equipment to allow it to test imports for

31. EU 2003a.
32. Africa Centre for Biosafety et al. 2004.
33. Mulvaney 2004.

the presence of GMOs.[34] The government then held up a shipment of sorghum from the United States on the suspicion that it was genetically modified. After testing determined that it was not, the food aid was released.[35]

In 2004 the government of Angola announced plans to ban GM food aid, but it eventually settled on a policy of accepting the aid on the condition that it was to be milled first. Although this policy was no different from that taken a few years earlier by many countries in southern Africa, there was a backlash against Angola from both the United States and the WFP over its decision. The government of Angola had officially instituted the policy as a means to protect biodiversity in the country, and this measure was in compliance with the guidelines of the Advisory Committee on Biotechnology and Biosafety of the Southern African Development Community (SADC), which suggested that countries ensure that GMO food aid was milled to prevent it from being planted.

The WFP responded to the policy by stressing to the Angolan government that it would take longer and cost more to provide milled grain, and thus the country would ultimately receive less aid. The United States continues to refuse to provide milled food aid, which means that when countries request such aid, the WFP must arrange funding to cover the milling. The United States went on to stress that the country would face a significant drop in U.S. food aid if it persisted with the milling request.[36] It cut its funding to the WFP shortly after the Angolan announcement, and Angola's WFP aid was then halved days later.[37]

In response to this treatment of Angola and Sudan, more than sixty African and international NGOs teamed up and sent an open letter to the WFP asking it to respect restrictions on GM food aid and provide non-GM alternatives.[38] The World Food Programme denied that it had aimed to pressure Angola into accepting GM food aid.[39] This letter also called for an increase in cash donations to allow for local and regional purchase of food. This echoed the analysis of a group of NGOs on this issue that also called for procurement of food aid from within the region.[40] It pointed to an FAO report that assessed Sudan's harvest as a bumper crop and called upon the WFP to use surpluses available in Sudan in the first instance to address hunger in the country.

34. Moola and Munnik 2007.

35. BBC News 2007.

36. Africa Centre for Biosafety et al. 2004, 4.

37. Ibid., 9–10; Lieberman and Gray 2008, 404.

38. This open letter is posted at http://www.earthlife-ct.org.za/filemgmt_data/files/WFP_letter_%20African_NGOs_May_2004.pdf.

39. ICTSD 2004; Jones 2004.

40. African Centre for Biosafety et al. 2004, 5.

In 2005 a group of NGOs in Central America complained about GMOs in food aid to the region. These groups had gathered and tested a number of samples of maize and soy food aid delivered by the WFP to Nicaragua, Honduras, El Salvador, and Guatemala. All the aid samples tested positive for GMOs. One NGO representative noted, "In Nicaragua our farmers produce enough food and the WFP should buy any needed food within our country, instead of using imported food with GMOs." The NGOs, which included environmental, farmer, consumer, union, and human rights groups, held a simultaneous press conference across the region, blaming the WFP and the United States for allowing the spread of unwanted GMOs and calling for a recall of all food aid that contained them.[41] While local NGOs issued a press release about the discovery, the governments in the region did not respond and have remained silent on this issue.

GMOs in food aid sparked concerns of environmental groups once again in 2006, this time with the detection of an unapproved GMO variety of rice found in food aid in Sierra Leone and Ghana. The particular variety, LL601, had never been approved for commercial release in the United States and was abandoned in 2001 by the company (subsequently purchased by Bayer) that had experimented with it. In 2006, however, it was found to have widely contaminated the U.S. rice supply. The incident highlighted the extent to which GMOs not only can spread but can do so without anyone's being aware of it. In this case, because the variety had never been approved for commercial release, there was no available test for it, and it was discovered only when a subsidiary of the company that developed it went public with the finding that it was in their seed supply.[42] Tests were conducted in countries that import rice from the United States, and the variety was found to have been shipped around the world.

Shortly after this discovery, the U.S. government chose to retroactively approve LL601 for commercial release, a decision that was announced just days after the discovery of the GMO rice in food aid shipments to West Africa. NGO groups were offended by the U.S. decision to approve the variety, considering it to be a "blatant insult to African people." NGO groups issued an open letter to USAID and the WFP calling on them to provide adequate information to countries that receive food aid about the contents of those shipments. The letter also demanded an immediate recall of the food aid by USAID and that Bayer cover the costs.[43] In a separate report, the groups called on African governments to monitor imports and food aid.[44] But while countries in Europe suspended commercial imports of

---

41. Environmental News Service 2005.
42. Clapp 2008.
43. Friends of the Earth Nigeria et al. 2006.
44. Friends of the Earth Africa 2006.

rice from the United States because of the contamination, African governments that received the aid did not reject it and have remained silent on the issue.

New incidents could erupt at any moment. Ethiopia, for example, passed a new biosafety law in the summer of 2009 and several months later issued an international plea for emergency food aid for some 6.2 million people facing severe malnutrition as a result of drought. The Environmental Protection Authority in Ethiopia apparently did not see that potential conflict was just around the corner when it passed the legislation.[45] The United States is the largest donor of food aid to Ethiopia, and the aid it pledged for this crisis in 2009, more than 464,000 tonnes, did contain GMOs.[46] In its press release, USAID was clear that the aid might contain GMOs, but it also emphasized that its aid met U.S. food safety standards and that the United States does not send "viable modified organisms, such as corn or soy grain which could be planted if distributed as aid." Instead it sends corn-soy-blend and vegetable oil, which are processed forms of grains that may contain GMOs. USAID indicated that the new law was unlikely to keep U.S. aid from reaching hungry people in Ethiopia, while officials in Ethiopia indicated that enforcement of the law was still open to interpretation, with the focus likely to be on the biosafety aspect.[47]

These recurring episodes of GMOs in food aid suggest that the shipment of genetically modified grains in food aid is likely to remain common. Some countries require that the aid be milled first, while others are more vigilant in terms of not allowing in any genetically modified food aid. Yet others appear to be accepting the aid, whether it contains GMOs or not, with little or no resistance, despite the protests of NGOs operating within their borders. The United States, as the major donor of commodity food aid that contains GMOs, has also taken steps to ensure that it sends processed foods such as corn-soy-blend and vegetable oil rather than whole grain maize or soy to countries that refuse to accept living modified organisms. The WFP, for its part, has requested certain food products from the United States for certain recipients, such as sorghum for Sudan, to minimize the potential for GMOs to enter countries that have passed legislation banning their import.

# Explaining Political Responses to GMO Food Aid

The advent of genetically modified foods transformed and complicated debates over the role and form of international food aid. Earlier studies on the politics of

---

45. Heinlein 2009.
46. USAID 2009.
47. See Heinlein 2009.

food aid from the 1960s to the early 1990s focused on the impact of the Cold War and wrangling among grain exporters over surplus grain disposal. Because agricultural biotechnology had not yet become commercialized or used on a wide scale, earlier international relations scholars of food aid did not foresee the ways in which it would spark intense political debates over food aid. Diverging policies among donors—the United States and the EU in particular—over the role of in-kind, commodity-form food aid versus financial resources for procurement at the local and regional level focused attention on the issue in the early 2000s.

At the same time that the divergence of policies presented the problem of GMO food aid, debates over tying became entangled in broader political and scientific debates over genetic modification of foods. Further complicating the politics of the issue was the lack of clear international rules over the movement of GMOs, including food aid, across borders. And they were additionally complicated by the different economic interests of donors.

## The Scientific Debate over GMOs

In the media accounts of the GMO food aid incidents in southern Africa in particular, the scientific debate was prominent. At the same time, however, the EU, some recipients, and many NGOs also clearly linked the GMO food aid problem to tied aid. Further, they pointed out that stores of non-GM food were available in the region and could be used for local and regional purchase.[48] The United States, in responding only to the scientific issues surrounding GMOs, managed to avoid engaging in direct debate over the potential problems associated with tied food aid. This likely had much to do with its dispute with the EU over trade in GMOs and its plans to challenge the EU at the WTO over this issue.[49] In choosing to address only the scientific aspects of GMOs, the United States was able to shape the debate and use the incident in southern Africa to its benefit.

The intensity of the debate was linked to the two very different kinds of policies that emerged regarding risks associated with genetic modification of foods in North America on one hand and Europe and a number of developing countries on the other.[50] The North American position on GM foods and crops was that minimal risk is attached to them and that because of this a precautionary approach in their adoption was not warranted. In both the United States and Canada, regulatory procedures for GMOs were built on the notion that if the developer of a genetically modified crop or food can demonstrate that it is

---

48. See Zerbe 2004, 601.
49. See Brack, Falkner, and Goll 2003.
50. See Bernauer 2003.

"substantially equivalent" to a conventional counterpart, that crop or food does not require an extensive risk assessment prior to its approval.[51] Ongoing scientific uncertainty with respect to the risks of GMOs did not automatically invoke a precautionary approach in these countries. In this system, the benefits of GM crops in terms of higher yields and easier management of weeds were assumed to far outweigh the (known) risks associated with them.[52] The United States and Canada viewed their approach to the regulation of agricultural biotechnology as being firmly grounded in "sound science."

In the EU and many developing countries, the approach to regulating agricultural biotechnology products was very different from that adopted in North America. In the European Union, the GMO policies have been more precautionary in practice. The 1998–2003 de facto moratorium on GMO approvals in the EU has been attributed to disagreements between some EU member states—namely Denmark, France, Austria, Greece, Italy, Luxemburg, Belgium, and Germany—and the European Commission over the safety of and hence approval processes for GMOs.[53] While the moratorium was the result of a failure to resolve the political conflict over GMO authorizations within the EU, the EU approval process was already based on precaution as a key principle of risk assessment and risk management.[54] It was moving in an even more precautionary direction than that in North America when the EU adopted new regulations on GMO approvals in 2001 and 2003 that included more stringent procedures for risk assessment as well as provisions for traceability and labeling. After these new regulations were adopted, the EU was able to lift its moratorium in 2004 with the approval of some new GM crops.[55]

Many developing countries lacked a regulatory structure for approval of agricultural biotechnology products in the late 1990s and early 2000s. For some sub-Saharan African countries, adopting an EU-style approach was attractive because genetically modified crops were not being developed domestically and they did not have the means or expertise at the time to test them for safety or develop legislation to govern them. Countries that were the centers of origin for certain crops adopted precautionary approaches to those crops, such as Mexico and Nicaragua for maize. Other developing countries have since the mid-2000s put legislation into place regarding agricultural biotechnology and biosafety.[56]

---

51. Prakash and Kollmann 2003, 625.
52. Paarlberg 2000.
53. Rosendal 2005; Levidow, Carr, and Weild 2005; Falkner 2007b.
54. Isaac and Kerr 2002, 1086–90; Prakash and Kollman 2003, 626.
55. Rosendal 2005.
56. Gupta and Falkner 2006.

The different interpretations of the science and risks of GMOs and the policies attached to them in the early 2000s go some way to explaining the widely divergent positions with respect to GM food aid among the United States, the EU, and the recipient countries. The hostility of the United States toward those countries that rejected the GM food aid and placing of the blame on Europe are partly products of these different policy approaches to the issue. The United States would much rather see its own regulatory style, rather than the EU approach, adopted in developing countries that currently lack a regulatory framework. This attitude can be seen in the comments made by Senator Chuck Grassley at a speech to the Congressional Leadership Institute in March 2003, just prior to the launch of the trade dispute against the EU: "By refusing to adopt scientifically based laws regarding biotechnology, the EU has fed the myth that biotech crops are somehow dangerous.... The European Union's lack of science based biotech laws is unacceptable, and is threatening the health of millions of Africans."[57]

The refusal of GM food aid by the southern African countries can also be seen as a reflection of their position in the scientific debate, as many of the comments made by African leaders when rejecting the aid made this specific link. For example, Zambian president Levy Mwanawasa expressed his concern that GM food aid was "poison," stating, "If it is safe, then we will give it to our people. But if it is not, then we would rather starve than get something toxic."[58] The Zambian government did authorize a scientific delegation to study the issue, which was sponsored by the U.S. government and several European countries. This delegation traveled to South Africa, several European countries, and the United States. The eventual report from the delegation, which came in the fall of 2002, cautioned against the acceptance of GMOs in Zambia, much to the disappointment of the United States.[59]

While the scientific debate over GMOs and their appropriateness in food aid was raging, the EU, recipient governments, and NGOs critical of GMOs in food aid continued to point out that tied aid was at the root of the GMO food aid problem. Greenpeace, for example, emphasized the importance of cash aid in its response to the southern African crisis, quoting WFP spokesperson Richard Lee on the WFP's preference for cash aid for local and regional purchase. Friends of the Earth's report on GMOs in food aid after the Southern African crisis also highlighted the benefits of local and regional purchases.[60]

---

57. Grassley 2003.
58. Dynes 2002, 12.
59. Carroll 2002; Hansch et al. 2003, 20.
60. See Greenpeace UK 2002; Friends of the Earth International 2003.

The EU's focus on local and regional purchase in its statement responding to the launch of the GMO dispute at the WTO highlighted its view that the issue was as much about the form of international food aid as about the role of GMOs in agriculture. In its reply to the launch of the challenge to EU regulations on imports of biotech products, the EU emphasized its own food aid policies:

> Food aid to starving populations should be about meeting the urgent humanitarian needs of those who are in need. It should not be about trying to advance the case for GM food abroad (while staying away from the international consensus such as the Cartagena Protocol), or planting GM crops for export, or indeed finding outlets for domestic surplus, which is a regrettable US food aid policy. European Commission policy is to source food for emergency situation [sic] as much as possible in the region, thus contributing to the development of local markets, providing additional incentives for producers and ensuring that products distributed closely match local consumption habits.[61]

The United States did not reply to these critiques and instead kept the discussion squarely on GMOs. It focused on scientific and food safety concerns probably because it wanted to emphasize this topic while it was part of a challenge to the EU at the WTO over GMOs. This strategy also enabled the United States to avoid having a broader discussion of its tied food aid policy.

The GMO trade dispute at the WTO was eventually settled in 2006. The WTO panel found that the EU's de facto moratorium was inconsistent with some aspects of WTO rules, including what it saw as undue delay in approving GMOs as a result of the moratorium. As noted above, the EU by that time had already lifted its moratorium on the import of genetically modified organisms after passing more stringent legislation. After the WTO ruling, the EU agreed to amend additional parts of its legislation to bring it into conformance with WTO rules. The United States saw the outcome as a victory, but many analysts see it as ambiguous.[62]

## Unclear Rules

The lack of scientific consensus on the safety of GMOs more broadly fed into lack of clarity in international rules regarding trade in GMOs. These unclear rules had important implications for commodity food aid movements between the mid-1990s and the mid-2000s, the period when political clashes over GMO food

---

61. EU 2003a.
62. Lieberman and Gray 2008.

aid were arguably the most intense. There was a lack of established norms on how GMOs in food aid should be handled by both recipients and donors. As both international and national policies and procedures with respect to GMOs became clearer after 2004, establishing clearer norms of behavior, the intensity of the exchanges over GMO food aid diminished somewhat, although the disagreements did not disappear entirely. While a significant degree of uncertainty over procedures and regulations continued, as exemplified by the case of Ethiopia in 2009, it appears as though awareness of the issue has prompted officials to preempt potential clashes before they occur.

When the southern African crisis erupted in mid-2002, only a few developing countries had any domestic legislation dealing with imports of GMOs, let alone specific regulations regarding GMO food aid. The only sub-Saharan African countries with biosafety laws in place at that time were South Africa and Zimbabwe, though others have since made serious efforts to develop policies dealing with the import of genetically modified organisms.[63] South Africa is the only sub-Saharan African country that has approved the commercial planting of genetically modified crops. In July 2001 the Organization of African Unity (OAU, now the African Union) endorsed a Model Law on Safety in Biotechnology, which takes a precautionary approach to biotechnology and calls for clear labeling and identification of imports of GMOs. This model legislation was designed as guidance for countries in formulating their own national laws on biosafety as well as a way to develop an Africa-wide system for biosafety. By 2011, most African countries had biosafety legislation either in development or in place.[64] Sudan, Ethiopia, Angola, and Zambia have adopted policies with a highly precautionary approach, while several others have been somewhat more permissive, particularly in allowing milled food aid grain.[65]

There have also been more regional approaches to biosafety policy development. In response to the southern African crisis in 2002, the Southern African Development Community established an advisory committee to set out guidelines for policy on GMOs in the region. These stipulate that "food aid that contains or may contain GMOs has to be delivered with the prior informed consent of the recipient country and that shipments must be labeled."[66] Other regional responses include efforts by the Common Market for Eastern and Southern Africa (COMESA) to develop a regional policy on GMOs, including food aid.

---

63. See Karenbu, Wafula, and Waithaka 2008; UNEP 2006.
64. See Biosafety Clearing-House website, http://bch.cbd.int/; see also Karembu, Wafida, and Waithaka 2008; UNEP 2006.
65. See Zepeda 2006, 1206; Karembu, Wafida, and Waithaka 2008.
66. Friends of the Earth International 2003, 9.

The African Union has called for a common approach to GMOs, including guidelines for handling them, though it noted that final decisions were ultimately up to individual countries.[67] These rules were developed in response to the crisis and thus were not available at the time it erupted. The absence of clear procedures within African countries was one of the reasons that the exchanges over GMO food aid had become particularly heated, as neither recipient nor donor knew exactly what norms should be followed.

At the international level, rules on biosafety and trade in GMOs were also not clear prior to 2003. The Cartagena Protocol on Biosafety, which governs trade in GMOs, was negotiated between 1995 and 2000 (when it was adopted). The agreement did not come into legal force, however, until September 2003.[68] The protocol's rules state that GMOs (living modified organisms—LMOs) intended for release into the environment (seeds) in the importing country, are to be subject to a formal advance informed agreement (AIA) procedure for the first international transboundary movement to a country. Exporting countries, in other words, must obtain consent from importing countries before shipping LMOs. Importing countries can reject them if they wish, on the basis of risk assessments. Genetically modified commodities (living modified organisms intended for food, feed, or processing—FFP) are exempted from the formal AIA procedure and instead are subject to a separate form of notification, by means of the Biosafety Clearing-House. This is an Internet database where exporters are required to note whether shipments of such commodities "may contain GMOs" and importers are encouraged to post information on domestic rules and regulations regarding GMOs. Importers can reject FFP shipments on the basis of risk assessments. In both cases, parties are given the right to make decisions on imports on the basis of precaution in cases where full scientific certainty is lacking.[69]

The food aid donations shipped before the protocol became effective were not covered by these rules. Now the rules apply only to countries that have signed and ratified the agreement. The United States and Canada—two of the major food aid donors, which grow significant quantities of GMOs—have not yet ratified the protocol and thus are not bound by its rules. Further, although these rules are now in place, some have argued that the onus has actually fallen on the importing countries to report their domestic regulations regarding GMOs that exporters can check before making shipments, rather than on exporters to post information before shipping.[70] This means that importing countries that

---

67. See African Union 2006; see also FAO 2006c.
68. For a history and analysis of these negotiations, see Bail, Falkner, and Marquard 2002.
69. Text of the Cartegena Protocol on Biosafety (http://bch.cbd.int/protocol/).
70. Gupta 2010.

do not post information about their policies on certain varieties of genetically modified crops could be interpreted as not banning them. If the importing country does not have the capacity to fully monitor and test its imports for GMOs, this could mean that they enter freely without being checked, even if that country is opposed to GMO imports.

The Codex Alimentarius Commission, which sets voluntary international guidelines on food standards, has attempted to address questions of biotechnology and food safety since the late 1990s. In 1999 it established a special task force on biotechnology to address the wider concerns expressed about biotechnology and food safety, especially those related to risk analysis. The task force did not release its guidelines until mid-2003. Although they are voluntary, the standards are considered a benchmark for international trade under the WTO. They include safety evaluations prior to marketing of GM products and measures to ensure traceability in case a product needs to be recalled.[71] But because these guidelines were not in place at the time of the food crisis in southern Africa, nothing was done to ensure that these guidelines were followed for food aid.

Even though it had been shipping GMOs in food aid for years, the WFP did not set an explicit policy on how to deal with them until mid-2003. Its policy has long been to give food aid to countries in food deficit if the food met requirements for food safety by both the donor and the recipient. But if neither the recipient nor the donor had a policy of notification, it was difficult for the WFP to keep track of GMOs. It defended its lack of a GMO policy prior to that date by stating that "none of the international bodies charged with dealing with foods derived from biotechnology had ever requested that the Programme handle GM/biotech commodities in any special manner for either health or environmental reasons."[72] Because of the media attention to the issue and claims by some NGOs that the WFP was negligent, the WFP decided to establish a formal policy for dealing with GMOs in food aid in 2002, which was finalized in 2003. The new policy asks recipient country offices of the WFP to be aware of and comply with national regulations regarding GM food imports. It also maintains its original policy that it will provide as aid only food that is approved as safe in both donor and recipient nations. Countries that clearly state that they do not wish to receive GM food aid will have their wishes respected. The WFP stated that it will still accept GM food aid from donors but will also respect the wishes of donors who give cash in lieu of in-kind aid if they request that the money not be spent on GM food.[73]

---

71. Codex Alimentarius Commission 2003.
72. WFP 2003, 5.
73. Ibid.

The Food Aid Convention does not give much guidance on the issue of GMOs, as it is not mentioned in the convention text. The FAC was in fact due to expire in 2002, at the height of the GMO crisis in southern Africa and has every year since then been renewed pending clarity with respect to the Doha Round of trade talks (see chapter 6). The FAC does, however, recognize that both donors and recipients have the right to set their own policies regarding food aid. The agreement, then, at least in principle would support recipient countries that choose to refuse food aid containing GMOs.[74] The issue of GMOs in food aid was discussed at the June 2003 Food Aid Committee Meeting. Delegates from the EU and United States agreed that recipients should ultimately be able to designate the type of food they accepted and FAC members further agreed that the committee need not discuss the issue again at future meetings.[75]

Donor governments also lacked clear policies and procedures with respect to GMOs in food aid at the time of the southern African crisis. The United States issued a guidance document in 2003 regarding GMOs for its program partners (grain firms, shippers, and NGOs) that handle food aid.[76] This document notes that while the United States is not a party to the Cartagena Protocol and thus cannot force exporters to comply with the documentation requirements— in particular to ensure that "may contain GMOs" labeling is on products containing living modified organisms—it encourages them to do so in any case in order to avoid unnecessary delays in food aid shipments. It notes, however, that aid that is processed, such as corn-soy blend, does not contain LMOs and thus does not require documentation.

In practice, the United States has addressed concerns over GM food aid largely by sending products that the recipient is likely to take, thus avoiding further controversies. But it has not tackled the issue head on, nor has it provided much assistance to recipient countries to develop clearer policies of their own. As one report on U.S. food aid notes, "While short-term fixes have been found to address recipients' policies on import of biotech grain in the form of food aid, other technical assistance has not been sufficient to enable countries to put into place appropriate policies that adequately address their concerns."[77] The United States in the meantime has continued to press countries to accept GMOs. As the USAID administrator, Henrietta Fore, said in 2008, "We will continue to urge countries to end restrictions to acceptance of biotechnology-based crops, either in commercial trade or food aid. As we have seen during past food crises,

---

74. See Consumers International, Africa Office 2004.
75. Food Aid Committee 2003.
76. This statement was updated in 2004. See USDA 2004.
77. Simmons 2007, 49.

distribution of food aid can be significantly complicated by barriers to biotech-nology crops."[78]

Before it untied its food aid in 2008, Canada had given assurances to NGOs such as Greenpeace that its food aid was not contingent on recipients' accepting GMOs,[79] but apart from that it had not issued any policy or guidance specifi-cally regarding the handling of GMO food aid. The EU had already switched to primarily cash food aid and thus saw that it was not likely to have to handle this thorny issue in its own food aid policy, apart from requesting that the WFP not spend the cash it donated on food containing GMOs.

## Economic Factors

Economic interests also help to explain the political exchanges between donors and recipients, and among donors over GMO food aid. Each of these players has strong commercial interests that are affected by the presence of GMOs. The U.S. response to the outcry over GMOs in food aid was most profoundly affected by the fact that its laws require that its food aid be domestically sourced, as discussed in the previous chapter. In the case of southern Africa, the United States was the only donor that gave food aid in kind rather than as financial assistance for local and regional purchase.[80] Because it was constrained by the domestic sourcing requirements, it had little choice but to defend the presence of GMOs, which were prevalent in U.S.-grown grains.

Beyond the impact of its tied aid policies, the United States has been keen to protect its markets for its maize and soy exports. The European moratorium on imports of GMOs meant a significant loss of foreign markets for U.S. grain. The United States had lost around $300 million *per year* in sales of maize to Europe, for example, between the late 1990s and the mid-2000s.[81] Some thirty-five coun-tries, composing half of the world's population, had rejected GM technology by the mid-2000s, and this closed market opportunities for GMO-producing countries to export their products. In addition to the European Union, Australia, Japan, China, Indonesia, and Saudi Arabia also did not approve most agricul-tural biotechnology for domestic use and import.[82] Having lost these markets, the United States was anxious not to lose others. This would explain why it was so adamant about the safety of its products and also would explain the timing of its

78. Fore 2008.
79. Office of the Auditor General of Canada 2003.
80. WFP official Richard Lee, quoted in Greenpeace UK 2002.
81. Brack, Faulkner, and Goll, 2003, 3; see also Zerbe 2004, 606.
82. Dauenhauer 2003.

challenge to the EU, directly after the southern African refusal of GMO food aid. Indeed, the inability to find export markets for its GM grain may well have fed into the U.S. insistence on maintaining a largely tied food aid program.

A further interest of the United States was its general support of the agricultural biotechnology sector, which is dominated by U.S. transnational corporations (TNCs).[83] The industry had experienced some losses in the early 2000s, particularly after the EU's imposition of the moratorium.[84] The U.S. Department of Agriculture, which is responsible for regulating biotechnology in the United States and oversees Title I food aid, works in close cooperation with the agricultural biotechnology industry.[85] USAID, which is responsible for Title II and Title III food aid, also actively promotes the adoption of agricultural biotechnology in the developing world through educational programs.[86]

Critics have argued that the United States is trying to pave the way for the introduction of pro-GM legislation to facilitate the export of GM crops and seeds around the world.[87] For many, the country's position on GMO food aid, especially its continued refusal to mill GM grain and its attack on Europe's regulatory structure, was a deliberate strategy not only to bolster its own biotech industry but also to spread GMOs as far and as wide as possible in order break the remaining resistance to the technology.[88] As the Consumers International Africa Office notes in a fact sheet on food aid and GMOs, "The use of GM food aid has added a new dimension to the debate because the provision of GM food aid is seen as providing an important back-door entry point for the introduction of [GMOs] in developing countries."[89]

Economic considerations in the EU must also be taken into account in explaining donor reactions to GMO food aid. The EU's position during the southern African crisis, for example, was very much linked to the pressure that the United States put on the EU over its moratorium on approvals of GM crops and foods. It is not surprising that the EU position was in opposition to that of the United States over the southern African crisis. Tied up in this broader dispute is the question of export markets for the EU. It may be that the EU is seeking to solidify trade relations with developing countries by creating a non-GM market that would exclude the United States. Indeed, as some argue, the EU's more

---

83. Noah Zerbe 2004 also makes this point.
84. Herrick 2008, 55–56.
85. Stapp 2003.
86. GM Food Aid 2003, 46.
87. Kuyek 2002; Consumers International, Africa Office 2004; Lieberman and Gray 2008, 40; Herrick 2008.
88. Glover 2003; Kneen 1999; Kuyek 2002; Mellen 2003.
89. Consumers International, Africa Office 2004.

precautionary approach to GMOs is largely a protectionist measure.[90] The EU has also been pushing for several years now for cash-only food aid to be written into WTO rules as part of the ongoing talks on the revision of the WTO's agreement on agriculture because it sees U.S. food aid practices as trade distorting.[91]

On the recipient side, economic considerations are also important in helping to explain their acceptance or rejection of food aid. The southern African countries were concerned about their export prospects with the EU if they accepted GM food aid in whole grain form.[92] African countries are economically much closer to Europe than they are to North America. Some 30 percent of cereal and oilseed exports from sub-Saharan Africa were exported to Europe in 2001, while less than 1 percent of its cereal exports went to North America.[93] Zambia, for example, exports some maize to European countries, and Zambia and other countries in the region did not want to close the door to potential future markets in Europe for GM-free maize exports.[94] The same might be said for Sudan and Ethiopia. But other countries were more accepting of GMO food aid, making relatively little fuss over it. Central American governments, for example, did not take up the call of NGOs in the region to reject GMO food aid. The fact that these countries were negotiating a Central American Free Trade Agreement with the United States at the time suggests that they were not willing to stand up to the United States over this issue.[95] The lack of concern about GMO rice aid among the governments in West Africa is likely tied to the fact that the EU had decided to allow in the imports of LL601 and that rice grains sent as aid could not be planted.

## Conclusion

Food aid has been repoliticized at the international level by GMOs in agricultural commodities. The political debate over GMOs in food aid has roots in debates over whether that aid should be given in kind or as financial resources as well as in questions about the safety of agricultural biotechnology. The broader debate over GMOs is still largely unsettled, despite the WTO's findings on the challenge to the EU moratorium. The debate over the appropriateness of GMOs as an agricultural strategy is still highly charged, with wide variation in viewpoints among

---

90. Lieberman and Gray 2008, 399.
91. Clapp 2004.
92. Clapp 2006.
93. Cited in Herrick 2008, 58.
94. Hansch et al. 2003, 18–19.
95. Clapp 2006.

different countries. The question of whether food aid should be tied or untied has become entangled in this broader debate.

Complicating these issues were unclear rules on the international trade in GMOs at the time of the southern African crisis. Because international-level policies and procedures were lacking in the early 2000s, domestic policies prevailed, but there were key divergences between countries. Economic interests played an important role in the political responses to GMO food aid incidents. The desire to protect export markets and to promote its agricultural biotechnology industry and in particular its trade dispute with the EU over GMO regulation appear to have been major influences on the United States' responses to GMO food aid. Similarly, the fact that the EU was under pressure from the United States over its more precautionary GMO food policies influenced its opposition to GMO food aid. Recipient countries for their part have been influenced by trade and aid opportunities from donor countries and have chosen policies on GMO food aid that tend to align with those of their major trade partners and aid donors.

# 6

# FOOD AID AT THE WTO

Clashes among donors and between donors and recipients in the context of the Doha Round of trade negotiations of the World Trade Organization after 2001 showed that in the international trade arena, food aid had become highly politicized. This chapter examines the debates in the Doha Round concerning the issue of food aid. In negotiations on the WTO Doha Round Agreement on Agriculture, the European Union pressed the idea of imposing trade disciplines, or strict rules, on such aid. It asserted that tied food aid, monetization, and concessional sales—all practiced by the United States—had the same overall effect as trade-distorting agricultural export subsidies. These practices, the EU argued, should be subject to the same strict trade rules that applied to other export subsidies. The EU was reluctant to accept trade disciplines on its own export subsidies—something it was under extreme pressure to do—unless the other WTO members, the United States in particular, faced similar disciplines. Thus it actively inserted food aid into the debate.

The issue became highly politicized when it became clear that the United States disagreed with the EU's assertions. The U.S. trade negotiators actively resisted the EU's claim that U.S. food aid programs distorted trade, and they defended the practice of tied food aid and monetization. They insisted that because international food aid made up only 1 to 2 percent of global agricultural trade, in-kind aid and concessional sales under the label of food aid could not possibly have the same trade-distorting impact as export subsidies imposed by the EU.

The differences between major donors on how they provide food aid—whether it is sold or given as a grant, whether it is tied or untied, and whether it is monetized—have been a key driving force behind the political clashes over the issue at the international level. Further, as food aid became caught up in broader debates over agricultural trade liberalization, donors began to use the issue as a bargaining chip for their broader negotiating positions in the agriculture talks. As with the case of GMOs, food aid became entangled in preexisting debates, with the differences on how to provide food aid adding a new layer of complexity.

## International Trade Impact of Food Aid

Food aid has long been considered a trade concern, but there is a substantial gray area between food aid and trade.[1] As noted in chapter 2, some aid is given in fully grant form and as such is essentially a gift to the recipient. Some is sold to recipients on concessional terms—i.e., on easier terms than those for commercial sales. Some donor countries sell agricultural products with export credits that give long periods for repayment or with credit guarantees, meaning that if the borrower defaults, the export credit agency (usually a government agency) will ensure repayment. Unlike concessional-sales food aid, export credits of this type are not technically food aid. They are, however, perceived by the selling countries to be a form of assistance to food-deficit countries.

There is general agreement in the economic literature that food aid shipments and monetization of food aid in recipient countries can and often do result in some displacement of commercial imports of food to the recipient country.[2] What this means in practice is that the aid does not merely add to the food consumed in the recipient country but in fact takes the place of some commercial food imports.[3] How much commercial food trade is actually displaced by food aid, however, is difficult to measure precisely. Moreover, the extent to which such displacement occurs depends on a number of factors, including the market conditions and crop mix in the recipient country, as well as the timing of the aid.[4] Less agreement exists on the impact of food aid and monetization on the functioning of domestic agricultural markets and on farmer production incentives in recipient countries, although the potential for disruptions of these sorts on domestic markets is widely understood.[5] The arrival of in-kind food aid that is monetized right at the time of a local harvest, for example, can result in lower prices received by local producers of similar food products.[6]

---

1. Shaw and Singer 1996, 452.
2. Barrett, 2002, 1.
3. FAO 2005, 5.
4. FAO 2006a, 2.
5. FAO 2005, 5.
6. Simmons 2009, 38.

Despite some divergence in views on the extent of commercial import displacement and domestic market disruption caused by food aid, there is wide agreement among economists that displacement of both local foods and imported foods will be greater if the aid is not targeted to those individuals with the most need.[7] In these cases, the leakage of food aid onto the local market can cause distortions. This type of leakage is most likely to occur with food aid that is sold on concessional terms and monetized rather than given in grant form and targeted to the neediest populations in emergencies. In emergency situations where food is simply not available in local markets, as in the case of a natural disaster or violent conflict, food aid is much less likely to disrupt either local or international markets and is much more likely to result in additional consumption.

The potential impacts of food aid on trade and local markets are generally understood by most donors. Indeed, food aid programs have often been openly promoted by donor governments on the grounds that they serve multiple functions, including the development of commercial markets for donor country agricultural exports. Title I of PL 480, for example, was established explicitly as an export promotion program.[8] The terms on which the food aid is sold under Title I generally have grace periods of up to five years, repayment periods of up to thirty years, and below-market interest rates. This type of arrangement closely resembles a straightforward export credit program.[9] Before it was scaled back after 2006, credit-based food aid from the United States regularly amounted to over $100 million annually in the early 2000s.[10]

Concern over the impact of food aid programs on commercial trade emerged early in the history of international food aid and prompted the establishment of the FAO Principles on Surplus Disposal overseen by the Consultative Subcommittee on Surplus Disposal in 1954, the same year that the United States enacted its PL 480 food aid programs. The main objective of the principles, as outlined in chapter 2, is to ensure that shipments of surplus food as aid do not displace commercial exports of food that would have taken place in the absence of the aid. The potential for such displacement was a particular concern for other exporting countries, who might lose export markets as a result of food aid programs that were clearly disposing of agricultural surpluses from donor countries. The Principles of Surplus Disposal call for the maintenance of usual marketing requirements in countries that receive food aid. In other words, recipient countries

---

7. FAO 2005; see also Barrett and Maxwell 2005.
8. USAID 1995; see also Young and Abbott 2005, 4.
9. Watkins 2003, 51.
10. GAO 2002, 6.

should not see a drop in commercial imports as a result of receiving food aid, because the aid is an addition to the imports.[11]

Awareness of the potential trade displacement effect of food aid also helps to explain why the 1967 Food Aid Convention was a product of the Kennedy Round of the General Agreement on Tariffs and Trade, rather than being a stand-alone treaty on humanitarian assistance. The FAC requires that donors carry out food aid transactions in a "manner that is consistent with the FAO 'Principles on Surplus Disposal and Consultative Obligations.'"[12] Neither the FAC nor the FAO Principles on Surplus Disposal, however, embody a binding enforcement mechanism.[13] Although the CSSD was active in its early years, with donors regularly reporting their food aid operations, by the late 1990s and early 2000s fewer than 5 percent of these transactions were being reported.[14]

The trade impacts of food aid were considered in the Uruguay Round Agreement on Agriculture negotiations, which set out requirements to reduce both domestic and export subsidies that distorted trade in agriculture. There are no strict disciplines, or restrictions, on food aid in the URAA. But article 10 does aim to prevent countries from circumventing their commitments for export subsidy reductions by spelling out that members should not use food aid or export credits to get around these commitments.[15] It also stipulates that food aid donors shall ensure that food aid is not directly or indirectly tied to commercial exports of agricultural products to recipient countries; that donations shall be in accordance with the FAO Principles of Surplus Disposal and Consultative Obligations, including, where appropriate, the system of UMRs to ensure that the aid results in additional consumption of food in the recipient country and does not disrupt commercial trade;[16] and that food aid, to the extent possible, be given in fully grant form or on terms that are no less concessional than those outlined in article VI of the 1986 Food Aid Convention. It also spells out that WTO members are to undertake work to develop internationally agreed disciplines on export credits.[17] The fact that article 10 of the URAA mentions the FAO Principles on Surplus Disposal and the FAC has important implications because adherence to the rules in these arrangements now in effect have become part of WTO member rights and obligations. Because the WTO does embody legally binding and enforcement mechanisms, these rules now carry more weight for signatories. But

---

11. See Cardwell 2008, 76.
12. Food Aid Convention 1999.
13. Konandreas 2005, 4.
14. Barrett and Maxwell 2006; Cardwell 2008, 76.
15. On the Food Aid Convention, see Benson 2000; Hoddinott, Cohen, and Barrett 2008.
16. Thompson 2001.
17. World Trade Organization 2004a.

at the same time, there is no formal requirement that the FAO and FAC report to the WTO Committee on Agriculture on donor compliance with these rules, and there is no clear course of action in cases of noncompliance.[18]

In addition to provisions in article 10, the members adopted the Marrakesh Decision at the conclusion of the Uruguay Round, in consideration of the expected impacts and needs of net food-importing developing countries under the URAA (due to subsidy reductions in rich countries that could lead to higher overall food prices on world markets). Anticipating a rise in food prices resulting from trade liberalization measures under the URAA, the Marrakesh Decision calls for WTO members to review food aid levels established by the FAC, and "to initiate negotiations in the appropriate forum to establish a level of food aid commitments sufficient to meet the legitimate needs of developing countries during the reform programme." It also calls for the adoption of guidelines to increase the share of food aid that is given in fully grant form or that is appropriately concessional, in addition to providing assistance to increase agricultural productivity.[19] The adoption of the Marrakesh Decision was an attempt to make the URAA more palatable for the world's poorest countries, particularly those in sub-Saharan Africa, who might be negatively impacted by the agricultural provisions.[20]

## Food Aid on the Doha Agenda

Food aid has been a contentious issue in the Doha Round of trade talks. These talks began in Doha, Qatar, in 2001, following the failure to launch trade talks at Seattle in December 1999. The aim of the round was in large part to rectify some of the imbalances in the Uruguay Round that had negatively affected developing countries. The Doha Round was initially expected to reach a conclusion by 2005 at the latest, but the talks have repeatedly collapsed over the past decade.

A cornerstone of the Doha trade talks, which were dubbed the "development round," was a revision of the URAA. Revisions were seen as necessary because it was evident early on that under the URAA very little progress had been made in the reduction of agricultural subsidies, as countries that made extensive use of them, primarily the United States and the EU, have found creative ways to continue to use them.[21] Indeed, even though subsidies as a percentage of GDP in

---

18. Konandreas 2007, 324
19. World Trade Organization 1994.
20. See Murphy 2005.
21. Madeley 2000.

OECD countries fell from 2.5 percent in 1986–88 to 0.9 percent in 2006–9, the absolute amount of total support to agriculture in OECD countries rose from $300 billion to $368 billion in that same period.[22] By the early 2000s, there was growing concern among NGOs, exemplified by the launch of Oxfam's Make Trade Fair campaign, about the rising absolute levels of agricultural subsidies in industrialized countries, which were seen by many to be responsible for outcompeting producers and contributing to poverty in developing countries.[23]

Even before the Doha Round was launched, those members with an interest in the food aid provisions of the agriculture agreement began to stake out positions regarding the extent to which they thought food aid should be subject to trade disciplines. In several papers issued on its positions on food aid and export competition, the European Union called for stronger trade disciplines on food aid since the URAA "has not been sufficient to stem the flow of subsidized exports which are clearly not genuine food aid but which have been diverted through the food aid complex."[24] Revisions to article 10.4, the European negotiators argued, needed to incorporate a prohibition on concessional sales of food aid and an elimination of all export credits for agriculture. The EU argued that these practices were at least parallel, or equivalent in their impact on trade, to export subsidies, if not worse in their effects (especially in that they raised the level of debt of borrowing countries). The EU claimed that the U.S. use of food aid in particular, with its explicit aim of increasing markets for commercial exports, was a misuse of food aid that prioritized export market development over humanitarian concerns while distorting trade. It noted that "to a certain extent, abuse of food aid is comparable to an export subsidy of 100 percent of the price of the product."[25]

The EU proposed that food aid should be given only in fully grant form, only in response to internationally declared emergencies, and preferably in the form of cash—financial assistance including the possibility of purchasing food in developing countries.[26] It also proposed a code of conduct covering food aid operations. The EU prominently noted that large swings in food aid, which increased with low prices and more availability, were clearly more about reducing surpluses than about providing genuine aid.[27] Food aid provided in kind, the EU argued, should be given only in response to requests from recipient countries and should be carefully targeted to the needs of the recipients rather than those

---

22. OECD 2009.
23. Oxfam International 2002b. See also Oxfam's Make Trade Fair Campaign, http://www.maketradefair.com/en/index.htm.
24. European Communities 2001.
25. European Communities 2000b.
26. European Communities 2000a, 2000b; see also Taylor and Pruzin 2004, 1011.
27. European Communities, 2000a, 2001.

of the donor.[28] The EU announced that it was willing to negotiate export subsidy reductions only if other forms of agricultural support that were equivalent to export subsidies, including what it considered the abuse of food aid, were treated on a "common footing."[29]

The positions taken by the EU regarding food aid and export credits put the United States on the defensive. In its own initial proposal for agricultural trade reform, it noted that it did not see the need to add any more disciplines to food aid than were already in place under the Uruguay Round. The U.S. negotiators argued that the provisions of article 10.4 of the URAA were "appropriate."[30] The U.S. justification for agricultural export credits and sales of concessional food aid was that these programs help promote food security in developing countries that find it difficult to obtain commercial credit for food imports. The United States pressured the EU to eliminate its export subsidies while downplaying any potential trade impacts from its own food aid programs. In comments in a Senate hearing on agricultural export programs in 2000, Senator Pat Roberts noted that "food aid and credit guarantee programs remain a cornerstone of our agricultural trade policy. Unfortunately, these programs have unfairly been subject to substantial scrutiny in the international arena. We need to fight to preserve these programs."[31] In that same hearing, Timothy Galvin, administrator in the Foreign Agricultural Service of the USDA stressed that the impacts of U.S. food aid programs on commercial displacement and depressing world commodity prices were "minimal" and not to be worried about because each shipment was analyzed as part of the U.S. reporting to the CSSD regarding UMRs.[32]

The African Group issued a proposal for the agriculture negotiations in March 2001. These countries expressed their view that all forms of export subsidies should be ended, including the subsidy element of export credit programs. The group considered these practices to be dumping of cheap food by the industrialized countries, which hurt the economies of developing countries. They added, though, that they wished to see the special conditions and needs of the net-food-importing and least developed countries taken into account when disciplines were imposed on export credits.[33] With respect to food aid, the African Group expressed regret that the Marrakesh Decision had not been operationalized. These countries did not want to see food aid ended, but they preferred that it be provided in fully

---

28. European Communities 2001.
29. See European Communities 2000b.
30. World Trade Organization 2000, 5.
31. Roberts, cited in United States Senate 2000, 1–2.
32. Galvin, cited ibid., 12.
33. WTO African Group 2001, 3; see also Mercosur 2001 and Dakar Declaration of Third LDC Trade Ministers' Meeting 2004.

grant form and that a mechanism be put in place at the WTO to ensure that the aid did not disrupt the domestic production of recipient countries.[34]

These initial positions on food aid by the key players were maintained after the Doha Round was officially launched in November 2001, and little headway was made in the early years of the negotiations regarding the issue. At the Ninth Special Session of the Committee on Agriculture, held in early December 2001, several "nonpapers" (unofficial statements) were presented on the topic of food aid, demonstrating a continuation of divergent views. Among the submissions were papers from a group of developing countries, the European Union, Japan, Mercosur (Common Market of the South whose members are Argentina, Brazil, Paraguay, and Uruguay), Namibia, and Norway.[35] Concern was expressed by some members that food aid donations had continued to follow a pattern of increasing when prices were low and falling when they were high. This pattern was seen to exacerbate the very problems identified in the Marrakesh Decision. Some members, such as the European Union, also expressed concern about domestic market disruption and commercial displacement caused by food aid. Stronger disciplines on food aid were proposed, including provisions to ensure that the aid responded more directly to assessed need and that it was targeted and demand driven, given in fully grant form, and not tied to commercial transactions.[36] While most of the members agreed that food aid should be given in fully grant form, the United States and Japan questioned this idea, arguing that such a requirement could reduce flexibility in food aid programming.[37]

Although U.S. trade negotiators were involved in the discussions at the WTO on food aid, and the White House flagged Title I food aid as needing to be reviewed in light of ongoing trade negotiations,[38] this did not result in any serious attempt to reform U.S. food aid programs in the early 2000s. Indeed, concern over EU proposals to discipline food aid at the WTO were not at the forefront of debates over the 2002 Farm Bill (as discussed in chapter 4). In congressional hearings in the run-up to that bill, the WTO negotiations were barely mentioned, except to note that the critiques of U.S. programs were unfair and that market-development programs such as food aid sales were an important part of U.S. agricultural policy and should be maintained.[39]

---

34. WTO African Group 2001, 4.

35. World Trade Organization 2002, 3–4

36. See World Trade Organization 2002; International Centre for Trade and Sustainable Development 2001.

37. International Centre for Trade and Sustainable Development 2001, 4.

38. United States Office of Management and Budget 2001.

39. See, for example, United States Senate 2001.

The 2002 Farm Bill incorporated few changes to food aid programs and increased the levels of domestic agricultural subsidies. It also provided for up to $5.5 billion annually for agricultural export credits through the end of 2007, including authorization for an additional $1 billion in credits to countries that were likely to become new markets for U.S. commercial agricultural exports and another $1.1 billion for the credit guarantee programs.[40] At the time that the 2002 Farm Bill was passed, there was widespread concern that it would seriously derail the Doha Round negotiations for at least the duration of that bill because it openly increased domestic subsidies after the United States had publicly committed to work toward a trade deal that reduced levels of farm support.[41]

## Stops and Starts in Drafting the Doha Food Aid Text

Discussions on a revised agriculture agreement, including provisions on food aid, continued at the WTO but did not see much progress. With a lack of convergence on these issues among members, the chair of the agriculture committee, Stuart Harbinson, presented a draft modalities text in February 2003 that contained a formula for tariff reductions and schedules for subsidy reductions and included language regarding disciplines on food aid. His aim was to arrive at a compromise text that could be approved by the end of March that year, a deadline for completion of the round that had been set when the talks were launched. Harbinson submitted the text in his personal capacity because the gulf between the members was too wide for him to presume it reflected all their views.[42]

With respect to food aid, Harbinson's text reflected the EU position more than that of the United States. It called for food aid to be given only in fully grant form and stated that nonemergency aid should be in the form of untied financial grants (rather than in-kind grants) unless channeled through the UN. The draft also called for more detailed reporting by donors regarding food aid shipments and for the elimination of agricultural export credits unless they were granted on fully market terms.[43] These measures on food aid were in the context of the broader agricultural modalities, which called for full elimination of export subsidies by 2012, as well as steep cuts to tariffs.

---

40. Hanrahan 2006, 6; Watkins 2003, 49.
41. Blustein 2009.
42. International Centre for Trade and Sustainable Development 2003a.
43. World Trade Organization 2003.

Although it reflected many of the EU's concerns regarding food aid, the Harbinson text was criticized from all sides. The United States felt that it did not go far enough with respect to tariff cuts and export subsidies, while the EU felt that the proposals did not go far enough with disciplines on export credits and food aid. Following the release of the paper, the EU farm commissioner at the time, Franz Fischler, expressed his frustration over the targeting of export subsidies without equivalent treatment of export credits and food aid:

> We have committed ourselves to reducing all forms of export subsidisation. The EU has respected our commitments from the URAA and we are asked to phase out completely this policy instrument, with a significant down-payment. But those that use other instruments to subsidise exports, from export credits to food aid, in a totally trade-distorting way, are not even asked to pay for the fact that the commitment of the previous round to discipline these forms of export support has not been fulfilled. On the contrary, significant loopholes are allowed in the future.[44]

For their part, developing countries felt that the text was heavily biased toward the concerns of the rich countries.[45] That concerns of southern nations were not incorporated into the draft text was also echoed by several studies of the original draft which estimated that the vast bulk of the gains from the proposal would accrue to the rich countries.[46] Although the March 31 deadline was missed, Harbinson vowed to continue to work toward an agreement in the run-up to the WTO ministerial meeting in Cancún in September 2003. But given the gulf between members, the talks were in serious jeopardy. Because of the inability to agree on concrete modalities, members decided to work toward a "framework" for the modalities (for instance, general goals without specific numbers) as a first step.[47]

Talks resumed prior to the meeting at Cancún in September 2003, but again no deal was reached on agriculture. The draft text for that meeting—referred to as the Derbez Draft after the meeting's chair, Luis Ernesto Derbez—called for the elimination of agricultural export subsidies and the subsidy element of agricultural export credits on a parallel schedule. It also called for disciplines on food aid programs to prevent commercial trade displacement. But these proposals were abandoned with the failure of the Cancún talks. A last-minute attempt

---

44. European Union 2003b.
45. International Centre for Trade and Sustainable Development 2003b.
46. Danish Research Institute of Food Economics 2003.
47. International Centre for Trade and Sustainable Development 2003c.

at a deal on the agriculture text, brokered between the EU and the United States with little input from the developing countries, precipitated a complete collapse of the talks. Developing countries, having recently formed their own negotiating groups—including two that focused on agriculture, the Group of Twenty (G20-WTO) and the Group of Thirty-Three (G33-WTO)—openly refused to agree to the deal presented to them by the industrialized countries.[48]

The failure at Cancún cooled the talks for months, but by early 2004 WTO members, including the United States and the EU, indicated that they were finally ready to work on a deal that would see the elimination of all forms of export subsidies, including both the "classic" export subsidies employed by the EU and the subsidy element of export credits and food aid.[49] The EU, which had the highest level of export subsidies and thus would have to reduce them the most, continued to insist that the United States also reduce the subsidy element of its export credits and food aid in return and maintained its position that food aid should be given only in grant form.[50] In the talks the United States made some concessions on food aid, showing a willingness to provide some flexibility on reducing its food aid sales, though it was quick to stress that only the subsidy element of such programs would be reduced, and it would not commit to removing in-kind food aid.[51]

In this stage of the talks, developing countries expressed their view that all forms of export subsidies should be ended, including the subsidy element of export credit programs. They added that it was important to consider the special conditions and needs of the net-food-importing developing countries (NFIDCs) and LDCs when disciplining export credits and food aid.[52]

Negotiations were tense and continued in the WTO Committee on Agriculture throughout July 2004. In the talks on export competition, all the elements under discussion within this pillar became linked. The EU insisted that any elimination of export subsidies be contingent on equivalent disciplines on food aid, export credits, and the ending of export monopolies in state trading enterprises (STEs). While the former demand was aimed at the United States, the latter was aimed at Canada and Australia, each of which has state trade enterprises for agricultural products. The United States, for its part, indicated a willingness to remove the subsidy element of its export credit and food aid programs, but this was contingent on the elimination of export subsidies and disciplines on STEs. For Canada and Australia, any reforms to STEs had to be matched by the elimination of

48. See Narlikar and Wilkinson 2004, 447–460.
49. Zoellick 2004.
50. BBC News 2005.
51. Pruzin, Yerkey, and Kirwin 2004, 808
52. Dakar Declaration of Third LDC Trade Ministers' Meeting 2004.

export subsidies and disciplines on export credits and food aid.[53] Australia, for example, although it had not untied its own food aid until 2004, issued a paper titled "Misuse of Surplus Disposal as Food Aid," showing its commitment to the idea of grant-only and untied food aid.[54] This tight linkage showed that food aid had effectively become a bargaining chip among the donor countries in the context of the broader agricultural trade negotiations.

The language on food aid in the framework document was fiercely debated. The July 16 version of the text included a statement that clarified the purpose of the disciplines on food aid: to ensure that the aid would not be used to dispose of agricultural surpluses and to prevent commercial trade displacement. But later the United States—along with several developing countries, including Sri Lanka, Mongolia, Honduras, and the Dominican Republic—insisted that the language on surplus disposal be removed, on the grounds that all food aid is essentially a disposal of surpluses.[55] A joint letter from the four developing countries noted that "the 16 July draft does not address the appeals and interventions of many developing and least developed countries in support of continued, adequate amounts of food aid and, alarmingly, takes a sharp step in opposite direction, placing the future of food aid in danger."[56] Although no African countries joined this request, and the issue of surplus disposal was one of the EU's principal arguments for why food aid should be disciplined, the final draft did not contain the wording on the need to prevent surplus disposal.

A framework document for relaunching the Doha Round was finally agreed to on July 31, 2004. The adoption of the framework followed heavy pressure to reach a deal, despite the fact that countries had very little time to consider the document before the deadline because of delays in its release caused by last-minute wrangling by the key players, including the United States and the EU, along with Australia, Brazil, and India. The framework reflected agreement that export subsidies would be eliminated on a "credible" schedule, with parallel elimination of export credits. It was also agreed that food aid would be disciplined, with the aim of preventing commercial displacement. The role of international organizations in the provision of food aid and the issue of food aid in fully grant form, as well as appropriate provisions for the LDCs and NFIDCs, were listed as items to be discussed, but no details beyond this were provided in the framework.[57] The specifics of these commitments were to be hammered out in the subsequent negotiations.

---

53. See Pruzin 2004.
54. See Australian Government 2004.
55. See Pruzin and Yerkey 2004, 1266; Rugaber 2004.
56. Mongolia 2004.
57. See World Trade Organization 2004b.

## Intensification of the Debate

In the year after the July 2004 framework was agreed on, there was little progress on putting detail into the agriculture modalities. Nonetheless, ambitions
were high that a final WTO deal would be struck in time to be adopted at the
December 2005 WTO ministerial meeting in Hong Kong. Media attention on
the round began to heat up in early 2005, as there was much work to be done if
the December deadline was to be met. International organizations such as the
OECD and NGOs such as Oxfam issued reports heavily criticizing the inefficiencies of and trade motivations behind tied food aid; these were no doubt timed for
consideration by WTO members as they negotiated the modalities on food aid.[58]
The reports largely took the side of the EU on the issue, making the case that tied
food aid, and especially aid that was sold by donors on credit at a discount, was
inefficient and potentially trade-distorting.

By mid-2005, WTO members began to put forward proposals regarding the
various aspects of the trade talks, including agriculture and in particular food
aid. Although the July 2004 framework package was somewhat vague on the
shape of the food aid provisions, there was general agreement that emergency
aid should not be hindered by the adoption of disciplines. This sentiment may
have been influenced by the fact that several UN agencies began to wade into the
debate around this time to make the case that humanitarian food aid in response
to emergencies should be preserved, whether it was tied or not.

James Morris, then director of the UN World Food Programme, warned WTO
members in a meeting with LDCs and African countries in May of that year not
to adopt disciplines on food aid that might curtail its supply. This was a particular concern for the WFP given that food aid had fallen from 15 million tonnes
in 1999 to just 7.5 million tonnes in 2004. In his comments Morris stressed that
in such a context, any disciplines that might result in reduced food aid could have
devastating consequences. He flatly dismissed arguments that in-kind food aid
was simply surplus disposal on the part of donors, noting that delivering food
aid was far most costly than other methods of surplus disposal: "[I]t's far cheaper
for an exporting country to use export subsidies or credits, sell commodities at
a reduced price for pet food or, as is still sadly the case, sometimes, just destroy
them.... The simple fact is that emergency food aid is an expensive business and
not a logical way to offload excess production."[59]

Morris stressed that it was not the task of the WTO to determine whether food
aid donations were from surpluses; what mattered was how they were used, and

---

58. Clay, Riley and Urey 2006; Oxfam International 2005.
59. Quoted in Pruzin 2005c.

in many instances, he noted, in-kind food aid had legitimate uses, particularly in contexts where there was simply no other food available. For this reason, he was opposed to any proposals for cash-only food aid.[60]

Soon after the WFP's intervention in the debate, then UN special rapporteur on the right to food, Jean Ziegler, issued a statement on the potential impact of the WTO negotiations on food aid. Ziegler stressed that it was imperative to ensure that these discussions did not harm the ability of relief agencies to reach hungry people. He warned that any requirement that donors provide food aid as financial resources only rather than in-kind aid would reduce the amount available to address hunger. Such a requirement would, he said "require an immediate and massive increase in the funds for development, especially funds for food aid, which seems to be out of the question for the moment."[61] He further stressed that any aid delivered through UN agencies such as WFP should be excluded from WTO disciplines.

In the midst of these UN interventions into the debate, the EU issued a non-paper on food aid in June, calling for an end date beyond which aid would be fully untied and provided in the form of financial resources only, in fully grant form. In-kind aid would be allowed only in "clearly defined exceptional emergency situations" and only for a limited period of time until the emergency could be addressed through untied, financial forms of food assistance. Such emergency situations, it noted, must be acknowledged by relevant international organizations. The proposal called for nonemergency aid to be provided in the form of untied financial grants to fund the purchase of food and for monetized food aid to be progressively converted to untied grant aid. Finally, it called on WTO members who were parties to the Food Aid Convention to confirm their commitment to provide adequate levels of international food aid.[62]

Canada issued its own proposal at the same time suggesting the creation of a "safe box" for food aid that was absolutely necessary for addressing humanitarian emergencies and was not considered to cause commercial displacement.[63] Food aid that was considered to be within the safe box would be exempt from disciplines, while the aid that fell outside the box would be subject to disciplines. Aid that was considered non-trade-distorting and could thus be placed within the safe box included aid that was demand-driven (based on assessed need), pledged in response to emergencies declared by a recognized agency, fully grant in form, untied, not linked to commercial market development of donor countries, and

---

60. See International Centre for Trade and Sustainable Development 2005; Williams 2005.
61. Pruzin 2005b.
62. See European Commission 2005.
63. Canadian Government 2005.

not reexported. Because Canada's food aid had increasingly become more emergency-focused by 2005, as noted in chapter 3, such change would not have a large impact on its own program. At the same time, the idea provided a compromise between the EU and U.S. positions on food aid. When it made this proposal, Canada was also engaged in internal decision making to partially untie its food aid, a decision that was announced in September 2005.[64]

In July the G20-WTO put forward a proposal on export competition issues, which stated that any new disciplines on food aid "should not compromise humanitarian emergency assistance and its effectiveness in situations that are well defined." Although it wanted to ensure that humanitarian assistance was not affected, it aligned with the EU on rules that should apply to food aid. It called for strict disciplines on "grey area operations" in order to prevent food aid from becoming surplus disposal and to ensure that food aid was in grant form only and fully untied. Also mirroring the EU, it called for members to confirm their commitments to food aid levels, in line with the commitments made as part of the Marrakesh Decision.[65]

The United States issued its own proposal on food aid in early October 2005, and although it had time to work with the other proposals that were converging on this issue, it took the discussion in a somewhat different direction. Rather than accepting the emergency/nonemergency language taken up by the other members, it put food aid into three categories: emergency, food aid provided to NFIDCs and LDCs, and all other food aid. It considered that food aid in the first two categories had little or no commercial displacement, and argued that in such cases the aid should be exempt from any disciplines. It then set out the criteria for emergencies and NFIDC and LDC food aid that included for the former, instances under which emergencies might arise, and for the latter, identification of a list of countries considered to be NFIDC or LDC. The proposal outlined that such aid should not be tied to commercial purchases from the donor country, should be demand-driven, should not be reexported, and should be subject to an objective analysis to determine whether it displaced commercial imports. It also called on members to commit to maintain food aid levels agreed on under the FAC.[66]

Although all the proposals discussed above contained similar elements regarding the acceptance of some in-kind food aid in emergencies and the need to maintain aid levels as agreed at the FAC, there were still wide divergences on some key points. The EU criticized the U.S. proposal for not going far enough, because if NFIDC and LDC food aid were exempt from disciplines, then there would be no

64. See Clapp 2010.
65. G20-WTO 2005.
66. See United States Government 2005.

changes for around 90 percent of U.S. aid. European agriculture commissioner Mariann Fischer Boel remarked, "This is unacceptable. We need more."[67]

Tensions over the issue ran high throughout the fall of 2005. The key divisions among key WTO members over how to handle food aid in the agriculture modalities were over where to draw the line between emergency and "other" food aid and also whether WTO members should provide the aid in the form of cash resources or in kind. These divisions remained deep right up to the eve of the Hong Kong meeting.

Also fanning the flames of the debate were further interventions by UN agency heads just before the opening of the meeting. In early December, the head of the WFP, the UN high commissioner for refugees, and the executive director of UNICEF (the former and the latter being U.S. appointees) issued a joint appeal to WTO members to put humanitarian concerns first when considering rules over food aid. They stressed that the WTO should not adopt rules that would constrain the flow of in-kind food aid outside emergencies. In their statement they noted that more than 90 percent of deaths from hunger and malnutrition occurred outside classic emergency situations and that it was unlikely that monetary equivalents to the in-kind aid would be forthcoming, especially from new donors within the developing world. Further, they pointed out that 45 percent of food aid was delivered to countries that were not members of the WTO, indicating that recipient countries were not being given a voice in the decision over the rules governing food aid.[68] The UN rapporteur on the right to food, Jean Ziegler, also issued a second statement on the issue, asking, "Will the aid keep coming if we outlaw food donations? I doubt it. Who suffers then?...The Doha Round should not discourage food aid. We need the WTO to promote commerce with a conscience—or millions of hungry children could pay the price."[69]

## The Hong Kong Ministerial

Even before the Hong Kong meeting officially opened, trade officials from the key countries acknowledged that it was unlikely that agreement on export competition, including food aid, would come during the course of the meeting. They set March 1, 2006, as a deadline for agreeing on draft modalities.[70] Postponing the date to settle differences on food aid and its relationship to other export

---

67. Quoted in Kirwin 2005.
68. WFP 2005b.
69. WFP 2005a.
70. Pruzin 2005a.

competition issues did not prevent further heated exchanges over food aid from taking place. On December 13, the opening day of the meeting, the UN WFP and special rapporteur on the right to food cosponsored an advertisement in the *Financial Times* warning that putting strict disciplines on food aid donated through UN agencies could leave children hungry.[71] On the same day, the U.S. trade representative, Rob Portman, expressed his frustration with the European Union's "obsession" with U.S. food aid policies, which he believed was misplaced in comparison with the gravity of other issues on the table.[72] The EU's trade commissioner, Peter Mandelson, remarked in response, "I find it surprising that a commitment entered into by the United States last year…should now be described as an obsession of the European Union."[73]

In a press conference the following day, Mandelson said, "I find it shocking that the United Nations agencies should be financing an advertisement in the Financial Times that is designed to support the US' trade distorting policies on food aid."[74] He went on to note that while food aid could be an important tool for development and emergency response, the U.S. food aid program was designed to support U.S. agricultural producers. The United States replied by issuing press briefings and statements noting that the European Union's move to provide its food aid as untied cash resources for local purchase had resulted in a decline in its levels of assistance and that U.S. food aid, because it averaged less than 2 percent of agricultural exports, could not possibly be trade-distorting.[75] The USAID administrator, Andrew Natsios, held a press briefing on December 14 on the issue of food aid, in which he stressed the decline in EU food aid since it had adopted a local purchase policy in the mid-1990s. "The fact of the matter is the European Union does some very good work in development, but in terms of food assistance, they are missing in action."[76]

Despite this wrangling, some progress was made at the meeting, albeit incremental. The final declaration noted the differences that remained:

> There are proposals that in the disciplines a distinction should be made between at least two types of food aid: emergency food aid and food aid to address other situations. However, there is not yet a common understanding where emergency food aid ends and other food aid begins, reflecting concerns that this distinction should not become a

71. Yerkey 2005.
72. Ibid.
73. Quoted in *Financial Express* 2005.
74. European Union 2005.
75. See, for example, Natsios 2005a; see also United States Trade Representative 2005.
76. Natsios 2005a.

means to create a loophole in disciplines. A fundamental sticking point is whether, except in exceptional, genuine emergency situations, Members should (albeit gradually) move towards untied, in-cash food aid only, as some Members propose but other Members strongly oppose.[77]

Despite the major disagreement on where to draw the line between emergency and other food aid, it was agreed that food aid disciplines should not hinder emergency aid and other genuine aid operations. The final declaration reflected Canada's earlier proposal by calling for the creation of a safe box for bona fide food aid, which would minimize chances of unintended negative impacts on emergency assistance from disciplines on food aid. It further noted that members would work toward eliminating commercial displacement caused by food aid that was outside the safe box, and placement of disciplines on monetization and reexports. It was agreed that members would negotiate and finalize these disciplines by the end of April 2006.[78]

## Inching toward Draft Food Aid Modalities

Negotiations proceeded throughout early 2006 on defining precise modalities for food aid. Comments and proposals were submitted by the African and LDC groups, the G20-WTO, the European Union, and the United States. The proposal submitted by the African and LDC groups carried a significant amount of weight because those countries were major recipients of food aid. It called for the safe box to be limited to emergency situations, which would be defined by a relevant UN agency, declared as an emergency by authorities in the recipient country, and based on independent needs assessment; the aid would be provided only for the duration of the emergency. It proposed that food aid that fell outside the safe box be demand-driven, provided in fully grant form, and not tied to commercial exports of goods or services to the recipient country, and that it take into account local market conditions, address development objectives by targeting food aid to the most needy, not promote market development or donors, and allow monetization only if it was to fund the delivery of the food aid or procurement of agricultural inputs in recipient countries. Finally, it called for prohibiting reexportation of food aid.[79] The then chair of the agriculture negotiations, Crawford Falconer, indicated that this proposal would form the basis for negotiation.

---

77. World Trade Organization 2005.
78. See ibid.
79. WTO African and LDC Groups 2006.

The United States was reluctant to accept the African and LDC group proposal in full, as it did not agree with the fully grant form requirement for all food aid.[80] It submitted its own proposal that expanded the safe box by defining an emergency situation as one that was declared by the recipient, the UN, or nongovernmental humanitarian organizations.[81] Such a change would allow U.S. food-aid-delivery NGOs to determine what aid would fall into the safe box, rather than requiring both UN agency and recipient country declarations.

The European Union's proposal closely mirrored that of the African and LDC group with the addition that all untied food aid in the form of financial resources be included in the safe box in addition to aid for declared emergencies. Regarding disciplines for non-safe box food aid, it went further than the African and LDC proposal by calling for full conversion of in-kind food aid to "untied cash" for food assistance activities, including local and regional purchase, as well as the complete phaseout of monetization, all of which was to occur during an implementation period.[82] The G20-WTO group's comments on food aid echoed the EU proposal. It further stressed the need to reconfirm levels of food aid and their increase if possible.[83]

With these proposals on the table showing a considerable amount of overlap in terms of direction, WTO members were able to move toward establishing draft modalities for food aid.[84] But while they moved to draft modalities, some key differences remained, as reflected in the considerable number of square brackets in the text, indicating lack of agreement. The key areas of contention remained, including precise rules regarding what requirements needed to be met for food aid to be considered within the safe box, and in particular what agencies could declare emergencies that would fall within the box. The length of time that food aid operations would remain inside the safe box also remained contested. Regarding aid that fell outside the safe box, there was still disagreement over whether in-kind aid should be allowed under certain circumstances or phased out in favor of untied cash aid, and whether monetization would be eliminated or merely subject to stricter disciplines.[85] The negotiations stalled again in mid-2006 but picked up in 2008, in the midst of the food crisis.

The agriculture committee met in mid-2008 and made some progress on determining the final contours of the modalities, including with respect to food aid, but these were not finalized, and as of mid-2011 the round had not yet been

---

80. Pruzin 2006b.
81. Pruzin 2006a.
82. European Communities 2006.
83. G20-WTO 2006.
84. See World Trade Organization 2006a.
85. See World Trade Organization 2006b, 2007.

completed. In late 2008, the chair of the agriculture committee submitted Revised Draft Modalities for Agriculture. This text represented the chair's best estimate of the state of the negotiations, though he noted that "everything is conditional in the deepest sense."[86]

The issues that had previously been unresolved on food aid were addressed in the following way. Inside the safe box would be aid given in response to a declaration of an emergency by a recipient country or a UN agency or to an emergency appeal issued by the receiving country or a UN agency or internationally recognized NGO; in both cases there would be an emergency needs assessment that involved both UN agencies and the recipient country. Food aid in the safe box also could not be monetized, except in the case of the least developed countries, and then only to pay for transport and delivery of the food, provided it was carried out in a manner that avoided commercial displacement. Aid could continue to be considered in the safe box as long as the emergency lasted, subject to an assessment of continued genuine need by a relevant multilateral agency.

Rules for food aid that is outside the safe box are also specified. In-kind non-emergency aid would be allowed but must be based on targeted assessment of need, be provided only in food deficit situations, and be targeted only to identified food-insecure groups. It must also be provided with the consistent objective of preventing or at least minimizing commercial displacement. Monetization of food aid outside the safe box would not be allowed unless it met the criteria for in-kind aid outside the safe box. Even if it did meet this criteria, it could be used only: as a means to meet the direct nutritional requirements of the least developed countries and net-food-importing country members if it is necessary to fund the internal transportation of that aid, or to obtain agricultural inputs for low-income or resource-poor producers in those member countries.[87]

This outcome reveals compromise on both sides of the debate. Despite its pressure, the EU did not manage to convince members to adopt a phaseout of monetization or in-kind aid. But the establishment of stringent rules to eliminate the most trade-distorting aspects of food aid was adopted. For its part, the United States did not convince members to adopt a significantly expanded safe box that would allow it to continue business as usual, but it would be allowed to keep a good portion of its current in-kind food aid practices both inside and outside the safe box. The outcome of the December 2008 draft modalities may have been influenced by the food price crisis of 2007–8 and a sense among WTO members that there was a need to conclude the agriculture negotiations as a way to bolster global food security. The food aid modalities are only a part of the broader overall agriculture

---

86. World Trade Organization 2008, 1.
87. Ibid., 72–74 (Annex L).

negotiations, and although the debates have been fierce, this was the one issue on which the members were somewhat close to agreeing on final wording. It remains to be seen whether these draft modalities will ultimately be accepted by the WTO members, and indeed whether the Doha Round will even be completed.

## Conclusion

Food aid has become intertwined in the broader international political disputes over agricultural trade liberalization at the WTO, a context in which food aid had not previously been so hotly debated. Fueling the debates at the WTO have been differences in donor food aid policies—specifically whether it is tied, sold, and monetized or whether it is given in the form of grants of untied financial resources for local and regional purchase. These differences, though the product of internal donor policymaking processes, have been a key driving force of the political disagreements at the WTO among donors and between donors and recipients.

As food aid became politicized in this context, donors ended up using it as a bargaining chip for the broader discussions on agricultural trade liberalization. The EU was most forthright in its attempt to extract concessions out of the United States by making food aid disciplines a condition of its own export subsidy reductions. Canada and Australia also tried to use food aid as a bargaining chip in WTO negotiations by linking it to reforms on the issues that mattered to them. The United States continues to have a strong interest in tied food aid and fought hard to maintain it. Although it was on the defensive on the issue, it was able to use its hard stance to secure a food aid text that enabled it to maintain most of its existing policies and practices.

Although donor food aid policy is set domestically, changes to the rules at the WTO can have an important impact on policymaking processes in donor countries. The WTO does carry clout internationally because of its ability to enforce its rules, and thus an agreement within the WTO regarding food aid could put external pressure on the donors to change their domestic policies. Indeed, as discussed in chapter 3, Canada and Australia's food aid untying was in part a response to the debate over tied food aid in the WTO and a way to gain clout in the negotiations. The United States did in fact end its concessional sales of food aid in 2006, an indication that the debate at the WTO had had some influence on its policy. However, now that the draft text on food aid has been largely agreed on, subject to final approval and completion of the Doha Round, the outcome does not force the United States to make drastic changes to its program. If the Doha Round is not completed, the fate of international food aid rules is unclear. Under this scenario, the Food Aid Convention may well be the place where such rules are articulated.

# 7

# THE 2007–2008 FOOD CRISIS AND THE GLOBAL GOVERNANCE OF FOOD AID

Even before the WTO draft text on food aid was settled in late 2008, the landscape of the global food economy had shifted dramatically with the sharp rise in food prices over the 2007–8 period. This new reality had a profound impact on food aid practice and politics. International attention began to focus on how to reform global governance mechanisms to promote food security in the world's poorest countries. Much of this discussion at the international level has centered on funding initiatives through the Group of Eight (G-8) major industrial economies and Group of Twenty (G-20) leading economies to increase food production in developing countries.[1] Alongside the launch of these initiatives have been discussions on how to revitalize the food aid regime to be more responsive to the new global situation.[2] The politics of food aid in the aftermath of the food crisis became wrapped up in complex ways with broader debates to which it is linked, similar to its politicization in the context of broader debates on GMOs and trade liberalization as described in the previous two chapters. But while the latter debates were very polarized and carried out publicly through the media, the debates over how to reformulate the food aid regime in the broader food security governance architecture have been more subtle and less public.

This chapter examines the politics of food aid since the 2007–8 food crisis. That crisis revealed the weakness of the present food aid regime as a mechanism

1. Clapp 2009c.
2. E.g., Clay 2010.

to respond to a rapid and sharp increase in world hunger.[3] As food prices climbed rapidly, it became difficult for donors to respond with the speed and efficiency needed to ensure that those most in need received sufficient food assistance. Both tied direct-transfer food aid and untied cash resources for food assistance proved to be problematic in the face of the crisis. Tied food aid could not reach the hungry within the time frame required, and its provision was limited as prices for both food and transportation shot up quickly, making it much more expensive for donors to provide. But cash resources for local purchases, while more efficient and flexible, had a limited and diminishing power to command sufficient amounts of food aid at that time as food prices climbed to unprecedented levels. Locally purchased food aid, in other words, became very expensive, as food prices climbed faster in many developing countries than in industrialized countries. Food aid and the food aid regime suffered a serious setback.

The World Food Programme was caught in the middle of the dilemma as it scrambled to raise funds to meet the feeding targets it had already set for 2008, not including those pushed into more severe hunger as a direct result of the food crisis. Requests by the WFP brought increased contributions from donors in 2008, but these were scaled back the following year, a situation that imposed considerable strain on the organization and a scaling back of rations and operations. The crisis in the food aid regime was also demonstrated by the fact that the Food Aid Convention did not feature prominently in the global response to the crisis. Although the overall levels of aid provided by the FAC signatories were maintained in 2008 when prices were suddenly higher, global deliveries fell again in 2009, a pattern of decline that had begun a decade earlier.

The challenges to the food aid regime as felt through the WFP and the FAC fed into broader political debates about the future of global food security governance. The food crisis has sparked serious discussion at the international level about the institutional structure, funding, and functions of the various organizations and agreements that seek to promote global food security. There are two key questions at the center of the current debate. First, with an increasingly volatile world food market, how will the risk of rapidly rising food prices be dealt with, particularly if some donors who have untied their food aid aim to express their commitments to the FAC in cash terms? And second, what is the place of food aid in the broader architecture of global food security governance? In 2010 donors began discussions with a view to renegotiating the Food Aid Convention, and thus far these questions have dominated the talks. The debate has only just begun, and it is unclear what its outcome will be.

---

3. Clark 2009; Hopkins 2009.

# The Food Crisis and the World Food Programme

The food crisis of 2007–8 was spurred by sharp increases in the price of food on both international and domestic markets.[4] The prices of key staples, such as wheat, soybeans, rice and corn, doubled in that period, while the IMF price index of internationally traded food commodities climbed 56 percent from January 2007 to June 2008.[5] As prices climbed, access to food was abruptly diminished for the world's poorest people, who spend some 50 to 80 percent of their income on food. In early 2008, riots over the high price of food erupted in more than thirty developing countries, many of which rely on food aid to meet a significant portion of their food needs. The crisis pushed millions of people into the category of food-insecure, and between 2007 and mid-2009 the number of hungry people on the planet rose from approximately 850 million to over 1 billion.[6] Riots across the developing world, from Haiti to the Philippines to Mozambique, galvanized international media attention on the issue.

By late 2008, just as international financial markets were thrown into turmoil, food prices on world markets fell by 50 percent from their highs earlier that year.[7] But despite this reprieve, world hunger only continued to climb. Food prices within many developing countries remained stubbornly high, in part because of decreased access to credit for low-income food-importing countries in the midst of the global financial crisis.[8] Complicating this precarious situation has been continued volatility on world food markets into 2011. Although in 2010 the FAO lowered its estimate of the number of undernourished people in the world to 925 million, by early 2011 the FAO food price index had surpassed its 2008 level.[9]

International food aid provision faltered in this period. Rapidly climbing prices for both food and fuel have affected the amount of aid donors were able to provide. By 2007 food aid levels, at 5.9 million tonnes, were at their lowest point since 1961, when records on food aid deliveries began.[10] That year marked the low point in the steady decline in food aid levels since 1999, when the total reached 15 million tonnes. With rising food prices coupled with increased numbers of hungry people, the situation was dire. A World Bank study published in mid-2008

---

4. For an overview of the crisis, see Clapp and Cohen 2009; Heady and Fan 2008.
5. Mitchell 2008.
6. FAO 2009b.
7. FAO 2008.
8. FAO 2009b.
9. See FAO website, http://www.fao.org.
10. WFP 2008a, 1.

estimated that some 73 to 105 million people had been pushed below the poverty line as a result of rising food prices, 30 million of those in Africa alone.[11]

Multilateral food aid provided by the WFP was deeply affected by the crisis. Because the WFP relies entirely on voluntary contributions (it does not receive regular guaranteed funding from the UN), it was in a particularly vulnerable situation. Food prices began to escalate and resources became less certain just as a new executive director, Josette Sheeran, joined the organization. In this context, the WFP fully embraced the idea of local procurement of food aid and other forms of food assistance in developing countries—not only as a cost-saving measure but as a means by which to promote local economies and reduce hunger. This move reflected a shift that had already taken place in the EU toward LRP as well as cash transfers and vouchers as primary tools of food assistance. The WFP had already been under pressure from European Union countries, Germany and the UK in particular, to increase its use of cash resources for local and regional purchase.[12] Although the WFP had been procuring some of its food aid in developing countries for thirty years, when Sheeran took the helm of the organization, she began to promote it forcefully and sought to make LRP an integral part of the WFP's strategic plan.

Because the United States is the largest donor to the WFP, the organization's reputation is that it is merely an extension of U.S. bilateral food aid programs.[13] The executive director of the WFP is typically an American, and the organization has tended to follow policies that fit well with that of its principal donor. The food crisis and the growing use of local purchase by other donors and the WFP posed an interesting dilemma for the organization because although the United States was just beginning to experiment with local purchase programs in 2008–9, the bulk of that country's food aid, including most of what it channeled through the WFP, was tied to U.S.-procured grain. Still, the WFP charted a new direction under Sheeran's leadership by making local purchase a central part of its strategy, marking a very different course from that of the previous WFP executive director, James Morris, who in the context of the WTO negotiations had been a strong supporter of tied aid (see chapter 6). The timing of their appointments may explain their different positions. Morris had been appointed in 2002, before President George W. Bush's attempts to push the agenda of food aid untying in Congress. Sheeran, formerly undersecretary for economic, energy, and agricultural affairs at the United States Department of State, had been appointed to her

---

11. World Bank 2008, 2.
12. Interview with Marc Cohen, senior research fellow, IFPRI, October 17, 2007.
13. Wahlberg 2008.

post in 2007 after Bush's request to untie a portion of U.S. food aid had been turned down several times by Congress (see chapter 4).

As food prices began to rise steadily throughout 2007, the WFP saw a 14 percent decline in the aid it could deliver that year.[14] With around 50 percent of the WFP's budget supplied by donors in the form of financial resources, this was not a surprising impact of rising food prices.[15] WFP's budget at the start of 2008 stood at $2.9 billion, but it quickly became aware that it could not fulfill its plan to feed seventy-three million people in 2008, including as many as three million in Darfur.[16] The cost of procuring food rose sharply in early 2008.[17] Sheeran explained the severity of the situation in blunt terms: "During the past five years, from 2002 to 2007, WFP saw a 50 percent increase in the cost to procure basic foods for our program. From June 2007 until February 2008 we saw another 50 percent increase. And we are not out of the woods yet. . . . This has rocked WFP to its core, and it has rocked many nations and villages too."[18]

In early 2008 the WFP began to make plans to ration food aid in the event that donors would not step up with additional resources for the agency.[19] To be planning cuts to food aid rations just as people were being priced out of the food market was difficult for the organization. As Sheeran noted to the press, "These are very heartbreaking kinds of decisions to make."[20] In March 2008, the WFP issued an extraordinary emergency plea to donors to provide an additional $500 million by May 1, 2008, to help meet its budget shortfall and to avoid the need to cut rations.[21] By mid-April, with food prices continuing to climb, the amount requested by the WFP had risen to $755 million. The WFP had specifically asked donors for untied or unearmarked financial donations to "give WFP greater flexibility for procuring and pre-positioning food for the hungry."[22]

Several countries came forward with additional donations in response to the appeal. On top of providing an additional $50 million to WFP, Canada announced that it would also untie 100 percent of its food aid (see chapter 3). The United States increased its contribution by several hundred million dollars as part of its food crisis supplemental appropriation (discussed in chapter 4), to bring its total contribution to the WFP for 2008 to just over $2 billion. A small amount of

14. Blas 2008.

15. Interview with Patrick Webb, dean and professor, Friedman School of Nutrition Science and Policy, and former chief of nutrition, WFP, November 13, 2007.

16. Ban Ki Moon 2008.

17. Beattie 2008.

18. Sheeran 2008.

19. Blas and Tett 2008.

20. Sheeran, quoted in Blue 2008.

21. WFP 2008d.

22. WFP 2008e.

this additional support from the United States was in the form of cash for local purchase, but the vast bulk of it was in-kind aid and all of it was earmarked for specific programs.[23] In late May, the appeal gained a substantial boost when Saudi Arabia provided a $500 million cash donation. This was the largest single donation in response to the appeal, and it was completely flexible and not earmarked. In total, twenty-eight countries responded to the extraordinary appeal, providing $1 billion, which enabled WFP to maintain its rations and programs in 2008 and to increase the number of people it could feed that year.[24]

Food security issues were placed on the G-8 agenda in the midst of the price crisis. World Bank president Robert Zoellick issued a letter to G-8 governments on the eve of the group's 2008 summit in Hokkaido, Japan, stressing that the WFP's budget would have to increase from the $3 billion annually that it had been in recent years to $6 billion for the foreseeable future. He urged the governments to increase their regular funding to the WFP and to consider mandating it as part of UN contributions and also to provide those funds unearmarked and untied. Echoing the WFP's new embrace of local purchase, he stressed that funding to the WFP would be most useful if it could include local and regional purchase, particularly in times of high food and fuel prices: "At a minimum, the Group of Eight should work with the UN to call on governments around the world to ensure access to local purchases for the WFP and for humanitarian purposes," which should be exempt from export restrictions and taxes.[25] The G-8 statement on food security, agreed to in July 2008, referred to these requests:

> We are determined to take all possible measures in a coordinated manner, and since January 2008 have committed, for short, medium and long-term purposes, over US$10 billion to support food aid, nutrition interventions, social protection activities and measures to increase agricultural output in affected countries. In the short-term, we are addressing urgent needs of the most vulnerable people. In this regard, we welcome the contributions which others have made to address the global food crisis. We call on other donors to participate along with us in making commitments, including through the World Food Programme (WFP), to meet remaining immediate humanitarian needs and to provide access to seeds and fertilizers for the upcoming planting season. We will also look for opportunities to help build up local agriculture

---

23. See also Ramachandran, Leo, and McCarthy 2010, 18.
24. See WFP 2009d, 37.
25. Zoellick 2008.

by promoting local purchase of food aid. We underline the importance of strengthening the effective, timely and needs-based delivery of food assistance and increasing agricultural productivity.[26]

With increased funds and political support from the G-8 in principle, including on the issue of local and regional purchase, the WFP stepped up its promotion of the organization's use of local procurement of the food aid it delivered. It promoted its "80–80–80 solution"—the aim to procure 80 percent of its food in developing countries, contract 80 percent of the transportation locally, and hire 80 percent of its staff locally. If the food and services for its delivery are procured locally, benefits from the operation flow to developing countries rather than to the donor countries. In advancing this approach, Sheeran said it was part of a revolution in food aid that was no longer reliant on the disposal of rich-country agricultural surpluses, stressing, "[T]his is not your grandmother's food aid."[27] The WFP strategic plan for 2008–2011 included a continuation of its local purchase practices: "Priority must be given to local purchases when this does not conflict with other requirements of WFP operations, namely the provision of adequate and timely food and nutrition assistance."[28]

In September 2008 the WFP launched its Purchase for Progress (P4P) program. Funded partially from private foundations and partially by donor states, P4P is a five-year pilot project in twenty-one countries that aims to improve the ability of the WFP's local food procurement to boost the incomes of low-income, small-scale farmers in developing countries.[29] Although 80 percent of the WFP's purchases are made in developing countries, the majority are purchased on large commodity exchanges. The P4P project aims to benefit small-scale farmers directly—farmers who may not otherwise have access to the larger markets where WFP buys. The project was a new direction for WFP, as it did not previously have the capacity to identify and carry out smaller purchases with farmer cooperatives. The WFP does not expect the P4P project to form the bulk of its purchases because of its small-scale nature, but it does aim to make around 10 percent of its purchases from small farmers. The economic crisis of 2008–9, however, has been a challenge for the project because food prices in many developing countries are higher than those on international exchanges.[30]

---

26. Group of Eight 2008.

27. Sheeran 2008.

28. WFP 2008b, 30.

29. WFP 2010b. The P4P program is funded by the Bill and Melinda Gates Foundation, the Howard G. Buffett Foundation, the European Commission, and the governments of Belgium, Canada, Ireland, Luxembourg, the United States, and Saudi Arabia.

30. Interview with Allan Jury, director, WFP U.S. Relations Office, November 4, 2009.

By the end of 2008, the WFP was able to provide food aid to 102 million people with a budget of $5.1 billion.[31] Although it had raised significant additional funds in 2008 when food prices were at record highs, it again faced funding shortfalls after food prices declined when the global financial crisis hit in late 2008 and early 2009. This situation was exacerbated not only by the cuts in aid programs in 2009 as a result of the global economic recession but also by a shift among donor countries away from financing food aid to funding longer-term agricultural development instead. Secretary of State Hillary Clinton remarked in a speech in mid-2009 that the United States was revising its approach to fighting hunger: "[F]or too long, our primary response has been to send emergency aid when the crisis is at its worst. This saves lives, but it doesn't address hunger's root causes. It is, at best, a short-term fix." The comment was printed in a July 6 article in the London *Telegraph* during the G-8 summit held in L'Aquila, Italy, in 2009, at which donors pledged to increase funding for agriculture and food security rather than for food aid.[32] Clinton's comments no doubt influenced Sheeran to issue a press statement the following day: "It's a false logic for the world to say that we will either invest in tomorrow's agriculture or today's urgent food needs. There is no question that we must do both."[33]

But donor contributions to the WFP in 2009 were not forthcoming at the same rate as they had been in the previous year, and the organization was forced to cut rations and close some of its food aid operations. The WFP had raised less than $1.5 billion by early June 2009, out of a requested budget of $6.4 billion, and by September of that year the funding shortage stood at around $3 billion.[34] Some donors suggested that the WFP should scale back operations and make efficiencies, even as the broader economic crisis was leading to increased requests for food aid due to credit shortages and stubbornly high food prices in developing countries.[35] The WFP funding shortfall continued into 2010–11, although the Haiti earthquake and Pakistan floods that year did lead to at least temporarily increased donations for food aid operations for these particular emergencies.

## Rethinking the Food Aid Convention

Throughout 2007–9, when food prices were highly volatile, hunger was on the rise, and the WFP faced serious funding shortfalls, the Food Aid Convention

---

31. WFP 2009d.
32. Clinton 2009. Quoted in London *Telegraph* July 6, 2009.
33. WFP 2009b.
34. WFP 2009a.
35. Blas 2009.

was rarely mentioned by donor countries and the WFP in official responses to the food crisis. Although food aid demand increased during the crisis, the role of the FAC in ensuring adequate food aid levels escaped media attention almost entirely. The FAC, as outlined in chapter 2, sets out minimum tonnage commitments for food aid that donors must provide each year. The aim of the convention is to provide a basic minimum floor of food aid donations on an ongoing basis in order to ensure that aid levels do not decline dramatically if prices rise sharply. However, as some analysts have pointed out, and as is discussed below, the minimum tonnage commitments made by the donors in the FAC agreement are today so low as to be almost meaningless, such that food aid levels can and do fluctuate widely, even if they are above the guaranteed minimum amount.[36]

The low commitment level for donor countries is shown by the fact that FAC members have collectively met their tonnage commitments under the convention since 1999 even though overall food aid levels fell by more than half from 1999 to 2007. The amount provided in 2007 was still above the combined annual commitment total of approximately 5.4 million tonnes agreed to under the 1999 FAC. The fact that donors' provision of this resource could change so dramatically—from 15 million to 5.9 million tonnes[37]—over the course of a decade without any recognized changes in FAC rules or commitments suggests that the agreement does little in practice to ensure a genuinely steady or reliable level of international food aid.

The weakness of the FAC as a global instrument to promote food security has prompted some observers to suggest that the agreement should be reformed.[38] This idea is not entirely new but has again been advanced in the broader context of discussion on rethinking and revamping the institutional framework for global food security governance in the aftermath of the 2007–8 food crisis. Recognizing that the crisis was a mix of both volatile markets that are now predicted to be a permanent feature of the global food system and longer-term structural trends of rising demand for food exacerbated by unstable agricultural futures markets,[39] a growing number of voices are calling for changes to the existing food security governance framework.[40]

These changes have already begun to take place and are shaping the broader international policy context.[41] In the midst of the crisis, the UN established the High-Level Task Force on the Food Security Crisis (HLTF), which developed a

---

36. Benson 2000.
37. See FAC data.
38. See Hoddinott, Cohen, and Barrett 2008; Maxwell 2007; Oxfam International 2009; ETC Group 2009; Clay 2010; Clapp and Clark 2010.
39. Von Braun et al. 2008.
40. Oxfam International 2009; ETC Group 2009.
41. See Harvey et al. 2010.

major document, the Comprehensive Framework for Action (CFA), that sets out policy directions to address the crisis.[42] In 2009 the UN substantially revamped the Committee on World Food Security, which is housed at the FAO. The revised CFS elevates that body to be a central node of coordination within the UN system on food security governance initiatives and also provides for a governance structure that is more open to participation by civil society actors.[43] Endorsed at the World Summit on Food Security in Rome, 2009, the revamped CFS is poised to take a greater role in shaping the future of the global food security governance architecture.[44] In 2008, the WFP also adopted a new strategic plan, as noted above. The G-8 endorsed a food security statement in 2008,[45] as mentioned above, and in 2009 G-8 governments pledged $20 billion over three years for agricultural development initiatives.[46] The G-8 pledge was subsequently endorsed by the G-20 group of leading economies meeting later that year. In early 2010 the World Bank set up the Global Agriculture and Food Security Program (GAFSP), which is poised to receive funding, including pledges from both the G-8 and the G-20 group of leading economies, to boost agricultural production in developing countries.[47]

The question of how to reform the international food aid regime has become part of this broader dialogue about needed changes to the global food security governance architecture. Because food aid is no longer reliant on donor-country surpluses and today is more of a humanitarian tool than a trade outlet (accounting for less than 2 percent of global agricultural trade), it is not at all clear that the Food Aid Convention, with its origins in a different era, is adequate in its current form. The FAC was last renegotiated in 1999, and that agreement was originally due to expire in 2002.[48] It has in the words of John Hoddinott, been "limping from extension to extension" since 2002 with the expectation that renegotiation would need to take place soon.[49] There was in fact an attempt to renegotiate the convention in 2004, but donors abandoned that effort in favor of waiting for the Doha Round of trade talks to be completed as rules regarding food aid are part of the agriculture text (see chapter 6).[50] But because the Doha talks have been stalled indefinitely since their breakdown in 2008 (and the food aid disciplines seem

---

42. United Nations High-Level Task Force on the Global Food Security Crisis 2008.
43. FAO 2009c.
44. FAO 2009a.
45. Group of Eight 2008.
46. Group of Eight 2009.
47. World Bank 2010.
48. See Hoddinott, Cohen, and Barrett 2008, 283.
49. Interview with John Hoddinott, senior research fellow, IFPRI, October 11, 2007.
50. See FAC website, http://www.foodaidconvention.org/en/index/aboutthefac.aspx.

largely decided) and in the wake of the food crisis, in 2009 donors again began to consider undertaking renegotiation of the convention.

In 2010 Canada assumed the chair of the governing body of the FAC, the Food Aid Committee. Canada also hosted the G-8 meetings that same year. In advance of the main G-8 summit in 2010, the G-8 development ministers met in Halifax. Signaling a move under Canada's leadership to discuss finally revamping the agreement, the chair's summary of the development ministers' meeting noted that "[m]inisters believe in a Food Aid Convention (FAC) for the 21st century that focuses on providing appropriate and effective food assistance to vulnerable populations. Ministers agreed to do further work."[51] Informal talks on renegotiating the agreement were launched in June 2010 when the Food Aid Committee met in London. Formal negotiations on a renewed treaty began in December 2010 and are expected to be completed in late 2011.

There are two main areas of the FAC that analysts have stressed are in need of reform, and these are currently under discussion by the convention's members. One is the set of rules governing donor countries' food aid commitments as articulated in the agreement. Commitments have historically been counted in tonnes of wheat equivalent, a metric that is seen by many to be outdated and unworkable for the current context.[52] Further, other rules regarding commitments have not provided adequate incentive to deliver aid to where it is needed most. The other aspect of the FAC that is in need of reform is its governance arrangements. Housed at the International Grains Council and having only donors as members, the FAC has been criticized for not being transparent and for lacking in effective consultation with stakeholders, having weak coordination with other bodies, and lacking meaningful monitoring and evaluation.[53]

Debates over the future of the food aid regime and the FAC in particular have not been as public or as openly heated as the food aid debates over GMOs and the WTO negotiations, although they have, at least in the past, been polarized.[54] As negotiations are ongoing through a process that is less than transparent, donor country governments have kept their positions largely to themselves. But these discussions are extremely important, as how they are resolved will determine the future direction and effectiveness of the international food aid regime. The range of options that are on the table for the revised convention range from abandonment of the agreement to minimalist tinkering with the existing text to a major overhaul of the key components.

---

51. Group of Eight Development Ministers 2010.
52. See Clay 2010, 9; Clark 2009.
53. See Clapp and Clark 2010; Clay 2010; Hoddinott, Cohen, and Barrett 2008.
54. Hoddinott interview, October 11, 2007.

## Donor Commitments under the FAC

A major weakness of the rules of the FAC is that the agreement does little to counteract the basic problem that food aid tends to be countercyclical with prices and procyclical with supply. In other words, when food prices are high and supply is tight, food aid levels tend to decline—at exactly the time when it is most needed; when food prices are low and food is in abundant supply, the provision of food aid tends to rise. Thus the risk of changes in grain prices is passed on to the recipient countries, which face fluctuating amounts of food each year, according to trends in grain markets. When food prices rise and food aid falls sharply, recipients have little to fall back on: food aid typically falls sharply and procuring food on markets is difficult because of higher prices. Adjusting to higher prices and lower aid levels is especially a problem if those countries had become dependent on food aid after a long period of low grain prices, as had been the case for much of the 1980s and 1990s.

The FAC originally aimed to address the tendency of food aid to fluctuate with prices and supply by setting a minimum combined commitment level for all donors that would provide a guaranteed floor below which food aid levels would not drop. Food aid is also counted under the FAC in terms of wheat equivalents measured in tonnes. The measurement of food aid in this way is a product of the fact that nearly all food aid was originally tied to grain—primarily wheat—procured in donor countries. Because some donors—e.g., Japan and the UK—did not have surplus grain at the time they joined the FAC, it has always allowed donors to provide cash to purchase grain, although their commitments had to be expressed in terms of tonnes of wheat equivalent. Following pressure from the European Union once it untied its food aid (see chapter 3), the expression of commitments was relaxed in the 1999 FAC, allowing donors to express commitments in wheat equivalent, value in monetary terms, or a combination of wheat equivalent and value.[55] Those member countries that express their commitments in value, however, must also provide a guaranteed annual tonnage.[56]

Over the years the FAC has gradually expanded its list of eligible food commodities from wheat to other food items, including rice, pulses (edible seeds such as beans, peas, lentils, and chickpeas), cooking oil, skimmed milk powder, and root crops, as well as some nutritional supplements. The FAC's Rules of Procedure set out the formulas by which various commodities and cash are converted into wheat equivalent for the purpose of donor reporting to the FAC. These

---

55. See Benson 2000; see also Overseas Development Institute 2000, 2.

56. See article III of the 1999 Food Aid Convention (http://www.foodaidconvention.org/en/index/faconvention.aspx).

formulas are typically based on the prevailing prices of wheat and other com-modities on international markets but are different for each commodity.[57]

Critics have pointed out that measuring commitments in wheat equivalent is not ideal, as it is an overly complex way of counting what is actually delivered as food aid, particularly for donors who have untied their aid.[58] Edward Clay, for example, argues that tonnes of wheat equivalents counted by the FAC are in fact quite different from actual tonnes of grain when the calorie content of each is considered. He shows that when one looks at actual calorie content, or energy, of the food aid provided under the FAC over time, it becomes clear that the calories have fallen sharply as prices have risen and vice versa, even while tonnes of wheat equivalent reported to the FAC have fluctuated very little by comparison.[59] John Hoddinott, Marc Cohen, and Christopher Barrett also critique the wheat equiva-lent measure, pointing out that FAC conversion formulas based on prevailing prices serve only to negate the intention of providing a guaranteed minimum fixed quantity of food aid because they create incentives for donors to delay ship-ments of food aid when prices are high until they have fallen again.[60]

The total combined commitments are also seen by many to be very low com-pared with global need, meaning that in effect the greater share of the price risk is again passed on to recipients. The total annual commitments agreed to in the 1999 FAC were approximately 5.4 million tonnes per year. But this amount was only half of what the global community agreed was needed at the 1974 World Food Conference. At that time, when prices were high and food aid levels fell, there was broad agreement that at least 10 million tonnes of aid should be pro-vided every year by donors. For most of the 1970s, the FAC commitments stood at only 4 million tonnes per year. The 1980 FAC revised the minimum upwards, to 7.6 million tonnes, but the total commitment was reduced again in the 1995 and 1999 FAC agreements. The sharp reduction in 1995 from 7.6 million to 5.4 million tonnes was a response to higher grain prices in 1995, which prompted the United States to reduce its commitments by 2 million tonnes, a 44 percent decline. The total combined commitment was not raised again in the 1999 FAC, even though grain prices had fallen substantially when compared with their level in the mid-1990s.[61] Although food aid shipments have often been over the mini-mum combined commitment level, the fluctuations even above that level have been stark and closely linked to grain prices. Charlotte Benson notes that food aid

57. See the Food Aid Convention Rules of Procedure (http://www.foodaidconvention.org/en/index/faconvention.aspx).

58. Clark 2009; Hoddinott and Barrett 2007.

59. Clay 2010, 9.

60. Hoddinott, Cohen, and Barrett 2008, 287.

61. Benson 2000, 103, 117.

flows have fluctuated by as much as 20–25 percent between years.[62] This has led many to argue that the minimum guaranteed floor is too low to be meaningful for recipients.[63]

The problem of fluctuating levels of food aid from year to year is exacerbated by the fact that there are no sanctions against donors that do not meet their food aid commitments in any given year. Donors are required to make up shortfalls in subsequent years, but this only highlights the fact that food aid is countercyclical with prices since the rules encourage donors to underprovide aid in high-price years and make up any shortfalls when prices are low. This happened in the mid-1990s, when the United States failed to meet its commitments for several years, and in the early 2000s, when Canada was in a similar position. Although in principle the rules that set out tonnage requirements of donors seek to ensure that they bear the bulk of the price risk, in practice the rules of the convention allow much of that risk to be transferred to recipient countries.

There are other problems with the FAC's rules on how donors can count food aid toward their commitments that work against effective food aid provision. The FAC does not allow donors to count expenditures on transportation for other donors' food aid, for example, as part of their own commitments. Such transactions could help to allow FAC members to "twin" with new, primarily developing-country donors of food aid who might have food but might not have the funds for its transportation. The rules also place some restrictions on the amount of micronutrients such as nutritional supplements that can be counted as part of a donor's commitments.[64]

The FAC has not waded fully into the debate over tied food aid, monetization, or food aid provided as an export credit. Echoing WTO rules agreed on in 1994, the 1999 FAC does not allow donors to count food aid that is tied to *commercial* exports to recipient countries. But the convention does not place any restrictions on in-kind, direct-transfer food aid that is tied to procurement in the donor country. It also allows donors to count untied forms of food aid, such as cash, as part of their commitments. The FAC encourages donors to give food aid in grant form and requires all aid to least developed countries to be in the form of grants, stipulating that 80 percent of donors' commitments should be in that form. However, the FAC does allow donors to count sales of food aid on long-term credit to non-LDC countries as part of their commitments, provided the credit rate charged is below the commercial rate. Monetization of food aid in recipient countries is also allowed under the FAC. As the international food aid

62. Ibid., 108.
63. Benson 2000; Clay 2010; Hoddinott, Cohen, and Barret 2008, 288.
64. Clark 2009; Hoddinott, Cohen, and Barrett 2008, 287; TAFAD 2010c.

regime shifts toward more fully grant and increasingly untied aid, and with mon-etization allowed only under certain circumstances under the proposed WTO text (outlined in chapter 6), some of the above aspects of the current rules are now clearly outdated.

In the present context, critics and some donors have argued that change to the FAC rules regarding commitments is needed. At the broadest level, many have argued that the FAC should be restructured so as to be needs-based rather than driven by the availability of donor resources.[65] Structuring the rules of the treaty around what hungry people in recipient countries need rather than what donor countries are seeking to provide would likely improve the ability of the agreement to respond more effectively to emergency food-deficit situations as they arise.

More specifically, most agree that moving away from wheat equivalent com-mitments probably makes sense. However, it is not clear what would be the most appropriate replacement. It is important that the new measure be easy to under-stand and transparent, to avoid the types of problems that the wheat equivalents brought about.[66] Counting commitments in terms of monetary value is likely to be attractive for only certain donors, especially those who have untied their food aid: Canada, the EU, and Australia. Because most donors set food aid budgets in monetary value terms in any case, such a metric has wide appeal, and it is easy to understand. But it is not clear that commitments only expressed in financial terms would do much, if anything, to reduce the transfer of the price risk to recipient countries. It would certainly make that transfer of risk to developing countries more transparent. If donors agree to provide only a fixed amount of financial resources over the length of the agreement, food aid levels would likely drop under a scenario of rising prices and rise with falling prices, as they have done in the past. Because the 1999 FAC has been in place for over a decade, dur-ing which a major increase in food prices has occurred, it is important to ensure that any commitments expressed in financial value terms are at the very least updated on a regular basis between FAC negotiations or adjusted annually based on a food price inflation index.[67]

The Transatlantic Food Assistance Dialogue (TAFAD), a consortium of food-aid-programming and delivery NGOs in North America and Europe, has sug-gested that donor commitments, however they are expressed (cash or otherwise), should be sufficient to feed a certain number of people each year. The current com-mitment level in grain terms is equivalent to food for approximately 23 million

---

65. TAFAD 2010a; Hoddinott, Cohen, and Barrett 2008, 300.
66. This point is echoed in Clay 2006, 122.
67. See Gaus et al. 2011.

people per year. Given that food needs have risen since the 1999 FAC was agreed on, especially in the wake of the food crisis, TAFAD considers that this amount should be increased by 30 percent, to approximately 30 million people. Counting donor commitments in terms of caloric food needs for a certain number of people per year is a more transparent and needs-based approach to commitments than the current method.[68]

Along similar lines, Clay has suggested that measuring food aid deliveries in coarse grain equivalent tonnages would better capture the caloric value of the food aid, or alternatively could be expressed as "total persons who could be provided with a basic ration over one year."[69] Likewise, Hoddinott and Barrett have suggested that wheat equivalent tonnes be converted not by price value, as they are currently calculated, but rather by caloric value and that these should be weighted more in cases of severe and acute hunger and when dispatched quickly in response to emergency appeals.[70] These various alternatives to wheat equivalents would give a better indicator of the role of food aid in fighting hunger because they focus on the nutritional value of food rather than its price value.

In addition to counting tonnage differently, the various proposals noted above see the usefulness of continuing to allow donors to meet some of their commitments in the form of cash to cover costs that are essential for local procurement and/or delivery of the aid plus expenditures on nutritional supplements. These funds could be channeled through the WFP or food aid delivery NGOs.[71] But the proposals note that certain rules should apply to the use of the cash, and equivalences should be carefully calculated. Clay proposes, for example, developing an eligible list of activities that the money could go toward and reassessing commitments expressed in financial terms on a regular basis (more frequently than the FAC is renegotiated) to take commodity and transportation price shifts into account.[72] Hoddinott and Barrett propose that donors should not be allowed to spend financial commitments within developed donor countries (that is, financial commitments should be spent in developing countries) and that the monetary value provided should be adjusted according to level of need and speed of provision (i.e., faster contributions and those directed toward emergencies should count for more). They also argue that new rules should be put in place to enable the financial donations to cover expenses such as twinning that are not now counted as donor commitments.[73]

---

68. See TAFAD 2010b.
69. Clay 2010, 12.
70. Hoddinott and Barrett 2007, 9–10.
71. Barrett and Maxwell 2006, 110–111.
72. Clay 2010. See also Gaus et al. 2011.
73. Hoddinott and Barrett 2007, 10–11.

THE 2007–2008 FOOD CRISIS

Regarding tying, Oxfam has argued that a revised FAC should allow only untied aid.[74] The proposals for reform all suggest that no matter how donors express their commitments, local and regional purchase of food aid should be encouraged. There is growing support as well for counting only grant aid as part of FAC members' commitments. TAFAD has argued that nongrant and program food aid should not be counted toward donor commitments and that the practice of monetization should be phased out of commitments completely.[75] It also proposes that food aid should, wherever possible, be procured close to recipients.[76]

In addition to the issue of how to count individual donor commitments within a renewed FAC, the overall amount provided collectively by donors is also a major concern, particularly for NGO groups such as TAFAD. As noted above, commitments were only increased following the 1970s food crisis in the 1980 FAC once donors knew they had surplus grain on which to draw. Donors today are not in that situation. Rather, the opposite conditions hold: continued uncertainty about the future world food supply and tight aid budgets in donor countries. This signals that the likely direction of overall commitment may well be downward.

It is as yet unclear how the members of the FAC will resolve these problems. Determining what donors can count as food aid as part of their commitments is one of the biggest issues on the table in the current negotiations, but it is also very thorny because of the lack of clarity on what metric would be acceptable to the donors *and* provide a meaningful and transparent level of commitment that does not transfer the greater part of the price risk back to recipients. The United States has not been active in trying to replace the wheat equivalent metric in the FAC because it must provide a minimum of 2.5 million tonnes of grain in any case, as mandated by the U.S. Farm Bill. It might support a new method to count commitments if it is easy to implement and does not require a drastic change in U.S. policies or reporting procedures. The EU, having untied its aid, already expresses part of its commitment in monetary value terms. Most of its food assistance goes toward emergency aid, and it has pushed in the negotiations for commitments to be in the form of cash to cover items necessary for humanitarian response, including those that go beyond food. It is likely that the commitment structure in a renegotiated agreement will contain a combination of monetary value and another metric, possibly based on tonnes of grain equivalents or number of persons fed. Whether it will count commitments from donors for monetary donations to cover items beyond food, however, is as yet unclear. Moreover, if donors cannot agree on a common metric for counting

---

74. Oxfam International 2009, 9.
75. TAFAD 2007; TAFAD 2006.
76. TAFAD 2006.

their commitments, reaching agreement on a collective level of donations may not even be possible.

## Governance Arrangements of the FAC

Beyond the problems with the way in which donor commitments are counted under the convention, criticisms have also been made of the FAC's current governance arrangements. As noted in chapter 2, the FAC secretariat is housed in the International Grains Council in London. This arrangement is a product of the FAC's early history. The original Food Aid Convention was adopted alongside the Wheat Trade Convention in 1967 as part of a broader International Grains Arrangement under the Kennedy Round of the GATT. The two agreements are linked, as concessions in one agreement were made in exchange for concessions in the other. The original agreements were thus deeply entrenched in trade concerns of the members. With food aid taking on more of a humanitarian function, particularly over the past decade, the question of whether the secretariat of FAC still belongs in the more trade-oriented IGC has been put on the table as part of the reform discussions.[77]

On another issue not completely separate from that of the location of the FAC secretariat, critics have noted that the governance functions of the agreement have been very weak. As a donor-only agreement, in practice its operation and meetings have not been very transparent. Before 2009, the FAC did not even have its own website,[78] and there was very little publicly available information on the agreement at all, apart from a brief mention of the existence of the agreement on the IGC website. The provision of information on the convention improved greatly in 2009 with the new website, which was launched on the occasion of the hundredth meeting of the Food Aid Committee. The text of the convention and the rules of procedure, previously difficult to obtain, are now posted publicly, as are brief minutes of the FAC meetings.

The donor-only membership of the FAC has also meant a lack of participation on the part of other food aid stakeholders—namely recipients, international food security organizations, and civil society organizations. The agreement's governing body is the Food Aid Committee, which normally meets twice per year, in June and December. The June meetings are typically held in London at the same time as the IGC annual conference. Participants must pay a hefty fee (over $900) to attend the conference, but even attendance there does not enable one to attend the Food Aid Committee meetings, which are normally closed

---

77. See Clapp and Clark 2010; Oxfam International 2009; Clay 2010.
78. Food Aid Committee 2009, 6.

sessions. Recipient country governments are rarely invited to attend these meetings. Recipient voices are useful in terms of ensuring appropriate food aid interventions and verifying needs. Representatives from international organizations, such as the WFP, FAO, WTO, and OECD, important for coordinating efforts, are also sometimes invited to attend parts of the meetings.[79] Civil society has even less access to the deliberations. Unless they are part of a government delegation, it is virtually impossible for NGOs to attend the meetings unless invited to give a presentation at informal sessions,[80] which makes the FAC very different from other UN convention meetings, where observers are welcome. This relative lack of participation on the part of a wide range of food aid stakeholders has meant that the convention remains donor-oriented in both focus and process, and this only contributes to its lack of transparency.

Coordination between the FAC and other food security bodies has also been poor. There is little discussion between the various relevant organizations apart from occasional participation by representatives of international organizations in FAC meetings and the participation of donor representatives on the executive board of the WFP. With the FAC secretariat housed in an organization focused on the trade in grains, this lack of coordination with other organizations that touch on food aid and emergency assistance is not surprising. The lack of proximity with the WFP and FAO, both based in Rome, and the OECD, based in Paris, complicates the coordination issue further. The increased emergency response nature of food aid has made it imperative to have effective coordination between the FAC and other bodies that address food security and humanitarian assistance.

As a small office located within the IGC, the FAC secretariat lacks sufficient staff and food aid expertise to carry out effective monitoring and evaluation of individual donor contributions and overall effectiveness of the convention. Donors self-report their contributions and the FAC secretariat maintains these records, but this does not constitute any kind of meaningful or systematic critical evaluation of donor and treaty performance.[81] While the WFP might seem to be an obvious place to relocate the FAC secretariat, because it does have the expertise required to monitor and evaluate the agreement and includes recipient-country voices, the fact that it is also a food aid operational agency means that donors do not consider it a neutral body.[82] Further, because the United States is by far the largest donor, as noted above, many other donors believe that it dominates the WFP.

---

79. See Hoddinott, Cohen, and Barrett, 289.
80. This occurred in 2007 and in 2010.
81. See Benson 2000; Barrett and Maxwell 2005.
82. Hoddinott, Cohen, and Barrett 2008, 301.

Several proposals have been put forward to reform the current governance arrangements of the FAC, taking into account the question of the location of the FAC secretariat and the weakness of the various governance functions it performs. Oxfam, for example, has argued that the Food Aid Committee should be moved out of the IGC and placed under the reformed CFS, based in Rome. TAFAD has also argued for a strengthened linkage with the CFS.[83] The rationale for this closer linkage is that the CFS is mandated by the UN to take on the role of coordinating global food security activities at the international level, and donor commitments to provide food assistance should naturally be placed under its domain. Such a move would bolster the coordination of the FAC with other food security bodies, including the FAO and WFP, both of which are also located in Rome. Housing the Food Aid Committee under the CFS would also go some way toward improving stakeholder participation in FAC deliberations. According to Oxfam, the "CFS Bureau and Advisory Group should facilitate the involvement of recipient governments, UN agencies and civil society in the FAC governance mechanism."[84] The CFS could also take a role in coordinating monitoring and evaluation of donor and treaty performance, as it has more access to expertise on food aid than does the IGC.[85] There may be some pushback, however, to relocating the secretariat in Rome, especially from donors who may be reluctant to open themselves to greater scrutiny from a wider group of stakeholders.

Clay has argued that instead of moving the FAC secretariat and Food Aid Committee to Rome, housing them under the OECD Development Assistance Committee (DAC) could be fruitful as an alternative reform model.[86] Because some of the present and potential future members of the FAC are not OECD members (for example, Argentina, Brazil, India, China, and South Africa), he suggests that the model be considered a "DAC Plus" group. Relocating the FAC to Paris under the OECD DAC would have the effect of situating food aid more fully within the framework of international development assistance organizations. Because food aid has become largely humanitarian in nature, Clay argues, this move makes sense. The Food Aid Committee could be an OECD DAC working group and include participation from other UN food security and humanitarian agencies, including the CFS and the WFP. The FAC would also have member status at these other organizations, further boosting coordination. Monitoring and evaluation would be conducted by the OECD working in close collaboration with the WFP, which already collects data on international food aid flows, as well

---

83. TAFAD 2010a.
84. Oxfam International 2009, 9.
85. Clapp and Clark 2010.
86. Clay 2010.

as by an OECD-type peer review process. There would also be close collaboration with the FAO to monitor the global food security situation. This model would help to improve transparency, monitoring and evaluation, and coordination. But being housed in the OECD, the FAC would retain a donor focus and would not include much civil society participation.[87]

These recent proposals pick up on some aspects of an earlier suggestion put forward by Christopher Barrett and Daniel Maxwell for a "Global Food Aid Compact" during the height of the WTO negotiations on the food aid text.[88] Their idea called for greater recipient country participation in the food aid regime and external monitoring by a Food Aid Council with technical expertise, made up of representatives from a variety of organizations. They also proposed a greater role for the WTO in setting out rules and in settling disputes between donors over food aid—but this aspect has not been reflected in the more recent proposals outlined above.[89] How the governance question will be resolved in a renegotiated FAC remains to be seen. Proposals are being refined and discussed among stakeholders, and the final outcome may include a hybrid of the various models put forward.[90] TAFAD has argued that, at the very least, there should be some multistakeholder mechanism for reviewing performance of the FAC and its members, in the form of a technical advisory committee.[91]

There remains the possibility that the discussions will not lead to a new agreement, which may be the outcome if donors are not interested enough to keep the FAC as a global mechanism.[92] The United States has indicated its willingness to support a renegotiated agreement, although it is unclear whether there is broad support for extensive rather than minimal reforms. The European Union has made clear that it would prefer to see major reform over minor tinkering. It has expressed support for reworking the FAC to become a Food Assistance Convention with a broader scope than the current agreement and stronger ties to the broader governance architecture for both food security and humanitarian assistance.[93] Some FAC members, including Norway and Argentina, have not attended recent meetings of the Food Aid Committee, however, and it is uncertain whether they would wish to be members of a reformed FAC.

---

87. On the degree of the OECD's inclusivity in its aid governance arrangements, see Killen and Rogerson, 2010.

88. Barrett and Maxwell 2006.

89. For a critique of that proposal, see Clay 2006.

90. See Clapp and Clark 2010.

91. See TAFAD 2006; TAFAD 2010c.

92. Clay 2010, 11.

93. Noted in Clay 2010.

## Conclusion

Food aid has yet again become politicized in the international arena in the wake of the 2007–8 food crisis and the ongoing situation of food price volatility. It has become entwined within the broader debates over how best to reform global food security governance in a new era marked by high and volatile food prices and rising levels of hunger. Although food aid is just one piece of the food security governance picture, its place is important. Emerging tensions over the most appropriate place for food aid have been exacerbated by the fact that some donors have untied their aid while others have not. This divergence has created some tensions for the WFP, especially at the height of the food crisis. The WFP has embraced food assistance as a concept, and local purchase in particular, following the lead of donors who have untied their aid and moved toward the use of alternative tools to assist hungry people to access food. But by far its largest donor is the United States, which still has a primarily tied food aid program. This will no doubt continue to lead to tensions and funding shortfall issues for the WFP.

At the same time, the launch of talks on renegotiating the Food Aid Convention has brought the weaknesses of the existing convention into sharper view, prompting a number of proposals for reform. Differences among the major donors regarding how they provide their food aid, whether tied or untied, has affected the nature of these debates. The question of how to count donors' commitments has been brought to the forefront of the discussions. The United States has not advocated major change away from the current system of counting commitments in terms of wheat equivalents. Other donors, however, including those that have untied their food aid, have been more open to exploring other metrics, including monetary value, while NGOs such as TAFAD have warned that moving to a monetary value-based commitment structure could result in further transferring the risk of price changes onto recipients. The question of where the FAC should be situated in the broader governance framework and how it should interface with other international organizations, including the WFP, has also become a subject of debate. Whether donors choose to relocate the FAC or retain its current placement with closer ties to the international trade architecture, will be telling.

# CONCLUSION

Prospects for the Future of Food Aid Politics

Through its various transformations over the decades, a constant feature of food aid is that it continues to be highly political, regardless of the conditions under which it is given and the form it takes. From its early days as a surplus disposal regime with foreign policy payoffs for donors to its more recent transformation toward a humanitarian assistance regime that provides food assistance in a variety of forms, its provision has continued to prompt debate, albeit in different ways.

In the early 1990s international relations scholars indicated that the shift toward a recipient-oriented and development-focused food aid regime was well under way. With East-West political tensions diffused, the assumption was that the old days of food aid as a political tool were numbered. Food aid, in other words, had become more functional in nature. The end of the Cold War did tone down some aspects of food aid politics at the international level as donors no longer blatantly used it as a carrot or stick for foreign policy purposes. But two decades after the end of the Cold War, food aid is still as political as ever. Different donor countries have not seen eye to eye on the question of how food aid should be provided—specifically whether or not it should be tied to commodities grown in the donor country. This disagreement occurred even as the function of food aid shifted toward development and then increasingly toward emergency relief goals. The differences between donors on this question has fueled considerable political debate about food aid over the past decade, both at the domestic level and internationally. The divergence in donor policies became stark by the late 1990s and the first decade of the 2000s.

Closer examination of food aid politics in this most recent period reveals that economic interests and institutional dynamics within the donors' own policy-making contexts are fundamental in shaping international debates on the subject. Previous studies on the international politics of food aid made the case that food aid had changed in the 1970s and 1980s from being based on donor self-interest to being more recipient-oriented, in large part due to the promotion of ideas on how to improve the effectiveness of food aid by international institutions such as the WFP and the FAC. The debates between donors that erupted at the international level in the past decade, however, show that differences between their policies, based on their unique domestic-level interests and institutional settings, feed into the international politics of food aid and subsequently shape the contours of the regime. In other words, within donor countries a complex mix of economic interests—including diverse actors such as business actors, NGOs, and government bureaucracies—and institutional dynamics have a deep influence on how policies on food aid and food assistance evolve. International institutions may embrace new ideas to make food aid more effective as a tool to address hunger. But international institutions still rely on donors to provide assistance, and thus donors and their policies remain fundamentally important in shaping international norms of food assistance.

Complicating the international politics of food aid is the fact that the issue became caught up in new international political contexts just as donors were diverging on the question of how to provide assistance. As the Cold War began to ease in the 1990s, many were relieved that food aid would no longer be entangled in that particular context. But food aid became a hotly debated topic in new contexts that were difficult to predict in the early 1990s. The emergence of international clashes over agricultural biotechnology politicized food aid in intense debates. The completion of the Uruguay Round of trade talks that brought about the WTO and the launch of the Doha Round unleashed yet more debate as the issues of food aid tying and monetization were challenged by some members and defended by others.

The food crisis of 2007–8 and the inability of the global community to act quickly enough to address it also brought food aid into the international spot-light and prompted calls for a reorientation of the food aid regime in the broader architecture of global food security governance. Differences in food aid policies among major donors, particularly with respect to tied food aid, have only pro-vided additional fuel to the debates in these new settings. This became especially apparent as the donors that untied their aid and the WFP moved toward accep-tance of the broader idea of food assistance, including local and regional pur-chase and greater use of vouchers and direct cash handouts to improve access to food, while the United States, as the world's largest donor of food aid, remained committed to a program based largely on direct transfers of food.

What does all this mean for the future of food aid? In the near term, food aid will likely remain political, despite any further changes that may take place in the international regime. The United States is likely to maintain its adherence to having at least a significant portion of its food aid sourced domestically. At the same time, other donors—the EU, Canada, and Australia—are unlikely to reverse their untying. To do so would be a major step, particularly as they have already staked out their viewpoints on the question at the international level. The likely continuation of this divergence among donors opens the door for future political clashes in new contexts that may alter the politics of food aid in significant ways.

There are a number of trends on the horizon and these may well be defining forces that will shape food aid and the political debates that surround it in the coming years. The first is the politicization of food aid in relation to yet another preexisting international debate: that of struggles over intellectual property rights with respect to products that are deemed essential for public health and well-being. The development of new food aid products, particularly ready-to-use foods for therapeutic purposes in situations of acute and chronic hunger, has raised questions about the appropriateness of patenting such products. Second is the emergence of new voices in the food aid regime, especially the growing role of new donors. The role of recipient and NGO voices in the governance of international food aid, which have long been relevant but also shut out of the discussions, is also set to bubble to the surface. Finally, today we face new economic conditions of global hunger that are enormously complex, characterized by higher and more volatile food prices that seem to be here to stay. In this new context, exacerbated by competing uses of grains for biofuels, weather variability due to climate change, and agricultural commodity speculation, hunger is on the rise. Each of these trends will have important implications for the future of food aid and may well feed into new divergences between donors not only over how to provide the aid but also over its role in promoting global food security.

## A New Political Battleground: Ready-to-Use Foods

The increased allocation of food aid for humanitarian emergency situations has encouraged the development and use of new kinds of food aid, including ready-to-use foods (RUFs) that are easy to administer. RUFs have grown in popularity for both therapeutic and supplemental use in situations of acute and chronic hunger, especially among children from the ages of six months to two years. One such product is Plumpy'nut—a nutritionally enhanced peanut and milk powder paste that is produced by the French firm Nutriset. Plumpy'nut is packaged in single-serve foil pouches and can be given to children easily at home. This is an enormous advantage over past treatments for severe acute malnutrition that required preparing liquid foods by combining blended fortified grain flours (for example, corn and soy blend) with water, as well as hospital stays during treatment. But while easier to use, it is also more expensive, costing around $60 per child for a two-month treatment, compared with around $10 per treatment of blended liquid food mixes. Although Plumpy'nut was first developed in the mid-1990s, its use has ballooned since 2005, when it was successfully used in Niger to treat forty thousand children suffering from malnutrition during a food crisis, with the result that 90 percent of the children treated recovered.[1] For this reason, some have referred to products such as Plumpy'nut as miracle foods.

But at the same time that the product is gaining accolades for its effectiveness in treating malnutrition, the production and sale of Plumpy'nut, as well as other RUFs, is hotly debated, with the battle only set to intensify in the coming years. There are several issues fueling tensions. One is linked to debates over intellectual property rights in the context of public health issues. Plumpy'nut is protected by a patent held by its manufacturer, Nutriset, which has a virtual monopoly on its sale. Nutriset has aggressively sought to defend its patent and prevent other firms from making a generic version of the peanut paste by threatening to sue firms that produce it without a licensing agreement with Nutriset.[2] It has licensed a number of small producers in Africa to make the peanut paste with local products but has been relatively closed to the idea of mass producing it in places like the United States. To date, Nutriset has only one licensed partner firm making Plumpy'nut in the United States. Several nonprofit organizations in the United States that wish to make similar types of nutritional food aid products have challenged Nutriset in U.S. court, claiming that the idea of mixing peanut paste with milk powder and micronutrients does not constitute a unique product worthy of a patent.[3] The international NGO Médicins Sans Frontières (MSF, Doctors Without Borders) issued a letter to Nutriset urging it to back off on its defense of its patent because public health is at stake.[4]

Another source of tension complicating the matter is the question of tied aid. U.S. rules regarding sourcing mean that the United States cannot easily purchase RUFs made outside the country. In the case of Plumpy'nut, because there is only one producer of the product, USAID can purchase the product only from that one firm. The United States is a large producer of peanuts, and the Peanut Institute,

---

1. Arie 2010.
2. Arie 2010; Rice 2010.
3. Arie 2010.
4. Rice 2010.

a major peanut lobby, has backed the U.S.-based nonprofit organizations that have launched the court challenge to Nutriset's patent.[5] The linking up of NGOs and corporate interests with respect to rules regarding tied food aid is not new, as outlined in chapter 4. Nutriset, a European company, complains that opening up production in the United States will not only drive the African producers out of business by flooding the market with cheap U.S.-produced product but harm African peanut farmers as well. There are some twenty-six million acute and severely malnourished children in the world, but only one to two million of them receive ready-to-use therapeutic foods.[6] Nutriset claims it has the capacity to supply the need and that its patents are not preventing those in need from receiving Plumpy'nut, but the NGOs challenging it in court disagree.

RUFs are also increasingly being used in different formulations as supplementary food interventions to reach a larger group of mildly malnourished people. Nutriset, for example, has developed a new product, Plumpy'Doz, also under patent, with the aim of making it available to food assistance agencies for wider application than Plumpy'nut. The Campbell Soup Company has also developed a new RUF, called Nourish, which is a prepared high-protein meal in a tin containing grains and vegetables fortified with micronutrients. Campbell's insists that the product was developed not to generate profits but rather as part of its broader corporate social responsibility efforts. Other corporations, including both PepsiCo and Unilever, are developing humanitarian food aid products, although it is not certain whether these products are being developed with the intention of making profits. The desire to cash in on the RUF trend, however, could be the driver. Nutriset's sales in 2009 topped $66 million, and it is estimated that the overall market for RUFs is around $200 million.[7] The WFP, meanwhile, is in talks with several private firms regarding the development and purchase of RUFs.[8] But some have expressed concern about the growing use of these products outside short-term interventions in situations of acute malnutrition. Some have warned, for example, that widespread and continued use could result in health problems associated with overnutrition, such as obesity and diabetes.[9]

With growing attention and demand for these products, the issue is set to generate further debate. Some are calling for the development of an international code of conduct, similar to that for infant formula, to govern the global distribution of RUFs.[10] The debate over RUFs, thus far, has been played out

5. Rice 2010.
6. Schofield 2010.
7. Rice 2010.
8. Leeder 2011.
9. Schofield 2010.
10. Leeder 2010.

largely between private-sector firms and nonprofit organizations, without much government involvement. Whether that debate stays in the private realm, or whether governments will choose to become involved, remains to be seen. In the meantime, the market for RUFs is large and growing.

## New Voices in the Food Aid Regime

The traditional donors of food aid—the United States, Canada, the European Union and individual European countries, Australia, and Japan, all of which are OECD Development Assistance Committee member countries—have dominated the delivery of food aid since its inception in the 1950s and 1960s. But since 2000 a number of new donors have arrived on the scene, and while their contributions are as yet small compared with those of the traditional donors— around 2 percent of the WFP's donations in 2009—the amount they provide has been steadily rising.[11] The main non-DAC new donors of food aid since 2005 include the BRIC countries (Brazil, Russia, India, and China), as well as South Korea and Saudi Arabia. All these countries, with the exception of Saudi Arabia, have historically been recipients of food aid themselves.

The new food aid donors are not currently members of the Food Aid Convention and thus are not bound by the international agreement to provide a certain minimum amount of food aid per year. These donors in fact have quite erratic records of food aid provision, and amounts provided change significantly from year to year. Saudi Arabia, for example, provided a massive $500 million donation to the WFP in 2008 at the height of the food crisis, but it has not come anywhere near matching that level in the years since. The variability in the amount of food aid provided by these new donors is likely due to conditions specific to each of them, including availability of resources and other factors. Over the five year period from 2007 to 2011, each of these new donors ranked anywhere from fifteenth to thirty-fourth in the amount of contributions to the WFP. Most of them also provide bilateral food aid, and so the exact amounts they provide are difficult to measure but not insignificant.

With the exception of Saudi Arabia, which donated to the WFP with unearmarked cash funds in 2008, the other new donors have tended to provide their food aid tied, in-kind, linked to availability of surplus on domestic markets. The aid is typically provided by these countries on a bilateral basis, usually to neighboring countries in their region.[12] Their bilateral food aid programs tend to be

---

11. WFP 2010c.
12. Harvey et al. 2010.

designed not just to offload surplus but also to advance their foreign policy and security agendas. India, for example, supplies food aid to Afghanistan, Pakistan, Nepal, and Sri Lanka. China and South Korea provide food aid mainly to North Korea, and Brazil has focused its aid programs on Latin American and Caribbean countries. After the earthquake in Haiti in 2010, for example, Brazil took a large role in the provision of humanitarian assistance, including food aid. The Russian Federation has focused its food aid on ex-Soviet Union countries such as Tajikistan, as well as on Cuba and African countries with which it has historically had close ties, including Ethiopia and Guinea.[13]

Beyond their bilateral food aid programs, it is as yet unclear whether these new donors will become heavy hitters in multilateral aid and food aid cooperation with other donors. The WFP has begun to focus on building linkages with the BRIC countries as donors, especially after their statement on food security adopted at the 2009 BRIC summit.[14] There is also the question of whether these countries would be willing and welcomed as regular donors to the Food Aid Convention. India, the Russian Federation, South Korea, and South Africa joined the FAC meetings in June 2010 as observers, which may indicate their interest in potentially joining the treaty in the future.[15] If these new donors become more prominent both as donors and in multilateral settings, it could change the international political dynamics around issues such as food aid tying.

At the same time that there is growing attention to new donors and their potential future role in the food aid regime, there is relatively little focus on recipients and NGOs as participants in the regime. The voices of recipient governments, particularly those that rely on food aid for a significant percentage of food imports, are virtually unheard in the governance and decision-making of international bodies such as the FAC. Similarly, although they have been increasingly relied on to deliver food aid, NGOs have been left out of FAC decision-making processes. Recipient and NGO voices have been more present in the WFP's executive board, but as noted in chapter 7, there is much room for improved coordination between that body and the FAC.

The lack of recipient country participation and the poor transparency with respect to donor decision making in the FAC is striking in a context where greater demands are being made for international aid operations to be more open and participatory. The Accra Agenda for Action, adopted in 2008 by a wide range of both donor and recipient countries, aims to strengthen the 2005 Paris Dec-

---

13. Russian Federation 2008.
14. See WFP 2010c.
15. Food Aid Committee 2010.

laration on Aid Effectiveness with respect to matters of aid transparency.[16] The agenda calls on signatories to facilitate and strengthen inclusive aid partnerships between donors and recipients, to deepen engagement with civil society organizations, to encourage more transparency and accountability, as well as the untying of aid.[17] If the renegotiation of the FAC does result in more transparency and enhanced participation of both recipient governments and NGOs, it could change the dynamics of future international food aid cooperation. If the FAC does not embrace transparency and participation in its governance as part of the treaty's renewal, this will reveal that food aid remains captive to donor self-interest. This outcome, too, could be the spark for future political clashes between donors and recipients.

# New Economic Conditions of Hunger

The 2007–8 food price crisis brought in a new era of high and volatile food prices, new conditions that appear to be here to stay, at least for the foreseeable future. Concern is widespread that another major food crisis is imminent. Food prices in early 2011 were some 36 percent higher than a year earlier. Prices for certain staple crops, such as maize and wheat, were 74 percent and 69 percent higher, respectively, than a year earlier.[18] World Bank head Robert Zoellick warned in April 2011 that the next food crisis is just "one shock away."[19] From mid-2010 to early 2011, rising food prices directly resulted in an additional forty-four million people falling below the poverty line of $1.25 per day. An additional 10 percent rise in food prices would push another ten million into poverty, according to the World Bank.[20] Developing countries have been particularly hard hit by food price inflation, with low- and low- to middle-income countries seeing higher food price levels than wealthier countries.

It is not just higher prices that are a concern but also the continued volatility of those prices over a sustained period. The unpredictable and sharp highs and lows in food prices can wreak havoc on farmer planning and incentives. The persistence of high and volatile food prices has been attributed to a range of factors, including increased investment in biofuels, financial speculation on

---

16. See OECD, Transparent and Responsible Aid, http://www.oecd.org/document/43/0,3746, en_2649_3236398_43385067_1_1_1_1,00.html; OECD 2008. To date, all the FAC signatories have signed on to the Accra Agenda for Action, as have the BRIC countries and many recipient countries.

17. OECD 2008b.

18. World Bank 2011, 1.

19. Quoted in Martin 2011.

20. World Bank 2011, 1.

agricultural commodity markets, rising demand for food, high energy prices, weather variability due to climate change, and the imposition of export restrictions by some grain-producing countries. High and volatile prices have in turn led to increased competition for land, including the emerging trend of large-scale foreign land acquisitions in developing countries. All these forces were important in the 2007–8 price spikes, but they now seem to have become normal features of the global food economy.

The future of food aid is uncertain in this new context. As food prices have risen dramatically, the ability of donors to maintain food aid levels has been severely challenged. There is a distinct possibility that the renegotiated FAC will result in a decline in overall commitments from the 5.4 million tonnes agreed to under the 1999 FAC. The trend of food aid donations to be procyclical with supply and countercyclical with prices will only be exacerbated by greater volatility in prices, meaning that amounts actually provided by donors are likely to spike and trough in concert with the sharp ups and downs of food prices. Such volatility creates problems for recipient countries by making forward planning difficult and by affecting local markets.

Two features of the new volatile food economy have direct implications for food aid. One is rising investments in biofuels, especially investment in maize (corn)-derived ethanol production in the United States. The United States is a major player in international maize markets, contributing on average approximately 40 percent of world production and 55 percent of world exports over the 2006–10 period.[21] A growing amount of U.S. corn production, however, is being diverted into biofuel production, as a result of policies that encourage investment in that sector. These include fuel mandates that require biofuels to make up a certain percentage of fuel consumption, as well as subsidies for ethanol production. As a result, the use of corn for biofuels in the United States has increased steadily from 20 percent of the country's total corn output in 2006 to 31 percent in 2008–9 to 40 percent in 2010–11.[22]

Because the United States gives a very high percentage of its food aid as in-kind donations, and because corn has traditionally been a key commodity in that aid, its diversion into biofuel production undermines the ability of the United States to provide it as food aid.[23] Given this diversion and rising prices, the United States is likely to find itself increasingly unable to provide the same levels of maize for food aid that it has in the past. If it continues with its biofuel policies even in the face of rising food prices and levels of world hunger, this linkage

21. USDA 2010.
22. For the 2006 figure, see Mousseau 2008; for the 2010 figure, see World Bank 2011, 2.
23. See Mousseau 2008.

between biofuel production and its ability to meet its food aid commitments is likely to spark considerable debate. Proposals have been put forward from a number of quarters to relax biofuel mandates when food prices exceed a certain threshold in order to reduce both prices and demand for food crops.[24]

Export restrictions in response to high and volatile world food prices also have direct implications for food aid. Many developing countries, including some large grain-exporting countries such as India, put export bans in place during the food price crisis of 2007–8. The idea of restricting exports is to insulate the country from world price changes by effectively keeping grain at home, which has the impact of lowering domestic prices. For some of these countries, the ban on grain exports remained in place for several years. Restrictions on agricultural exports are allowed under the World Trade Organization rules as temporary measures to address shortages of basic foodstuffs, and countries are thus able to impose them at their own discretion. In late 2010, for example, the Russian Federation placed restrictions on exports of wheat after a lower-than-expected harvest of the crop due to drought. Although such measures may reduce food prices in the countries that impose them, they also tend to spark price rises on world markets.[25]

International aid agencies have pointed out the potential conflict between food export bans and humanitarian food aid operations. The WFP might effectively be shut out of markets where it normally buys grain for food aid. This is a major concern for the WFP. In 2008, it had trouble accessing food for emergency operations and faced delays in some of its operations in Afghanistan and Somalia, particularly after Pakistan imposed a wheat export ban.[26] But in other cases countries have relaxed their export restrictions for humanitarian transactions. India, for example, allowed the WFP to get around its export ban in 2008, enabling it to buy thousands of tonnes of rice at prices well below world market levels.[27]

In a world where export restrictions are increasingly being used by grain-producing countries, there have been calls from a number of quarters, including the World Bank, the World Trade Organization, and various UN agencies, for a code of conduct to exempt humanitarian food aid from export bans.[28] The United Nations High-Level Task Force on the Global Food Security Crisis noted an "urgent need to remove impediments to the export, trans-shipment and import of humanitarian food aid in recipient and neighboring countries which

---

24. World Bank 2011, 8
25. Mitra and Josling 2009.
26. Ibid.
27. WFP 2009c.
28. Lynn 2011; Boschat 2011.

delay the ability to respond to urgent needs."[29] Measures to exempt humanitarian food aid from export restrictions are currently under consideration by the G-20 leading economies.

In the face of high and volatile food prices, proposals have also been made to establish an emergency grain reserve exclusively for the WFP. A proposal made by researchers at the International Food Policy Research Institute calls for a small, decentralized physical emergency reserve for humanitarian purposes of around 300,000–500,000 tonnes of grain (around 5 percent of annual food aid flows) that could be quickly accessed by the WFP for purchase of the grain at pre-crisis prices.[30] The grains held in this reserve would be managed by the WFP and placed in strategic locations in or near major regions in developing countries that typically receive food aid. The idea of a small emergency grain reserve was endorsed by World Bank president Robert Zoellick as a measure for the G-20 leading economies to implement.[31] In mid-2011 the G-20 agriculture ministers expressed support for the development of a small pilot project along these lines to be overseen by the WFP.[32] The emergency reserve is just one of three reserves outlined in the IFPRI proposal, which also includes a globally coordinated grain reserve and a "virtual" reserve that uses government funds to intervene in agricultural commodity futures markets as mechanisms to calm global grain prices in times of volatility. The issue of grain reserves, including those at the global and national levels, is currently being widely discussed in food security forums, although no clear consensus has yet emerged.[33]

The new global economic conditions of hunger have raised the stakes for international food assistance, whether in the form of food that is shipped halfway around the world, purchased locally, or purchased with cash or a voucher. The heightened vulnerability of the world's poor to food crises, on top of the already existing emergency situations that call out for assistance, poses a significant challenge for the international food aid regime. Levels of food aid have dropped off sharply in recent years as these new economic conditions constrain its availability. Food assistance is only one of many interventions available to address rising world hunger. Its aim is to meet the needs of the world's most destitute and vulnerable people, historically only around 10 percent of the world's hungry people, for whom its provision can make an enormous difference.[34]

---

29. United Nations High-Level Task Force on the Global Food Security Crisis 2008, 7.
30. Von Braun and Torero 2008; see also Von Braun, Lin, and Torero 2009.
31. Zoellick 2011.
32. Group of Twenty Agriculture Ministers 2011; See also FAO et al. 2011.
33. See, for example Murphy 2010, 2009; McCreary 2011; Mousseau 2009.
34. WFP 2010c.

How donors navigate the provision of food assistance for those people will likely continue to be highly contentious, particularly if the availability of food aid continues to fall. The global community has not prepared well for a world with significantly less food assistance, especially in conditions of rising hunger. There is a wide range of measures that need to be implemented to improve food security for the world's poorest people, measures that go far beyond food aid itself. They include more balanced international agricultural trade policies, greater investment in agricultural production in developing countries, and policies at both the global and domestic levels to improve access to food.[35] Until these broader issues are adequately addressed in a way that reduces the need for poor and vulnerable countries to rely heavily on outside sources of food, including that provided as aid, some sort of food assistance will likely continue to be a necessary international intervention to counteract hunger, especially in emergency situations. For this reason, resolving debates that surround the provision of food aid and food assistance remains deeply important for those people for whom hunger hangs in the balance.

---

35. Clapp 2009b.

# References

Abbott, Charles. 2010. U.S. Farm Supports May Need Change—Key Lawmaker. Reuters, April 21. http://www.reuters.com/article/idUSTRE63K64P20100421.

Abbott, Philip. 2007. Overview of the 2007 USDA Farm Bill: Food Aid and the Farm Bill. http://www.ces.purdue.edu/extmedia/EC/EC_750_W_Food_Aid.pdf.

ACDI/VOCA. 2003. *Genetically Modified Food: Implications for U.S. Food Aid Programs.* 2nd rev., April. Washington, DC: ACDI/VOCA.

ActionAid International. 2005. Power Hungry: Six Reasons to Regulate Global Food Corporations. http://www.actionaid.org.uk/_content/documents/power_hungry.pdf.

Ad Hoc Coalition in Support of Sustained Funding for Food Aid. 2007. Statement for the Hearing Record of the Subcommittee on Agriculture, Rural Development, FDA, and Related Agencies, Committee on Appropriations, U.S. House of Representatives. March 19. http://www.wheatworld.org/wp-content/uploads/foodaid-ad-hoc-coalition-statement-house-hearing-20070319.pdf.

Africa Center for Biosafety, Earthlife Africa, Environmental Rights Action, Friends of the Earth Nigeria, GRAIN, and SafeAge. 2004. GE Food Aid: Africa Denied Choice Once Again? May 4. Johannesburg: African Center for Biosafety. http://www.grain.org/research/contamination.cfm?id=102.

African Union. 2006. An African Position on Genetically Modified Organisms in Agriculture. Conference of African Union Ministers of Agriculture. http://www.africa-union.org/root/au/AUC/Departments/HRST/biosafety/DOC/level2/African PositionOnGMOs_EN.pdf.

Agricultural Food Aid Coalition (AFAC). 2007. Food Aid Principles for the 2007 Farm Bill. Submitted May 10. http://www.namamillers.org/FoodAidPrincipals07.html.

Alden, Edward. 2002. U.S. Beats Egypt with Trade Stick. *Financial Times,* June 29.

Allen, George. 1976. Some Aspects of Planning World Food Supplies. *Journal of Agricultural Economics* 27 (1): 97–120.

Alliance for Food Aid. 2007. Monetization and Barter Contribute to Food Security. August 21. http://www.globalfoodsecurity.info/Default.aspx?tabid=58&metaid=H9NK0915–7af.

Alpha, Arlène, Gérard Franéoise, Bénédict Hermelen, and Ann Wagner. 2006. Impact of Export Support Measures on Food Aid and Food Security. Groupe de recherche et d'échanges technologiques, study report. http://ec.europa.eu/agriculture/eval/reports/food_security/sum_en.pdf.

*American Maritime Officer.* 2006. 2007 Budget Proposal Would Cut Food Aid Programs, Damage U.S. Agricultural and Shipping Industries: Cargoes Traditionally Reserved for U.S.-Flagged Vessels Would be Replaced by Grants. March. www.amo-union.org/News/2006/200603/200603.pdf.

Anderson, Kym, and Will Martin. 2005. Agricultural Trade Reform and the Doha Development Agenda. *World Economy* 28 (9): 1301–1327.

Arie, Sophie. 2010. Hungry for Profit. *British Medical Journal* 341 (7776): 758–759.

AusAID (Australian Agency for International Development). 1997. *Review of AusAID's Food Aid.* Canberra: AusAID. http://www.ausaid.gov.au/publications/pdf/qas06.pdf.

————. 2006. Australian Aid: Approach to Food Security. http://www.ausaid.gov.au/publications/pdf/ausaid_food.pdf.

Australian Government. 2004. Misuse of Surplus Disposal as Food Aid. Department of Agriculture, Fisheries and Forestry.http://www.daff.gov.au/agriculture-food/wheat-sugar-crops/crops/market_access/misuse.

Bageant, Elizabeth, Christopher Barrett, and Erin Lentz. 2010. U.S. Food Aid and Agricultural Cargo Preference Policy. *Applied Economic Perspectives and Policy* 32 (4): 642–641.

Bail, Cristoph, Robert Falkner, and Helen Marquard, eds. 2002. *The Cartagena Protocol on Biosafety: Reconciling Trade in Biotechnology with Environment and Development?* London: Earthscan.

Ban Ki Moon. 2008. The New Face of Hunger. *Washington Post,* March 12. http://www.washingtonpost.com/wp-dyn/content/article/2008/03/11/AR2008031102462.html.

Barrett, Christopher. 2002. Food Aid and Commercial International Food Trade. Background paper prepared for the Trade and Markets Division, OECD. http://aem.cornell.edu/faculty_sites/cbb2/papers/BarrettOECDReportMar2002.pdf.

————. 2007. The United States' International Food Assistance Programs: Issues and Options for the 2007 Farm Bill. Working paper. http://aem.cornell.edu/faculty_sites/cbb2/Papers/US%20International%20Food%20Assistance%20Programs%20&%202007%20Farm%20Bill%20Feb%202007.pdf.

Barrett, Christopher, and Daniel Maxwell. 2005. *Food Aid after Fifty Years: Recasting Its Role.* London: Routledge.

————. 2006. Towards a Global Food Aid Compact. *Food Policy* 31 (2): 105–118.

BBC News. 2005. Final Push for World Trade Talks. December 17. http://news.bbc.co.uk/2/hi/business/4536958.stm.

————. 2007. Sudan's U Turn on "GM" Food Aid. 26 April. http://news.bbc.co.uk/2/hi/africa/6594947.stm.

Beattie, Alan. 2008. Boom Challenge for Food Aid. *Financial Times,* February 7.

Belfrage, Carl-Johan. 2006. Food Aid from the EU and the US—Its Consequences for Local Food Production and Commercial Food Trade. SLI Working Paper No. 3. http://www.sli.lu.se/pdf/SLI_WP20063.pdf.

Bennett, Jon. 2003. Food Aid Logistics and the Southern Africa Emergency. *Forced Migration Review* 18 (5): 28–31.

Benson, Charlotte. 2000. The Food Aid Convention: An Effective Safety Net? In *Food Aid and Human Security,* edited by Edward Clay and Olav Stokke, 102–118. London: Frank Cass.

Bernauer, Thomas. 2003. *Genes, Trade and Regulation: The Seeds of Conflict in Food Biotechnology.* Princeton: Princeton University Press.

Bernauer, Thomas, and Erika Meins. 2003. Technological Revolution Meets Policy and the Market: Explaining Cross-National Differences in Agricultural Biotechnology Regulation. *European Journal of Political Research* 42:643–683.

Blas, Javier. 2008. Food Aid Declines to near 50-Year Low. *Financial Times,* June 9.

————. 2009. Funds Crunch Threatens World Food Aid. *Financial Times,* June 11.

Blas, Javier, and Gillian Tett. 2008. UN Poised to Ration Food Aid as Prices Soar. *Financial Times,* February 25.

Blue, Laura. 2008. Food Aid Agency Feels the Crunch. *Time,* April 23. http://www.time.com/time/world/article/0,8599,1734218,00.html.

Blustein, Paul. 2009. *Misadventures of the Most Favored Nations: Clashing Egos, Inflated Ambitions, and the Great Shambles of the World Trade System.* New York: Public Affairs.

Borlaug, Norman. 2003. Science vs. Hysteria. *Wall Street Journal,* January 22.

Boschat, Nathalie. 2011. Zoellick Warns on Food, Oil Prices. *Wall Street Journal,* April 14.

Brack, Duncan, Robert Falkner, and Judith Goll. 2003. The Next Trade War? GM Products, the Cartagena Protocol and the WTO. Royal Institute of International Affairs Briefing Paper No. 8.

Bread for the World Institute. 2006. Feeding a Hungry World: A Vision for Food Aid in the 21st Century. http://www.bread.org/learn/global-hunger-issues/feeding-a-hungry-world-a.html.

Byerlee, Derek. 1987. The Political Economy of Third World Food Imports: The Case of Wheat. *Economic Development and Cultural Change* 35 (2): 307–328.

Canadian Government. 2005. Prevention of the Circumvention of Export Subsidy Commitments: A Safe-Box for Food Aid.

Canadian Foodgrains Bank. 2005. Canadian Foodgrains Bank Welcomes Changes in Federal Procurement Rules. Press release, 22 September.

Cardwell, Ryan. 2007. Food Aid as Surplus Disposal? The WTO, Export Competition Disciplines and the Disposition of Food Aid. Canadian Agricultural Trade Policy Research Network, Trade Policy Brief 2007-1. http://www.uoguelph.ca/catprn/PDF-TPB/TPB-07-01-Cardwell.pdf.

Cardwell, Ryan. 2008. Food Aid and the WTO: Can New Rules be Effective? *Estey Centre Journal of International Law and Trade Policy* 9 (1): 74–93.

CARE USA. 2006. White Paper on Food Aid Policy, June 6. www.care.org/newsroom/articles/2005/12/food_aid_whitepaper.pdf.

Carroll, Rory. 2002. Zambia Slams Door Shut on GM Food Relief. *Guardian* (London), October 30.

Carty, Bob, with the Canadian Council for International Cooperation (CCIC) 2006. From the Sideline to the Front Lines: The Campaign to Change Canada's Policy on Tying Food Aid. *In Telling Our Stories: Drawing Policy Lessons from Development Experience,* edited by Canadian Council for International Co-operation, 46–52. Ottawa: CCIC. http://www.ccic.ca/_files/en/what_we_do/002_capacity_bldg_stories_complete.pdf.

Cathie, John. 1982. *The Political Economy of Food Aid.* Aldershot, UK: Gower Publishing.

———. 1990. Some Contrasts between European and U.S. Food Aid Policies. *Food Policy* 15 (6): 458–460.

———. 1997. *European Food Aid Policy.* Aldershot, UK: Ashgate.

Charlton, Mark. 1992. *The Making of Canadian Food Aid Policy.* Montreal: McGill-Queen's University Press.

———. 1994. Continuity and Change in Canadian Food Aid. In *Canadian International Development Assistance Policies,* edited by Cranford Pratt, 55–86. Montreal: McGill-Queen's University Press.

Christensen, Cheryl. 2000. The New Policy Environment for Food Aid: The Challenge of Sub-Saharan Africa. *Food Policy* 25 (3): 255–268.

CIDA (Canadian International Development Agency). 2005. Canada Opens Food Aid Purchases to Developing Countries. September 22. http://www.acdi-cida.gc.ca/acdi-cida/ACDI-CIDA.nsf/eng/JER-32714474-R82.

Clapp, Jennifer. 1997. *Adjustment and Agriculture in Africa: Farmers, the State and the World Bank in Guinea.* London: Macmillan.

———. 2004. WTO Agricultural Trade Battles and Food Aid. *Third World Quarterly* 25 (8): 1439–1452.

———. 2005. The Political Economy of Food Aid in an Era of Agricultural Biotechnology. *Global Governance* 11 (4): 467–485.

———. 2006. WTO Agriculture Negotiations: Implications for the Global South. *Third World Quarterly* 27 (4): 563–577

———. 2008. Illegal GMO Releases and Corporate Responsibility: Questioning the Effectiveness of Voluntary Measures. *Ecological Economics* 66 (2–3): 348–358.

———. 2009a. Corporate Interests in U.S. Food Aid Policy: Global Implications of Resistance to Reform. In *Corporate Power in Global Agrifood Governance,* edited by Jennifer Clapp and Doris Fuchs, 125–152. Cambridge, MA: MIT Press.

———. 2009b. Food Price Volatility and Vulnerability in the Global South: Considering the Global Economic Context, *Third World Quarterly* 30 (6): 1183–1196.

———. 2009c. The Global Food Crisis and International Agricultural Policy: Which Way Forward? *Global Governance* 15 (2): 299–312.

———. 2010. Responding to the Food Crisis: The Untying of Canadian Food Aid. In *Canada Among Nations 2009–2010: As Others See Us,* edited by Paul Heinbecker and Fen Hampson, 360–367. Montreal: McGill-Queens University Press.

Clapp, Jennifer, and C. Stuart Clark. 2010. Improving the Governance of the Food Aid Convention: Which Way Forward? CIGI Policy Brief No. 20. http://www.cigionline. org/sites/default/files/Policy_Brief_20_0.pdf

Clapp, Jennifer, and Marc J. Cohen, eds. 2009. *The Global Food Crisis: Governance Challenges and Opportunities.* Waterloo, Ont.: Wilfrid Laurier University Press.

Clark, C. Stuart. 2002. Briefing on the Food Aid Convention. Canadian Foodgrains Bank. April. http://www.foodgrainsbank.ca/uploads/fja_convention.pdf.

———. 2009. The Food Aid Convention: A Primer for Supporters of the Foodgrains Bank. Canadian Foodgrains Bank. September. http://www.foodgrainsbank.ca/uploads/ The%20Food%20Aid%20Convention%20Primer%20-%20September%2009.pdf.

Clay, Edward. 1983a. Is European Community Food Aid Reformable? *Food Policy* 8 (3): 174–177.

———. 1983b. European Community Responses to the "Problem of World Hunger": Food Aid, Food Security, Food Strategies and All That. *IDS Bulletin* 14 (3): 13–20.

———. 2003. Responding to Change: WFP and the Global Food Aid System. *Development Policy Review* 21 (5–6): 697–709.

———. 2004. European Food Aid: Untying and Budgetary Flexibility. Unpublished research note. December 16.

———. 2006. Food Aid and the Doha Development Round: Building on the Positive. Overseas Development Institute (ODI) Background Paper. February. http://www. odi.org.uk/resources/download/2251.pdf.

———. 2010. A Future Food Aid or Food Assistance Convention? Overseas Development Institute Background Paper on Food Aid No. 6. July. www.odi.org.uk/ resources/download/4941.pdf.

Clay, Edward, and Charlotte Benson. 1990. Aid for Food: Acquisition of Commodities in Developing Countries for Food Aid in the 1980s. *Food Policy* 15 (1): 27–43.

Clay, Edward, Sanjay Dhiri, and Charlotte Benson. 1996. *Joint Evaluation of European Union Programme Food Aid: Synthesis Report.* London: ODI.

Clay, Edward, Matthew Geddes, Luisa Natali, and Dirk Willem te Velde. 2008. Thematic Study, The Developmental Effectiveness of Untied Aid: Evaluation of the Implementation of the Paris Declaration and of the 2001 DAC Recommendation on Untying ODA to the LDCs. Phase I Report. Copenhagen. http://www.oecd.org/ dataoecd/5/22/41537529.pdf.

Clay, Edward, and Mark Mitchell. 1983. Is European Community Food Aid in Dairy Products Cost Effective? *European Review of Agricultural Economics* 10 (2): 97–121.

Clay, Edward, Nita Pillai, and Charlotte Benson. 1998. *The Future of Food Aid: A Policy Review.* London: Overseas Development Institute.

Clay, Edward, Barry Riley, and Ian Urey. 2006. *The Development Effectiveness of Food Aid: Does Tying Matter?* Paris: OECD.

Clay, Edward, and Olav Stokke, eds. 1991. *Food Aid Reconsidered: Assessing the Impact on Third World Countries.* London: Frank Cass.

———. 2000a. The Changing Role of Food Aid and Finance for Food. In *Food Aid and Human Security,* edited by Edward Clay and Olav Stokke, 13–51. London: Frank Cass.

———. 2000b. *Food Aid and Human Security.* London: Frank Cass.

Clinton, Hillary Rodham. 2009. Secretary Clinton's Remarks at 2009 World Food Prize Ceremony: Ethiopian-American scientist Gebisa Ejeta named World Food Prize winner. June 11. http://www.america.gov/st/texttrans-english/2009/June/2009061 2091231eaifas0.7548944.html.

Codex Alimentarius Commission. 2003. *Report of the Fourth Session of the* Ad Hoc *Intergovernmental Task Force on Foods Derived from Biotechnology ALINORM 03/34A.* Rome: Food and Agriculture Organization of the United Nations (FAO) and World Health Organization (WHO).

Cohn, Theodore. 1979. *Canadian Food Aid: Domestic and Foreign Policy Implications.* Denver: University of Denver, Graduate School of International Studies.

———. 1990. *The International Politics of Agricultural Trade: Canadian-American Relations in a Global Agricultural Context.* Vancouver: University of British Columbia Press.

Coleman, Rebecca. 2006. Agricultural Community Reacts to Food Aid Paper. Wheat Letter (U.S. Wheat Associates). October 26. http://www.uswheat.org/newsEvents/wheat Letter/archive/doc/BE670E8E1EE0B3528525766A0055F4C3?OpenDocument#.

Consumers International, Africa Office. 2004. Fact Sheets on Biotechnology and Bio-safety. Harare, Zimbabwe. http://www.corecentre.co.in/Database/Docs/DocFiles/factsheet.pdf.

Coulter, Jonathan, David J. Walker, and Rick Hodges. 2007. Local and Regional Procurement of Food Aid in Africa: Impact and Policy Issues. *Journal of Humanitarian Assistance.* http://jha.ac/2007/10/28/local-and-regional-procurement-of-food-aid-in-africa-impact-and-policy-issues.

CRS (Catholic Relief Services). 2007. CRS Testimony on Food Aid and the Farm Bill. House Foreign Affairs Committee, Subcommittee on Africa and Global Health. May 24. http://www.crs.org/about_us/newsroom/speeches_and_testimony/releases.cfm?ID=40.

Dakar Declaration of Third LDC Trade Ministers' Meeting. 2004. Dakar, Senegal. May 4–5.

Danish Research Institute of Food Economics. 2003. Note on the Harbinson Draft on Modalities in the WTO Agriculture Negotiations. http://www.ictsd.org/issarea/atsd/Resources/docs/note_harbinson.pdf.

Dauenhauer, Katrin. 2003. Health: Africans Challenge Bush Claim That GM Food Is Good for Them. *SUNS: South-North Monitor,* June 23.

Delgado, Christopher, and Cornelia Miller. 1985. Changing Food Patterns in West Africa: Implications for Policy Research. *Food Policy* 10 (1): 63–74.

Denny, Charlotte, and Larry Elliott. 2003. French Plan to Aid Africa Could Be Sunk by Bush. *Guardian,* May 23.

Diven, Polly. 2001. The Domestic Determinants of U.S. Food Aid Policy. *Food Policy* 26 (5): 455–474.

Dugger, Celia. 2005. Food Aid for Africa Languishes in Congress. *International Herald Tribune,* October 13.

———. 2007a. CARE Turns Down Federal Funds for Food Aid. *New York Times,* August 16.

———. 2007b. Charity Finds That U.S. Food Aid for Africa Hurts Instead of Helps. *International Herald Tribune,* August 14. http://www.nytimes.com/2007/08/14/world/americas/14iht-food.4.7116855.html?pagewanted=1.

———. 2007c. For the Hungry in Zambia, U.S. Law May Hinder Urgent Food Aid. *International Herald Tribune,* April 6. http://www.nytimes.com/2007/04/06/world/africa/06iht-web0406-zambia.5175503.html?_r=1&pagewanted=1.

———. 2007d. U.S. Rethinks Foreign Food Aid. *International Herald Tribune,* April 22. http://www.nytimes.com/2007/04/22/world/americas/22iht-food.4.5392898.html.

Dynes, Michael. 2002. Africa Torn between GM Aid and Starvation. *Times* (London), August 6, 12.

Environmental News Service. 2005. Banned as Human Food, StarLink Corn Found in Food Aid. February 16. http://www.ens-newswire.com/ens/feb2005/2005–02–16–09.html.

ETC Group. 2009. Who Will Govern? Rome's Food Summit May Determine Who Decides Who Will Eat. Communique, issue103.http://www.etcgroup.org/upload/publication/pdf_file/ETCCom103GovernanceDec2009_15Nov09.pdf.

European Commission. 2005. *Food Aid.* Nonpaper submitted to WTO. June 18. http://www.iatp.org/tradeobservatory/library.cfm?refID=73273.

European Communities. 2000a. EC Comprehensive Negotiating Proposal, G/AG/NG/W/90. Special session of the WTO Committee on Agriculture. December 14.

———. 2000b. European Communities Proposal, Export Competition, G/AG/NG/W/34. Special session of the WTO Committee on Agriculture. September 18.

———. 2001. Food Aid. Note by the European Communities. Special session of the WTO Committee on Agriculture. December 3–5.

———. 2006. European Communities Contribution on Food Aid, JOB (06)/122. Special session of the WTO Committee on Agriculture. April 25.

European Union (EU). 2003a. European Commission Regrets U.S. Decision to File WTO Case on GMOs as Misguided and Unnecessary. Press Release IP/03/681. May 13.

———. 2003b. WTO and Agriculture: "Harbinson Draft Won't Bridge the Gaps," EU Farm Commissioner Fischler Says. Press Release IP/03/231. February 13. http://ec.europa.eu/agriculture//newsdigest/2003/35.htm#book2.

———. 2005. Food Aid: EU Urges US Reform. Press Release MEMO/05/481. (December 14). http://europa.eu/rapid/pressReleasesAction.do?reference=MEMO/05/481&format=HTML&aged=0&language=EN&guiLanguage=en.

Evans, David. 2007. International Food Aid Programs. Statement of David Evans, vice chair of the Alliance for Food Aid. Hearing of the Agriculture, Rural Development, Food and Drug Administration and Related Agencies Subcommittee of the House Appropriations Committee. October 2.

Executive Office of the President. 2002. President's Management Agenda. Executive Office of the President, Office of Management and Budget. http://www.whitehouse.gov/omb/budget/fy2002/mgmt.pdf.

Falkner, Robert. 2000. Regulating Biotech Trade: The Cartagena Protocol on Biosafety. *International Affairs* 76 (2): 299–313.

———. 2007a. International Cooperation against the Hegemon: The Cartagena Protocol. In *The International Politics of Genetically Modified Food: Diplomacy, Trade and Law,* edited by Robert Falkner, 15–33. Basingstoke, UK: Palgrave Macmillan.

———. 2007b. The Political Economy of "Normative Power" Europe: EU Environmental Leadership in International Biotechnology Regulation. *Journal of European Public Policy* 14 (4): 507–526.

FAO (Food and Agriculture Organization). 2001. Reporting Procedures and Consultative Obligations under the FAO Principles of Surplus Disposal: A Guide for Members of the FAO Consultative Subcommittee on Surplus Disposal. ftp://ftp.fao.org/docrep/fao/007/y1727e/y1727e00.pdf.

———. 2005. Food Aid in the Context of International and Domestic Markets and the Doha Round. FAO Trade Policy Technical Notes No. 8. ftp://ftp.fao.org/docrep/fao/007/j5072e/j5072e00.pdf.

———. 2006a. Food Aid in the Context of International and Domestic Markets and the Doha Round. FAO Trade Policy Briefs (8). ftp://ftp.fao.org/docrep/fao/007/j5072e/j5072e01.pdf.

———. 2006b. Food Security. Policy Brief No. 2. ftp://ftp.fao.org/es/ESA/policybriefs/pb_02.pdf.

———. 2006c. Policy and Regulation of Biotechnology in Food Production. Twenty-Fourth Regional Conference for Africa. ARC/06/INF/5.ftp://ftp.fao.org/unfao/bodies/arc/ 24arc/J6967E.pdf.

———. 2007. *The State of Food and Agriculture 2006: Food Aid for Food Security?* Rome: FAO.

———. 2008. Food Outlook. November. Rome. ftp://ftp.fao.org/docrep/fao/011/ai474e/ai474e00.pdf.

———. 2009a. Declaration of the World Summit on Food Security. November. Rome. www.fao.org/fileadmin/templates/wsfs/Summit/Docs/Final_Declaration/WSFS09_Declaration.pdf.

———. 2009b. More People than Ever are Victims of Hunger. FAO Media Centre. June 20. http://www.fao.org/fileadmin/user_upload/newsroom/docs/Press%20release%20june-en.pdf.

———. 2009c. Reform of the Committee on World Food Security. CFS:2009/2 Rev.1 October. Rome. ftp://ftp.fao.org/docrep/fao/meeting/017/k3023e3.pdf.

FAO Committee on Commodity Problems. 2010. Consultative Subcommittee on Surplus Disposal (CSSD) Forty-Third Report to the CCP. http://www.fao.org/docrep/meeting/018/K7806E.pdf.

FAO, IFAD, IMF, OECD, UNCTAD, WFP, the World Bank, the WTO, IFPRI, and the UN HLTF. 2011. Price Volatility in Food and Agricultural Markets: Policy Responses. June 2. http://www.ifad.org/operations/food/documents/g20.pdf.

*Financial Express.* 2005. EU Blasts U.S. Food Aid, Says Reform Key to WTO. December 14. http://www.financialexpress.com/news/eu-blasts-us-food-aid-says-reform-key-to-wto/75987/0.

Food Aid Committee. 2003. Summary of 88th session of the Food Aid Committee. June.

———. 2009. Food Aid Committee Activities in 2008/09. http://www.foodaidconvention.org/Pdf/activities/0809.pdf.

———. 2010. Meeting of the Food Aid Committee, London, June 4, 2010. Press Release. June 11. http://www.foodaidconvention.org/Pdf/p_r/prfacjun10.pdf.

Food Aid Convention (FAC). 1999. http://www.foodaidconvention.org/en/index/faconvention.aspx.

Fore, Henrietta. 2008. U.S. Response to the Global Food Crisis: New Approaches. Statement before the Foreign Relations Committee May 14. http://foreign.senate.gov/testimony/2008/ForeTestimony080514a.pdf.

Friedmann, Harriet. 1982. The Political Economy of Food: The Rise and Fall of the Post-war International Food Order. In Marxist Inquiries: Studies of Labor, Class, and States, edited by Michael Burawoy and Theda Skocpol. *American Journal of Sociology* 88, Supplement: S248–286.

———. 1993. The Political Economy of Food. *New Left Review* 197: 29–57.

Friends of the Earth Africa. 2006. Africa Contaminated by Unapproved GM Rice from the United States. November 23. http://www.eraction.org/publications/FoEAfrica_briefing01.pdf.

Friends of the Earth International (FOEI). 2003. Playing with Hunger: The Reality behind the Shipment of GMOs as Food Aid. April. Amsterdam. http://www.foei.org/

en/resources/publications/food-sovereignty/2000–2007/playing_with_hunger 2.pdf.

Friends of the Earth Nigeria et al. 2006. Africa Will Not Accept Being the Dumping Ground for GMOs: Contaminated Food Aid Must Be Recalled from Africa. Open Letter to the United States Agency for International Development (USAID) and the World Food Programme (WFP). December 4. http://www. eraction.org/publications/open_letter.pdf.

G20-WTO. 2005. G20 Proposal on Export Competition. July 7. http://www.tradeobservatory. org/library.cfm?RefID=76159.

———. 2006. *G20* Comments on Food Aid. JOB (06)/150. Special session of the Committee on Agriculture. May 19.

GAO (Government Accountability Office). 2002. Food Aid: Experience of U.S. Programs Suggests Opportunities for Improvement. GAO-02–801T. June. http://www.gao. gov/products/GAO-02–801T.

———. 2007. Foreign Assistance: Various Challenges Impede the Efficiency and Effectiveness of U.S. Food Aid. http://www.gao.gov/new.items/d07560.pdf.

———. 2009. International Food Assistance: Local and Regional Procurement Can Enhance the Efficiency of U.S. Food Aid, but Challenges May Constrain Its Implementation. May. http://www.gao.gov/new.items/d09570.pdf.

Gaus, Alexander, Julia Steets, Andrea Binder, Christopher Barrett, and Erin Lentz. 2011. How to Reform the Outdated Food Aid Convention. GPPI—Cornell University United on Food Assistance Project, Policy Brief No. 1. March.

Gentilini, Ugo. 2007. Cash and Food Transfers: A Primer. Rome: WFP. http://www.wfp. org/sites/default/files/OP18_Cash_and_Food_Transfers_Eng%2007.pdf.

George, Susan. 1976. *How the Other Half Dies.* Harmondsworth, UK: Pelican.

Gillies, David. 1994. Export Promotion and Canadian Development Assistance. In *Canadian International Development Assistance Policies,* edited by Cranford Pratt, 186–209. Montreal: McGill-Queen's University Press.

Gillis, Chris. 2004a. U.S.-Flag Vessel Operators Torn by Market. *American Shipper,* May. Available at: http://www.americanshipper.com/paid/MAY04/US_flag_frm.asp Accessed July 27, 2010.

———. 2004b. U.S. Food Aid Volumes Promising: U.S.-Flag Vessel, PVO Lobbies to Work More Closely Together on Mutual Concerns. *American Shipper,* January. http://www.americanshipper.com/paid/JAN04/US_food_aid.asp.

Glover, Dominic. 2003. GMOs and the Politics of International Trade. Democratising Biotechnology: Genetically Modified Crops in Developing Countries Briefing Series, Briefing 5. Brighton, UK: Institute of Development Studies.

GM Food Aid. 2003. *Ecologist* 33 (2): 46.

Goldfarb, Danielle, and Stephen Tapp. 2006. How Canada Can Improve Its Development Aid: Lessons from Other Aid Agencies. CD Howe Institute, Commentary No. 232. April. http://www.cdhowe.org/pdf/commentary_232.pdf.

GRAIN (Genetic Resources Action International). 2002. Better Dead Than GM Fed? *Seedling,* October 2002. http://www.grain.org/seedling/?id=208.

Grassley, Chuck. 2003. Salvation of Starvation? GMO Food Aid to Africa. Remarks of Senator Chuck Grassley to the Congressional Economic Leadership Institute. March 5. http://grassley.senate.gov/releases/2003/p03r03–05a.htm.

Greenpeace UK. 2002. USAID and GM Food Aid. http://www.greenpeace.org.uk/ MultimediaFiles/Live/FullReport/5243.pdf.

Group of Eight. 2008. G-8 Leaders' Statement on Global Food Security. Hokkaido Toyako Summit. July 8. http://www.g7.utoronto.ca/summit/2008hokkaido/2008-food.html.

————. 2009. "L'Aquila" Joint Statement on Global Food Security: L'Aquila Food Security Initiative (AFSI). http://www.g8italia2009.it/static/G8_Allegato/LAquila_Joint_Statement_on_Global_Food_Security%5B1%5D,0.pdf.

Group of Eight Development Ministers. 2010. G-8 Development Ministers' Meeting Chair's Summary. http://g8.gc.ca/6599/g8-development-ministers-meeting-chairs-summary.

Group of Twenty Agriculture Ministers. 2011. Action Plan on Food Price Volatility and Agriculture. 22–23 June. http://agriculture.gouv.fr/IMG/pdf/2011-06-23_-_Action_Plan_-_VFinale.pdf.

Grünewald, François, Domitille Kauffmann, Bonaventure Gbetoho Sokpoh. 2009. Evaluation of the DG ECHO Food Aid Budget Line: Evaluation Report. Group URD for the European Commission. http://www.reliefweb.int/rw/RWFiles2009.nsf/FilesByRWDocUnidFilename/SODA-7WRNWA-full_report.pdf/$File/full_report.pdf Accessed September 30, 2010.

Gupta, Aarti. 2000. Governing Trade in Genetically Modified Organisms: The Cartagena Protocol on Biosafety. *Environment* 42 (4): 22–33.

————. 2010. Transparency to What End? Governing by Disclosure through the Biosafety Clearing House. *Environment and Planning C: Government and Policy* 28 (1): 128–144.

Gupta, Aarti, and Robert Falkner. 2006. The Influence of the Cartagena Protocol on Biosafety: Comparing Mexico, China and South Africa. *Global Environmental Politics* 6 (4): 23–55.

Haas, Peter. 1992. Introduction: Epistemic Communities and International Policy Coordination. *International Organization* 46 (1): 1–35.

Haider, Rizvi. 2006. Senate Resisting Food Aid Reforms That Could Save Money, Lives, Says Top U.S. Official. *OneWorld.net.* January 5.

Hall, Kenji. 2008. How Japan Helped Ease the Rice Crisis. *Business Week,* May 22. http://www.businessweek.com/globalbiz/content/may2008/gb20080522_132137.htm?campaign_id=rss_daily.

Hanrahan, Charles. 2003. Agricultural Export and Food Aid Programs. CRS Issue Brief for Congress. Congressional Research Service, Library of Congress.

————. 2006. Agricultural Export and Food Aid Programs. CRS Issue Brief for Congress. Congressional Research Service, Library of Congress.http://www.au.af.mil/au/awc/awcgate/crs/ib98006.pdf.

————. 2008. International Food Aid and the 2007 Farm Bill. CRS Report. Congressional Research Service, Library of Congress. Updated January 25. http://www.nationalaglawcenter.org/assets/crs/RL34145.pdf.

Hansch, Steven, Andrew Schoenholtz, Alisa Beyninson, Justin Brown, and Don Krumm. 2004. *Genetically Modified Food in the Southern Africa Food Crisis of 2002–2003.* Washington, DC: Institute for the Study of International Migration and Georgetown University School of Foreign Service.

Harris, David. 2007. *Food Aid and Agricultural Trade Reform.* Barton, Australia: Rural Industries Research and Development Corporation.

Harris, Mike, and Preston Manning. 2007. International Leadership by a Canada Strong and Free. Fraser Institute. http://www.fraserinstitute.org/research-news/display.aspx?id=13119.

Harvey, Paul. 2007. Cash-Based Responses in Emergencies. Humanitarian Policy Group Report 24. London: ODI.

Harvey, Paul, Karen Proudlock, Edward Clay, Barry Riley, and Susanne Jaspars. 2010. *Food Aid and Food Assistance in Emergency and Transitional Contexts: A Review of Current Thinking.* London: ODI Humanitarian Policy Group (HPG).

Heady, Derek, and Shenggen Fan. 2008. Anatomy of a Crisis: The Causes and Consequences of Surging Food Prices. *Agricultural Economic,* 30 (S1): 375–91.

Hedges, Stephen. 2007. U.S. Food Aid Reform Plan Has Stout Foes. *Chicago Tribune,* May 31. http://articles.chicagotribune.com/2007–05–28/news/0705280091_1_ food-crisis-food-shortage-food-last-year.

Heinlein, Peter. 2009. Ethiopia Biodiversity Law Threatens Food Aid Shipments. Voice of America News. November 2. http://www.voanews.com/english/news/a-13–2009– 11–02-voa47.html.

Herrick, Clare. 2008. The Southern African Famine and Genetically Modified Food Aid: The Ramifications for the United States and European Union's Trade War. *Review of Radical Political Economics* 40 (1): 50–66.

Ho, Melissa, and Charles Hanrahan. 2010. International Food Aid Programs: Background and Issues. CRS Report for Congress. Congressional Research Service, Library of Congress. http://www.fas.org/sgp/crs/misc/R41072.pdf.

Hoddinott, John, and Chris Barrett. 2007. Counting Commitments in the Food Aid Convention. April 13. http://www.foodgrainsbank.ca/uploads/commitments_ paper_17_april_07.pdf.

Hoddinott, John, Marc Cohen, and Christopher Barrett. 2008. Renegotiating the Food Aid Convention: Background, Context and Issues. *Global Governance* 14 (3): 283–304.

Hopkins, Raymond. 1992. Reform in the International Food Aid Regime: The Role of Consensual Knowledge. *International Organization* 46 (1): 225–264.

———. 1993. The Evolution of Food Aid: Towards a Development-First Regime. In *Why Food Aid?* edited by Vernon Ruttan, 132–152. Baltimore: Johns Hopkins University Press.

———. 2009. Responding to the 2008 "Food Crisis": Lessons from the Evolution of the Food Aid Regime. In *The Global Food Crisis: Governance Challenges and Opportunities,* edited by Jennifer Clapp and Marc J. Cohen, 79–93. Waterloo, Ont.: Wilfrid Laurier University Press.

IDS/CEAS. 1982. *The Community's Cost of Food Aid Study.* 2 vols.). Institute of Development Studies and Centre for European Agricultural Studies. Brighton, UK.

International Grains Council (IGC). 2004. *IGC Annual Report.* London: IGC.

———. 2009. International Grains Council: 60 Years of Successive Agreements. GEN(08/09) 4. http://www.igc.int/en/downloads/brochure/gen08094.pdf.

International Centre for Trade and Sustainable Development (ICTSD). 2001. Agriculture: Members Discuss Environment, Food Aid and Preferences. *Bridges Weekly Trade News Digest,* December 12.

———. 2003a. Agriculture: Harbinson Circulates First Modalities Draft, *Bridges Weekly Trade News Digest,* February 12.

———. 2003b. Agriculture: Harbinson's Modalities Draft Receives Mixed Reactions, *Bridges Weekly Trade News Digest,* February 19.

———. 2003c. Agriculture Negotiations at the WTO: Post-Cancun Outlook Report, 9. Geneva: ICTSD.

———. 2004. African NGOs Voice Concern to Food Aid Donors. *Bridges Weekly Trade News Digest,* May 14.

———. 2005. WTO Food Aid Disciplines Could Increase Hunger, Warns UN Agency Chief. *Bridges Weekly Trade News Digest,* May 11.

Isaac, Grant, and William Kerr. 2002. Genetically Modified Organisms at the World Trade Organization: A Harvest of Trouble. *Journal of World Trade* 37 (6): 1083–1095.

Isenman, Paul. J., and Hans Wolfgang Singer. 1977. Food Aid: Disincentive Effects and Their Policy Implications. *Economic Development and Cultural Change* 25 (2): 205–237.

IWC (International Wheat Council). 1974. Report by the Executive Committee. Seventy-First session. London, November 25–28. CL71/8. Photocopy on file with the author.

IWC Secretariat. 1991. Food Aid Convention of the International Wheat Agreement: A Note by the Secretariat of the IWC. London: IWC.

Jackson, Tony. 1982. *Against the Grain: The Dilemma of Project Food Aid*. Oxford: Oxfam.

———. 1983. A Triumph of Hope over Experience: An Assessment of the Recent Evaluation of the EEC Food Aid Program. *IDS Bulletin* 14 (2): 53–55.

James, Clive. 2003. Preview: Global Status of Commercialized Transgenic Crops: 2003. Executive Summary. ISAAA Briefs No. 30: 3–4. International Service for the Acquisition of Agri-Biotech Applications (ISAAA). Ithaca, NY. http://www.isaaa.org/resources/publications/briefs/30/default.html.

Jones, Gillian. 2004. Africa GM Food Aid Claims are "Rubbish." *Mail and Guardian,* May 4.

Josling, Tim, and Dale Hathaway. 2004. This Far and No Farther? Nudging Agricultural Reform Forward. International Economics Policy Briefs, No. PB04–1 Washington, DC: IIE. http://www.iie.com/publications/pb/pb04–1.pdf.

Karenbu, M., D. Wafula, and M. Waithaka. 2008. Status of Biotechnology Policies and Biosafety Legislation in the COMESA Region. http://programs.ifpri.org/pbs/pdf/statuscomesa.pdf.

Killen, Brenda, and Andrew Rogerson. 2010. Global Governance for International Development: Who's in Charge?" OECD Development Brief (2), June. http://www.oecd.org/dataoecd/34/63/45569897.pdf.

Kinetz, Erika. 2010. Massive Wheat Stockpile Rots in India. *Globe and Mail,* August 6. http://www.theglobeandmail.com/report-on-business/massive-wheat-stockpile-rots-in-india/article1664176.

Kirwin, Joe. 2005. EC Retains Doha Negotiating Mandate as French Plan to Monitor Offers Fails. *International Trade Reporter,* October 20.

Kneen, Brewster. 1999. *Farmageddon.* Gabriola Island, BC: New Society Publishers.

Konandreas, Panos. 2005. Multilateral Mechanisms Governing Food Aid and the Need for an Enhanced Role of the CSSD in the Context of the New WTO Disciplines on Agriculture. Rome: FAO. http://www.fao.org/fileadmin/templates/loge/Speeches_and_statements/BackroundPapers/CSSD-January2005.pdf.

———. 2007. WTO Negotiations on Agriculture: A Compromise on Food Aid is Possible. In *WTO Rules for Agriculture Compatible with Development,* edited by Jamie Morrison and Alexander Sarris, 313–332. Rome: FAO.

Kripke, Gawain. 2009. The Uses of Crisis: Progress on Implementing U.S. Local/Regional Procurement of Food Aid. In *The Global Food Crisis: Governance Challenges and Opportunities,* edited by Jennifer Clapp and Marc J. Cohen, 113–126. Waterloo, Ont.: Wilfrid Laurier University Press.

Kuyek, Devlin, 2002. Past Predicts the Future—GM Crops and African Farmers. *Seedling,* October 2002. http://www.grain.org/seedling/seed-02–10–3-en.cfm.

Lean, Geoffrey. 2000. Rejected GM Food Dumped on the Poor. *Independent* (London), June 18.

Leeder, Jessica. 2011. Campbell's Nourish Brand Tackles Hunger through Canada's Food Banks. *Globe and Mail,* February 26.

Levidow, Les, Susan Carr, and David Wield. 2005. European Union Regulation of Agri-biotechnology: Precautionary Links between Science, Expertise and Policy. *Science and Public Policy* 32 (4): 261–276.

Levinson, Ellen. 2007. Written Testimony of Ellen S. Levinson before the Committee on Agriculture, Subcommittee on Specialty Crops, Rural Development, and Foreign Agriculture Programs, U.S. House of Representatives. May 10. http://www.allianceforfoodaid.com/IssuesandPress/Testimony/tabid/84/Default.aspx.

Lieberman, Sarah, and Tim Gray. 2008. GMOs and the Developing World: A Precautionary Interpretation of Biotechnology. *British Journal of Politics and International Relations* 10 (3): 395–411.

Lillis, Mike. 2008. Few Friends on Hill for Bush's Food Aid Plan: Congress Certain to Block Plan to Buy from Foreign Farms. *Washington Independent,* February 8. http://washingtonindependent.com/2358/few-friends-on-hill-for-bushs-food-aid-plan.

Loewenberg, Samuel. 2008. Bush in Food Aid Fight with Congress. *Politico,* February 6. http://www.politico.com/news/stories/0208/8378.html.

Lynn, Jonathan. 2011. WTO Chief Urges Alternatives to Food Export Curbs. Reuters, January 22. http://www.reuters.com/article/2011/01/22/trade-food-idUSLDE 70K1TK20110122.

Madeley, John. 2000. *Hungry for Trade: How the Poor Pay for Free Trade.* London: Zed Books.

Madich, Jim. 2005. Food Aid Programs. Statement of Jim Madich, vice president, Horizon Milling, Wayzata MN, on behalf of the North American Millers Association. Hearing before the Subcommittee on Specialty Crops and Foreign Agriculture Programs of the Committee on Agriculture. June 16. http://agriculture.house.gov/hearings/109/10910.pdf.

Madrid, René. 2004. Thematic Evaluation of Food-Aid Policy and Food-Aid Management and Special Operations in Support of Food Security. Evaluation for the European Commission. Vol. 2. http://ec.europa.eu/europeaid/how/evaluation/evaluation_reports/reports/sector/951657_vol2_en.pdf.

Margulis, Matias. 2005. Changing Canadian Food Aid Rules Only First Step, *Toronto Star,* September 27.

Martin, Eric. 2011. World's Poor "One Shock" from Crisis as Food Prices Climb, Zoellick Says. Bloomberg, April 16. http://www.bloomberg.com/news/2011–04–16/zoellick-says-world-economy-one-shock-away-from-food-crisis-1-.html.

Maxwell, Daniel.2007. Global Factors Shaping the Future of Food Aid: The Implications for WFP. *Disasters* 31 (S1): S25–S39.

Maxwell, Simon J., ed. 1982. An Evaluation of the EEC Food Aid Programme. Institute of Development Studies. Brighton, UK: IDS.

Maxwell, Simon, and Hans W. Singer. 1979. Food Aid to Developing Countries: A Survey. *World Development* 7 (3): 225–247.

McCreary, Ian. 2011. Protecting the Food Insecure in Volatile International Markets: Food Reserves and Other Policy Options. Canadian Foodgrains Bank Occasional Paper. http://www.foodgrainsbank.ca/uploads/Food%20Security%20Price%20Volatility%20and%20Policy%20Responses-%20final%20-%2025%20March%2011.pdf.

Mellen, Matt. 2003. Who Is Getting Fed? *Seedling,* April 2003. http://www.grain.org/seedling/?id=231.

Mercosur. 2001. Export Credits for Agricultural Products, G/AG/NG/W/139. Special session of the WTO Committee on Agriculture. March 21.

Ministry of Foreign Affairs of Japan. 2007. Comments of the Government of Japan on 2007 National Trade Estimate Report. http://www.mofa.go.jp/region/n-america/us/economy/date/nte2007.pdf.

Mitchell, Donald. 2008. A Note on Rising Food Prices. Policy Research Working Paper No. 4682. Washington, DC: World Bank.

Mitra, Siddhartha, and Tim Josling. 2009. Agricultural Export Restrictions: Welfare Implications and Trade Disciplines. International Food & Agricultural Trade Policy Council. IPC Position Paper. http://www.agritrade.org/documents/ExportRestrictions_final.pdf.

Mongolia. 2004. Permanent Mission of Mongolia. Letter to Tim Groser July 27.

Moola, Shenaz, and Victor Munnik. 2007. *GMOs in Africa: Food and Agriculture Status Report 2007*. Johannesburg: African Centre for Biosafety.

Morris, James. 2002. Lift a Tragic Blockade on Aid: Biotech Food Can Save Millions of African Lives. *International Herald Tribune*, September 19. http://www.nytimes.com/2002/09/19/opinion/19iht-edjames_ed3_.html.

———. 2003. Statement by the Executive Director of World Food Programme to the 25th Anniversary Meeting of the IFAD Governing Council. 19 February. http://www.ifad.org/events/gc/26/speech/wfp.htm.

Mousseau, Frederic. 2005. Food Aid or Food Sovereignty: Ending Hunger in Our Time. http://www.oaklandinstitute.org/pdfs/fasr.pdf.

———. 2008. The Status of International Food Aid Negotiations: An Update to Food Aid or Food Sovereignty: Ending Hunger in Our Time. http://oaklandinstitute.org/pdfs/Food_aid_update.pdf.

———. 2009. From Food Handouts to Integrated Food Policies. 2009. In *The Global Food Crisis: Governance Challenges and Opportunities*, edited by Jennifer Clapp and Marc J. Cohen. Waterloo, Ont.: Wilfrid Laurier University Press.

Mulvaney, Patrick. 2004. The Dumping Ground: Africa and GM Food Aid. *Open Democracy*, 28 April. http://www.opendemocracy.net/globalization-trade_economy_justice/article_1876.jsp.

Murphy, Sophia. 2005. Food Aid: What Role for the WTO? Minneapolis: Institute for Agriculture and Trade Policy. http://www.iatp.org/iatp/publications.cfm?accountID=451&refID=77567.

———. 2009. Strategic Grain Reserves in an Era of Volatility. Minneapolis: Institute for Agriculture and Trade Policy. http://www.iatp.org/tradeobservatory/library.cfm?refid=106857.

———. 2010. Trade and Food Reserves: What Role Does the WTO Play? Minneapolis: Institute for Agriculture and Trade Policy. http://www.iatp.org/iatp/publications.cfm?refid=107697.

Murphy, Sophia, Ben Lilliston, and Mary Beth Lake. 2005. WTO Agreement on Agriculture: A Decade of Dumping. Minneapolis: Institute for Agriculture and Trade Policy. http://www.tradeobservatory.org/library.cfm?refid=48532.

Murphy, Sophia, and Kathy McAfee. 2005. U.S. Food Aid: Time to Get it Right. Minneapolis: Institute for Agriculture and Trade Policy. http://www.tradeobservatory.org/library.cfm?refid=73512.

Narlikar, Amrita, and Rorden Wilkinson. 2004. Collapse at the WTO: A Cancun Post-mortem. *Third World Quarterly* 25 (3): 447–460.

Natsios, Andrew. 2005a. Briefing by USAID Administrator Andrew Natsios and Deputy U.S. Trade Representative Karan Bhatia, WTO Hong Kong Ministerial. December 14. http://ustraderep.gov/Document_Library/Transcripts/2005/December/Briefing_by_USAID_Administrator_Andrew_Natsios_Deputy_US_Trade_Representative_Karan_Bhatia,_WTO_Hong_Kong_Ministerial.html.

———. 2005b. Keynote address: Can Food Aid Be a More Effective Development Tool? Centre for Global Development, December 9. http://www.cgdev.org/content/calendar/detail/5164.

———. 2005c. Remarks by Andrew Natsios, Administrator, U.S. Agency for International Development: The Local Purchase Initiative. Kansas City Export Food Aid Conference. May 3. http://www.usaid.gov/press/speeches/2005/sp050503.html.

Newell, Peter, and Ruth Mackenzie. 2000. The 2000 Cartagena Protocol on Biosafety: Legal and Political Dimensions. *Global Environmental Change* 10 (4): 313–317.

Nichols, John. 2005. Critics Call for Changes to U.S. Food Aid Policy: Transcript from television program *Market to Market*, April 18. http://www.iptv.org/mtom/archivedfeature.cfm?fid=289.

OECD (Organisation for Economic Cooperation and Development). 1987. *1987 DAC Guiding Principles for Associated Financing and Tied and Partially Untied Official Development Assistance.* Paris: OECD.

———. 2005. *The Paris Declaration on Aid Effectiveness.* Paris: OECD.

———. 2007. *Canada: Development Assistance Committee (DAC) Peer Review.* Paris: OECD. http://www.oecd.org/dataoecd/48/61/39515510.pdf.

———. 2008a. *DAC Recommendation on Untying ODA.* Paris: OECD. http://www.oecd.org/dataoecd/61/43/41707972.pdf.

———. 2008b. The Paris Declaration on Aid Effectiveness and the Accra Agenda for Action. Paris: OECD. http://www.oecd.org/dataoecd/30/63/43911948.pdf.

———. 2009. *Agricultural Policies in OECD Countries: Monitoring and Evaluation (Highlights).* Paris: OECD. http://www.oecd.org/dataoecd/37/16/43239979.pdf.

Office of the Auditor General of Canada. 2003. Petition pursuant to section 22 of the Auditor General Act Genetically Engineered (GE) Crops: World Trade Organisation, Biosafety Protocol, International Trade & Development and the Codex Alimentarius. Filed by Greenpeace Canada. http://www.oag-bvg.gc.ca/internet/English/pet_085_e_28797.html.

Overseas Development Institute. 2000. Reforming Food Aid: Time to Grasp the Nettle? ODI Briefing Paper. January. http://www.odi.org.uk/resources/download/1954.pdf.

Oxfam America. 2005. Food Aid Programs. Statement Oxfam America. Hearing before the Subcommittee on Specialty Crops and Foreign Agriculture Programs of the Committee on Agriculture. June 16. http://agriculture.house.gov/hearings/109/10910.pdf.

Oxfam Great Britain. 2006. *Cash-Transfer Programming in Emergencies.* London: Oxfam Publishing.

Oxfam International. 2002a. Crisis in Southern Africa. Oxfam Briefing Paper 23. http://www.oxfam.org.uk/resources/policy/conflict_disasters/downloads/bp23_africa.rtf.

———. 2002b. Rigged Rules and Double Standards: Trade, Globalisation, and the Fight against Poverty. http://www.cbnrm.net/pdf/oxfam_001_tradesummary.pdf.

———. 2005. Food Aid or Hidden Dumping: Separating Wheat from Chaff. Oxfam Briefing Paper No. 71. http://www.oxfam.org/en/policy/food-aid-or-hidden-dumping.

———. 2009. Bridging the Divide: The Reform of Global Food Security Governance. Oxfam Briefing Note. November 16. http://www.oxfam.org.uk/resources/policy/conflict_disasters/downloads/bn_bridging_the_divide_en_web_111109.pdf.

Paarlberg, Robert. 2000. The Global Food Fight. *Foreign Affairs* 79 (3): 24–38.

———. 2002. The Real Threat to GM Crops in Poor Countries: Consumer and Policy Resistance to GM Foods in Rich Countries. *Food Policy* 27: 247–250.

———. 2008. *Starved for Science: How Biotechnology Is Being Kept Out of Africa.* Cambridge, MA: Harvard University Press.

Parliament of Canada. 2007. Overcoming 40 Years of Failure: A New Roadmap for Sub-Saharan Africa. Report of the Standing Committee on Foreign Affairs and International Trade. http://parl.gc.ca/39/1/parlbus/commbus/senate/Com-e/fore-e/rep-e/repafrifeb07-e.pdf.

Parotte, John H. 1983. The Food Aid Convention: Its History and Scope. *IDS Bulletin.* 14 (2): 10–15.

Partnership to Cut Hunger and Poverty in Africa. 2008. The 2008 Farm Bill: Implications for Food Aid. Policy Brief No. 3. http://www.partnership-africa.org/content/policy-brief-3.

Pearce, Fred. 2003. UN Is Slipping Modified Food into Aid. *New Scientist* 175 (2361): 5.

Prakash, Aseem, and Kelly Kollman. 2003. Biopolitics in the EU and the U.S.: A Race to the Bottom or Convergence to the Top? *International Studies Quarterly* 47 (4): 617–641.

Pratt, Sean. 2006. U.S. Wheat Associates Opposed to Food Aid Changes. *Western Producer,* February 9.

Promar International. 2010. *Impacts on the U.S.* Economy of Shipping International Food Aid. Report Prepared for USA Maritime. http://www.usamaritime.org/pdf/Promar_Study_Jun_2010_Jul_2010.pdf.

Pruzin, Daniel. 2001. United States Rejects Call for WTO Talks on New Disciplines for Food Aid Distribution. *International Trade Reporter* 18 (49): 1979.

———. 2004. Canadian Rejects U.S., EU Demands in WTO for Disciplines on State Trading Enterprises. *International Trade Reporter* 21 (21): 852.

———. 2005a. Key Ministers Set March Date to Resolve Farm Export Subsidy Issues in WTO Talks. *International Trade Reporter* 22 (48): 1989.

———. 2005b. U.N. Human Rights Official Warns Against WTO Restrictions on Food Aid. *International Trade Reporter.* 22 (29): 1195.

———. 2005c. U.N. Official Issues Warning on New WTO Food Aid Disciplines. *International Trade Reporter* 22 (19): 773.

———. 2006a. U.S. Offers New Initiatives on Green Box, Food Aid, State Trading Firms in Farm Talks. *International Trade Reporter* 23 (15): 556.

———. 2006b. WTO Wraps Up Disappointing Week of Agriculture Talks; No Advances Made. *International Trade Reporter* 23 (13): 479.

Pruzin, Daniel, and Gary Yerkey. 2004. Delays Occur in New WTO Framework Text; Ag Chair Warns Draft Is Substantially Revised. *International Trade Reporter* 21 (3): 1266.

Pruzin, Daniel, Gary Yerkey, and Joe Kirwin. 2004. EU Members Express Anger at Plan to Negotiate End of Export Subsidies. *International Trade Reporter* 21 (20).

Ramachandran, Vijaya, Benjamin Leo, and Owen McCarthy. 2010. Financing Food Assistance: Options for the World Food Programme to Save Lives and Dollars. Center for Global Development Working Paper No. 209. http://www.cgdev.org/files/1424053_file_Ramachandran_Leo_McCarthy_WFP_FINAL.pdf.

*Religion and Ethics News Weekly.* 2010. Andrew Natsios Extended Interview. February 19. http://www.pbs.org/wnet/religionandethics/episodes/february-19–2010/andrew-natsios-extended-interview/5720.

Renzaho, André M. N. 2002. Human Right to Food Security in Refugee Settings: Rhetoric versus Reality. *Australian Journal of Human Rights* 8 (1): 43–56.

Reutlinger, Shlomo. 1999. From "Food Aid" to "Aid for Food": Into the 21st Century. *Food Policy* 24 (1): 7–15

Rice, Andrew. 2010. The Peanut Solution. *New York Times,* September 7 http://www.nytimes.com/2010/09/05/magazine/05Plumpy-t.html?pagewanted=all.

Rosendal, Kristin. 2005. Governing GMOs in the EU: A Deviant Case of Environmental Policy-Making? *Global Environmental Politics* 5 (1): 82–104.

Rothschild, Emma. 1976. Food Politics. *Foreign Affairs* 54 (January): 285–307.

Rugaber, Christopher. 2004. U.S. Farm Groups Endorse WTO Framework Provisions on STEs, Food Aid. *International Trade Reporter* 21 (33): 1342.

Russian Federation. 2008. Russia-United Nations. Press release. http://www.un.int/russia/new/MainRoot/docs/off_news/130109/newen2.htm.

Ruth, Bart. 2005. *Food Aid Programs.* Statement of Bart Ruth, past president, American Soybean Association. Hearing before the Subcommittee on Specialty Crops and Foreign Agriculture Programs of the Committee on Agriculture. June 16. http://agriculture.house.gov/hearings/109/10910.pdf Accessed July 28, 2010.

Ruttan, Vernon. 1993. The Politics of U.S. Food Aid Policy: A Historical Review. *In Why Food Aid?* edited by Vernon Ruttan, 2–38. Baltimore: Johns Hopkins University Press.

Salzman, Avi. 2008. U.S. Food Aid: We Pay for Shipping. *Business Week,* July 9. http://www.businessweek.com/bwdaily/dnflash/content/jul2008/db2008078_468803.htm.

Sandefur, Charles. 2007. Examining the Performance of U.S. Trade and Food Aid Programs for the 2007 Farm Bill. Written Statement of Charles Sandefur, Alliance for Food Aid, before the Committee on Agriculture, Nutrition and Forestry. March 21. http://agriculture.senate.gov/Hearings/hearings.cfm?hearingid=2637&witnessId=6170.

Schofield, Hugh. 2010. Legal Fight over Plumpy'nut, The Hunger Wonder-Product. BBC News. April 8. http://news.bbc.co.uk/2/hi/europe/8610427.stm.

Schultz, Theodore. 1960. Value of U.S. Farm Surpluses to Underdeveloped Countries. *Journal of Farm Economics* 42 (2): 1019–1030.

Segarra, Alejandro E., and Jean M. Rawson. 2001. StarLink™ Corn Controversy: Background, CRS Report for Congress. Congressional Research Service, Library of Congress. http://www.ncseonline.org/nle/crsreports/agriculture/ag-101.cfm.

Sen, Amartya. 1981. *Poverty and Famines: An Essay on Entitlement and Deprivation.* Oxford: Oxford University Press.

Shaw, D. John. 2001. *The UN World Food Programme and the Development of Food Aid.* Basingstoke, UK: Palgrave Macmillan.

Shaw, D. John, and Edward Clay. 1993. *World Food Aid: Experiences of Recipients and Donors.* Rome: World Food Programme; London: James Currey.

Shaw, D. John, and H. W. Singer. 1996. A Future Food Aid Regime: Implications of the Final Act of the Uruguay Round. *Food Policy* 21 (4/5): 447–460.

Shaw, Ron, and Craig MacKay. 2006. An Analysis of PL-480 Title II Monetization Data 2001–2005: Impacts on Domestic Production, Local Marketing and Global Trade. World Vision and Save the Children. http://www.savethe children.org/publications/technical-resources/hunger-malnutrition/Monetization-Data-Study-Paper-Final-09-Feb-06.pdf.

Sheeran, Josette. 2008. Statement by Josette Sheeran, executive director UN World Food Programme. 11th ordinary session of the Assembly of the African Union. June 30.http://documents.wfp.org/stellent/groups/public/documents/news room/wfp182389.pdf.

Simmons, Emmy. 2007. Reconsidering Food Aid: The Dialogue Continues. Partnership to Cut Hunger and Poverty in Africa. http://www.partnership-africa.org/content/reconsidering-food-aid-dialogue-continues.

———. 2009. *Monetization of Food Aid: Reconsidering U.S. Policy and Practice.* Washington, DC: Partnership to Cut Hunger and Poverty in Africa.

Singer, Hans, John Wood, and Tony Jennings. 1987. *Food Aid: The Challenge and the Opportunity.* Oxford: Clarendon Press.

Singh, Simron Jit. 2009. Complex Disasters: The Nicobar Islands in the Grip of Humanitarian Aid. *Geographische Rundschau International Edition* 5 (3): 48–56.

Slayton, Tom, and C. Peter Timmer. 2008. Japan, China and Thailand Can Solve the Rice Crisis—But U.S. Leadership Is Needed. Centre for Global Development. http://www.cgdev.org/files/16028_file_Solve_the_Rice_Crisis_UPDATED.pdf.

Sobhan, Rehman. 1979. The Politics of Food and Famine in Bangladesh. *Economic and Political Weekly* 14 (48): 1973–1980.

Stapp, Katherine. 2003. Biotech Boom Linked to Development Dollars, Say Critics. *South-North Development Monitor (SUNS)*, December 5.

Steven, Andrew Schoenholtz, Alisa Beyninson, Justin Brown, and Don Krumm. 2004. *Genetically Modified Food in the Southern Africa Food Crisis of 2002–2003.* Washington, DC: Institute for the Study of International Migration and Georgetown University School of Foreign Service.

TAFAD (Trans-Atlantic Food Assistance Dialogue). 2010a. TAFAD Vision for a Renewed Food Aid Convention. http://www.partnership-africa.org/sites/default/files/TAFAD%20Vision%20for%20a%20New%20Food%20Assistance%20Convention.pdf.

———. 2010b. TAFAD's Proposals for a New Food Aid/Assistance Convention. September 8.

———. 2010c. Why Reform the Food Aid Convention? March 29 http://www.partnership-africa.org/sites/default/files/Why%20Reform%20the%20Food%20Aid%20Convention%20-%20March%202010.pdf.

Trans-Atlantic NGO Food Aid Policy Dialogue (TAFAD). 2006. *Proposals for a Renewed Food Aid Convention.* September. http://www.foodgrainsbank.ca/uploads/TAFAD_detailed_statement.pdf.

Trans-Atlantic NGO Food Aid Policy Dialogue (TAFAD). 2007. Letter to Mr. William Whelan, Chair of the Food Aid Convention. May 22. http://www.foodgrainsbank.ca/uploads/TAFAD_letter_may_07.pdf.

Tarnoff, Curt, and Larry Nowels. 2005. Foreign Aid: An Introductory Overview of U.S. Programs and Policy. CRS Report for Congress. Updated January 19. http://fpc.state.gov/documents/organization/45939.pdf.

Taylor, Ed, and Daniel Pruzin. 2004. Top Trade Officials Announce "Convergence" on Points Related to WTO Agriculture Talks. *International Trade Reporter* 21 (25): 1011.

Third World Network. 2002. GMO Food Aid: Ripple in the WSSD Corridors.http://www.twnside.org.sg/title/twr145g.htm.

Thirion, Marie-Ceclie. 2000. EU Food Aid and NGOs. In *Food Aid and Human Security,* edited by Edward Clay and Olav Stokke, 274–288. London: Frank Cass.

Thompson, Wyatt. 2001. Food Aid in the Context of the WTO Negotiations on Agriculture. http://www.fao.org/docrep/005/y3733e/y3733e06.htm.

Thurow, Roger, and Scott Kilman. 2005. Farmers, Charities Join Forces to Block Famine-Relief Revamp. *Wall Street Journal,* October 26.

Timmer, Peter. 2005. *Food Aid: Doing Well by Doing Good.* Washington, DC: Center for Global Development.

Tschirley, David, and Anne Marie del Castillo. 2007. Local and Regional Food Aid Procurement: An Assessment of Experience in Africa and Elements of Good Donor Practice. Michigan State University International Development Working Paper No. 91.

Tschirley, David, and Julie Howard. 2003. Title II Food Aid and Agricultural Development in Sub-Saharan Africa: Towards a Principled Argument for When, and When Not, to Monetize. Food Security International Development Working Paper 81. http://www.aec.msu.edu/fs2/papers/idwp81.pdf.

Tschirley, David, Cynthia Donovan, and Michael Weber. 1996. Food Aid and Food Markets: Lessons from Mozambique. *Food Policy* 21 (2): 189–209.

UNEP (United Nations Environment Programme). 2006. Africa Environment Outlook 2: Our Environment, Our Wealth. http://www.unep.org/dewa/africa/publications/AEO-2/aeo-2report.asp.

United Nations. 2002. United Nations Statement Regarding the Use of GM Foods as Food Aid in Southern Africa. 23 August. http://documents.wfp.org/stellent/groups/public/documents/newsroom/wfp076534.pdf Accessed May 1, 2010.

United Nations High-Level Task Force on the Global Food Security Crisis. 2008. Comprehensive Framework for Action. July. http://www.un.org/issues/food/taskforce/Documentation/CFA%20Web.pdf.

United States Government. 2005. Food Aid (Draft).

United States Office of Management and Budget. 2001. Blueprint for New Beginnings, A Responsible Budget for America's Priorities. http://www.gpoaccess.gov/usbudget/fy02/pdf/blueprnt.pdf.

United States Senate. 2000. U.S. Agriculture Export Programs. Hearing before the Subcommittee on Production and Price Competitiveness, of the Committee on Agriculture, Nutrition, and Forestry. July 18. http://frwebgate.access.gpo.gov/cgi-bin/useftp.cgi?IPaddress=162.140.64.183&filename=70092.pdf&directory=/diska/wais/data/106_senate_hearings.

———. 2001. *Review of the Trade Title of the Farm Bill*. Hearing before the Committee on Agriculture, Nutrition, and Forestry. April 25. http://frwebgate.access.gpo.gov/cgi-bin/getdoc.cgi?dbname=107_senate_hearings&docid=f:78561.pdf.

United States Trade Representative (USTR). 2005. Facts on Global Reform. Doha Development Agenda Policy Brief. December. http://ustraderep.gov/assets/Document_Library/Fact_Sheets/2005/asset_upload_file582_8531.pdf.

USAID (United States Agency for International Development). 1995. Food Aid and Food Security Policy Paper, PN-ABU-219.

———. 2003. United States and Food Assistance. Africa Humanitarian Crisis. July 3. http://www.usaid.gov/about/africafoodcrisis/bio_answers.html#8.

———. 2006. U.S. International Food Assistance Report 2006. http://www.usaid.gov/our_work/humanitarian_assistance/ffp/fy06_usifar.pdf.

———. 2007. U.S. International Food Assistance Report 2007. http://www.usaid.gov/our_work/humanitarian_assistance/ffp/fy07_usifar.pdf.

———. 2008. U.S. International Food Assistance Report 2008. http://www.usaid.gov/our_work/humanitarian_assistance/ffp/fy08_usifar_revised.pdf.

———. 2009. U.S. International Food Assistance Report 2009. USAID. http://www.usaid.gov/our_work/humanitarian_assistance/ffp/fy09.ifar.pdf.

———. 2010. A Report to Congress on the US75 Million FY09 Food Security Strategy: Targeted Agriculture Funds. http://www.usaid.gov/press/congressional/2009/cr_foodsecstrat_fy2009.pdf.

USDA (United States Department of Agriculture. 2004. Cartagena Protocol on Biosafety Update for U.S. Food Aid Program Partners. http://www.fas.usda.gov/info/regs/cpbupdate041504.htm (April 15).

———. 2007. USDA's 2007 Farm Bill Proposals. http://www.usda.gov/documents/07final fbp.pdf Accessed July 28, 2010.

———. 2009. The Use of Local and Regional Procurement in Meeting the Food Needs of Those Affected by Disasters and Food Crises. http://reliefweb.int/rw/lib.nsf/db900sid/SNAA-7X35DE/$file/usda-jan2009.pdf?openelement.

———. 2010. Grain: World Markets and Trade. December. http://www.fas.usda.gov/grain/circular/2010/12–10/grainfull12–10.pdf.

USDA Farm Service Agency. 1999. Commodity Credit Corporation Fact Sheet. United States Department of Agriculture. November. http://www.fsa.usda.gov/FSA/newsReleases?area=newsroom&subject=landing&topic=pfs&newstype=prfactsheet&type=detail&item=pf_19991101_comop_en_ccc.html.

USWA (U.S. Wheat Associates). 2007. Wheat Letter. May 3. http://www.uswheat.org/newsEvents/wheatLetter/archive/doc/482A95524A2583598525766A0055EBEA?OpenDocument#.

Uvin, Peter. 1992. Regime, Surplus and Self-Interest: The International Politics of Food Aid. *International Studies Quarterly* 36 (3): 293–312.

Von Braun, Joachim, Akhter Ahmed, Kwadwo Asenso-Okyere, Shenggen Fan, Ashok Gulati, John Hoddinott, Rajul Pandya-Lorch, Mark W. Rosegrant, Marie Ruel, Maximo Torero, Teunis van Rheenen, and Klaus von Grebmer. 2008. *High Food Prices: The What, Who and How of Proposed Policy Actions.* Washington, DC: International Food Policy Research Institute.

Von Braun, Joachim, Justin Lin, and Maximo Torero. 2009. Eliminating Drastic Food Price Spikes—A Three Pronged Approach for Reserves. IFPRI Note. Washington, DC: International Food Policy Research Institute. http://www.ifpri.org/sites/default/files/publications/reservenote20090302.pdf.

Von Braun, Joachim, and Maximo Torero. 2008. Physical and Virtual Global Food Reserves to Protect the Poor and Prevent Market Failure. IFPRI Policy Brief No. 4. Washington, DC: International Food Policy Research Institute.http://www.ifpri.org/sites/default/files/pubs/pubs/bp/bp004.pdf.

Von Helldorf, Klaus, with Ch. Bossard, P. Hoguet and A. Szarf. 1979. Food Aid Policy Report: Food Aid from the European Commission. In *The European Alternatives: An Inquiry into the Policies of the European Community,* edited by Ghita Ionescu And Alphen aan den Rijn. The Netherlands: Sijtoff and Noordhoff.

Wahlberg, Katarina. 2008. Food Aid for the Hungry? Global Policy Forum website (January). http://www.globalpolicy.org/component/content/article/217/46251.html.

Wallerstein, Mitchel B. 1980. *Food for War/Food for Peace: United States Food Aid in a Global Context.* Cambridge, MA: M.I.T. Press.

Watkins, Kevin. 2003. Northern Agricultural Policies and World Poverty: Will the Doha "Development Round" Make a Difference? Paper presented at the World Bank Annual Bank Conference of Development Economics (Paris). London: Oxfam. http://www.intermonoxfam.org/cms/HTML/espanol/452/Politicas_agrarias_norte_pobreza_mundial.pdf.

WETEC (Wheat Export Trade Education Committee), NAWG (National Association of Wheat Growers), and USWA (U.S. Wheat Associates). 2006. Keep the Food in Food Aid. http://www.wheatworld.org/wp-content/uploads/foodaid-keep-the-food-in-food-aid-20060209.pdf.

WFP (World Food Programme). 2003. Policy on Donations of Foods Derived from Biotechnology (GM/Biotech Foods).WFP/EB.A/2003/5-B/Rev.1 (May 29).

———. 2005a. Doha Round Must Deliver Commerce with a Conscience. Press release. December 8. http://www.wfp.org/stories/doha-round-must-deliver-commerce-conscience.

———. 2005b. UN Agencies Ask WTO to Protect Humanitarian Food Aid. Press release. August 12. http://www.wfp.org/news/news-release/un-agencies-ask-wto-protect-humanitarian-food-aid.

———. 2008a. Food Aid Flows 2007. http://documents.wfp.org/stellent/groups/public/documents/newsroom/wfp180471.pdf.

———. 2008b. Strategic Plan 2008–2011. http://www.wfp.org/sites/default/files/WFP_Strategic_Plan_2008–2011_0.pdf.

———. 2008c. Vouchers and Cash Transfers as Food Assistance Instruments: Opportunities and Challenges. http://home.wfp.org/stellent/groups/public/documents/communications/wfp200471.pdf.

———. 2008d. WFP Letter of Appeal to Government Donors to Address Critical Funding Gap. March 20. http://documents.wfp.org/stellent/groups/public/documents/newsroom/wfp174162.pdf.

———. 2008e. WFP Welcomes G8 Resolve to Tackle Hunger. Press release. July 10. http://www.wfp.org/node/165.

———. 2009a. Hunger in 2009: A Recipe for Disaster. http://documents.wfp.org/stellent/groups/communications_content/documents/webcontent/wfp207754.pdf.

————. 2009b. WFP Commends G8 Leaders' Focus on Food Security; Urges Support for Hunger Needs of World's Poorest. July 7. http://www.wfp.org/news/news-release/wfp-commends-g8-leaders-focus-food-security-urges-support-hunger-needs-worlds-poorest.

————. 2009c. WFP Food Procurement Chief Praises India for "Humanitarian Exception." Press release. http://www.wfp.org/stories/food-procurement-chief%20-india-humanitarian-exception.

————. 2009d. World Food Programme 2009 (Annual Report). http://documents.wfp.org/stellent/groups/public/documents/newsroom/wfp204445.pdf.

————. 2010a. Food Aid Flows 2009. http://www.wfp.org/content/food-aid-flows-2009-report.

————. 2010b. P4P Purchase for Progress.http://documents.wfp.org/stellent/groups/public/documents/communications/wfp223705.pdf.

————. 2010c. Resourcing for a Changing Environment: Informal Consultation. 12 January. http://home.wfp.org/stellent/groups/public/documents/resources/wfp214221.pdf

Williams, Frances. 2005. Move by WTO "Is Threat to Food Aid." *Financial Times,* May 10.

World Bank. 2007. *World Development Report 2008: Agriculture for Development.* Washington DC: World Bank.

————. 2008. The World Bank's Response to the Food Crisis. Washington, DC: World Bank. http://siteresources.worldbank.org/IDA/Resources/IDA-Food_Crisis.pdf.

————. 2010. The Global Agriculture and Food Security Program (GAFSP) Questions & Answers. http://siteresources.worldbank.org/NEWS/Resources/GAFSPQuestionsAnswers_ext042210.pdf.

————. 2011. Food Price Watch. April. http://siteresources.worldbank.org/INTPOVERTY/Resources/335642-1210859591030/FPW_April2011.pdf

WTO (World Trade Organization). 1994. Marrakesh Declaration of 15 April 1994. http://www.wto.org/english/docs_e/legal_e/legal_e.htm.

————, 2000. Proposal for Comprehensive Long-Term Agricultural Trade Reform, Submission from the United States. G/AG/NG/W/15. Special session of the WTO Committee on Agriculture. June 23. http://docsonline.wto.org/imrd/directdoc.asp?DDFDocuments/t/G/AG/NGW15.doc.

————. 2002. Committee on Agriculture, Special session—Summary Report on the Ninth Meeting of the Special session. December 7, 2001. Note by the Secretariat. G/AG/NG/R/9. http://docsonline.wto.org/DDFDocuments/t/G/AG/NGR9.doc.

————. 2003. *Negotiations on Agriculture.* First Draft of Modalities for the Further Commitments. TN/AG/W/1. Special session of the WTO Committee on Agriculture. February 17.

————. 2004a. Agreement on Agriculture, article 10. http://www.wto.org/english/docs_e/legal_e/14-ag_02_e.htm.

————. 2004b. Doha Work Programme. Decision adopted by the General Council on August 1. WT/L/579 2. http://www.wto.org/english/tratop_e/dda_e/ddadraft_31jul04_e.pdf.

————. 2005. Doha World Programme: Ministerial Declaration. WT/MIN(05)/DEC. December 22. http://www.wto.org/english/thewto_e/minist_e/min05_e/final_text_e.pdf.

————. 2006a. Chair's Reference Paper on Export Competition. Special session of the Committee on Agriculture. April 11. http://www.wto.org/english/tratop_e/agric_e/ref_paper_foodaid_e.pdf.

————. 2006b. Draft Possible Modalities on Agriculture. TN/AG/W/3. Committee on Agriculture. July. http://www.wto.org/english/tratop_e/agric_e/mod_ag_2006_e.htm.

———. 2007. Communication from the chairman of the Committee on Agriculture. Special session April 30. http://www.wto.org/english/tratop_e/agric_e/agchairtxt_30apr07_e.htm.

———. 2008. Revised Draft Modalities on Agriculture. TN/AG/W/4/Rev.4. Committee on Agriculture. December 6. http://www.wto.org/english/tratop_e/agric_e/agchairtxt_dec08_a_e.pdf.

WTO African Group. 2001. Joint Proposal on the Negotiations on Agriculture. G/AG/NG/W/142. Special session of the WTO Committee on Agriculture. March 23.

WTO African and LDC Groups. 2006. Joint Submission by the African and LDC Groups on Food Aid. Geneva: WTO. TN/AG/GEN/13. March 6.

Yerkey, Gary. 2005. USTR Portman Says EU "Obsessed" with Halting U.S. Food Aid in WTO Talks. *International Trade Reporter,* December 15.

Young, Linda, and Philip Abbott. 2005. The WTO Negotiations and Disciplines for Food Aid. *Bridges* 9 (5): 3–5. http://ictsd.org/downloads/bridges/bridges9-5.pdf.

Zepeda, Jose Falck. 2006. Coexistence, Genetically Modified Biotechnologies and Biosafety: Implications for Developing Countries. *American Journal of Agricultural Economics* 88 (5): 1200–1208.

Zerbe, Noah. 2004. Feeding the Famine? American Food Aid and the GMO Debate in Southern Africa. *Food Policy* 29 (6): 593–608.

Zoellick, Robert. 2004. A Strategic Opportunity for Trade. Speech given at the French Institute of International Relations. May 13. http://ustraderep.gov/Document_Library/USTR_Speeches/2004/A_Strategic_Opportunity_for_Trade.html.

———. 2008. Letter to Prime Minister Fukuda of Japan. July 1. http://siteresources.worldbank.org/NEWS/Resources/zoellick-fukuda-070108.pdf.

———. 2011. Free Markets Can Still Feed the World. *Financial Times,* January 5.

# Index